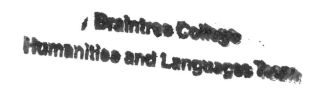
Talking Business French

Sandra Truscott and Margaret Mitchell

Stanley Thornes (Publishers) Ltd

First published in 1992 by:
Stanley Thornes (Publishers) Ltd
Old Station Drive
Leckhampton
CHELTENHAM GL53 0DN
England

British Library Cataloguing in Publication Data

Truscott, Sandra
    Talking business French. – (Talking business)
    I. Title   II. Mitchell, Margaret   III. Series
    448.3

    ISBN 0–7487–1376–X

Typeset by Tech-Set, Gateshead, Tyne & Wear
Printed and bound in Great Britain by Butler and Tanner, Frome, Somerset

Contents

Introduction

How to use this course

The course has several components which are described on p. vii. This coursebook consists of 15 units followed by a key. The different elements of each unit are described below.

Aims

Each unit starts by outlining what you should be able to achieve by the time you have completed it. You will be able to monitor your success by means of the **Progress check** (see below) at the end of the unit.

Time management

Time management is as important in language learning as it is in general business life/affairs. You should try to organise your time in such a way as to be able to do some language learning every day. Remember that we all learn at different speeds and have different learning styles. It is important, therefore, to be realistic about the time available to you and to pace yourself accordingly. It is generally felt that short, regular and frequent bursts of study are more effective than the occasional marathon. Try to schedule a 20-minute language learning slot into your daily routine.

Study tip

A brief **Study tip** has been included at the start of each unit. It is designed to help you find the most effective way to learn the language.

Dialogues

Each unit contains one or more dialogues which are recorded on the Presentation Cassettes. They should be listened to once or twice, without looking at the text. This gives you a feel for the sound and rhythm of the language without your being distracted by how it is spelt. Once you begin to recognise one or two words, listen again, this time with the English version (Units 1 and 2 only), in front of you. When you are ready, listen again with the French version so that you can begin to see how the words and phrases are divided. Once you feel you can understand the material, you are ready to study it more thoroughly.

Vocabulary, notes and key phrases

Each dialogue is accompanied by explanatory vocabulary, notes and key phrases. Any word which is not clear appears under **Vocabulary**. There is always an indication of whether a word is masculine (*m*), feminine (*f*), singular (*sing*) or plural (*pl*) – or you are given the article (**le** or **la**, **un** or **une**). The **Notes** are vital to understanding how the language is put together. You may want to make your own: we advise you to invest in a loose-leaf binder and to divide it up into several sections, such as vocabulary, verbs, grammar, etc. You will decide for yourself which information is important to you and how to organise it. The more active you are in your learning, the more quickly and efficiently you will learn. Language can be divided into what you need to produce (*active vocabulary*) and what you need to understand (*passive vocabulary*). Both are important, but you will find that your active vocabulary will soon be outstripped by your passive vocabulary. Try to distinguish between what is worth remembering and what is simply there as background. To help you, we have highlighted the **Key phrases** of every dialogue. Concentrate on these so that you can produce them yourself, quickly and accurately.

Practice exercises

Don't skip these! Practising the new language is vital if you are studying alone. Try to devise different ways of approaching the exercises, such as writing down the answers, reading them out loud and trying to remember them at odd times during the day. The more senses you use while learning, the more likely your new knowledge is to stick. We give you various ideas about how to do this as you work through the course. Answers to exercises appear in the **Unit key** at the end of the book.

Listening comprehension

Each unit includes at least one passage recorded on the Presentation Cassettes intended for 'gist' listening, that is, for understanding the general idea only. You are not expected to understand every word. This gives you practice in several skills: listening to native speakers at normal speed, coping with words and phrases you have not met before, sensitising yourself to accent and intonation. Listen to the passages as often as you like – the more the better! If you are really stumped, you will find a transcript at the back of the book, but don't forget that it is the general drift which is important, not each individual linguistic item.

Reading comprehension

Again, you don't need to understand everything in order to grasp the general idea. Try to get the broad outline first and then work down to individual words and phrases. The practice exercises will help you to do this. Translations of the reading passages are included in the key, but they should only be used as a last resort!

Language structures

In each unit, you will find a section called **Language structures**. Here we pull together the grammatical elements of the language and present them in graphic form. Try to remember that it is only an aid, a diagram to help you build up language as you might build a kitchen cabinet.

It will be helpful to know what certain grammatical terms mean, so we've included a glossary of the most commonly used words which you may or may not be familiar with already:

- *Noun* — the name of a person or thing (*John*, the *box*, my *wife*)
- *Pronoun* — a word that replaces a noun (*I, he, it, them*)
- *Preposition* — a word that links two nouns or pronouns (we paid *with* cash, I gave it *to* you, I put sugar *in* the coffee)
- *Adjective* — a word which describes a noun (*red, beautiful, small*)
- *Verb* — a doing word (you *are*, I *look*, he *ran*)
- *Infinitive* — the name of the verb. In English it is preceded by *to*, for example, *to see, to write*. In French you recognise it by the ending (either **er** as in **aimer**, **re** as in **repondre**, or **ir** as in **partir**)
- *Tense* — the form of the verb which expresses time – future, past, or present
- *Past participle* — second part of the verb indicating the past tense in phrases like 'I have *done*', 'he has *gone*'.

Pronunciation
Good pronunciation will come naturally if you listen carefully to and imitate what you hear on the cassettes. However, in each unit and on the Presentation Cassettes we have focused on one of the trickier or less obvious aspects of French pronunciation to help you sound as authentic as possible.

Cultural briefing
You may have acquired language skills, but can you strike the right note? These sections are designed to give you insights into the cultural context and to supply you with essential background information on how things are done in French-speaking countries.

Progress check
Each unit has a short self-assessment test. If you complete this successfully you can feel satisfied that you have learned the language points introduced in the unit. If you find it difficult, it would be a good idea to run through the material again before going any further.

Unit key
This includes answers to exercises, transcripts of listening comprehensions, translations of reading comprehensions. In addition, you will also find a **Summary of language functions**, a **Grammar summary** and a complete **Vocabulary list** at the back of the book.

Symbols

 When you see this symbol, you should listen to the appropriate material on the Presentation Cassettes.

Course components

Coursebook
This book, whose contents are described on pp. v–vii.

Presentation Cassettes 1 and 2
These are closely linked to the coursebook and contain dialogues, listening material, and pronunciation.

Consolidation Cassettes 1 and 2
These contain extensive and varied additional listening and practice material based on the key phrases, vocabulary and structures introduced in the Coursebook.

Teacher's Resource Book
Although this course is designed to be used for self-study purposes, most students will benefit greatly from even a limited amount of contact with a teacher and other language learners. This Teacher's Resource Book therefore provides notes for teachers whose students are using the *Talking Business* course, together with a wide range of photocopiable resources including role-plays, blank forms, realia, etc. designed for use in a class or study group. The book also contains transcripts of the listening comprehensions on the Consolidation Cassettes. The Teacher 's Resource Book can be ordered from your local bookshop or, in case of difficulty, direct from Stanley Thornes (Publishers) Ltd., Old Station Drive, Leckhampton, Cheltenham, Glos GL53 0DN.

Acknowledgements

The author and publishers wish to thank the following for permission to use material:

Berlitz Publishing for the extracts from the *Berlitz Guide de voyage – Paris* on pp. 96 and 101.
J. Allan Cash for the photos on pp. 48, 68 and 93.
C.C.E.A.A. for the advertisement on p. 95.
Thomas Cook for the photos on pp. 24 and 140.
Éditions La Route Robert for the extract on p. 119.
Femme Actuelle for the extract on p. 116.
French Railways for the photos on p. 37 and p. 46 (by Montchanin).
Keith Gibson for the photos on pp. 1, 4, 5, 10, 12, 13, 14, 42, 56, 62, 72, 73, 74, 84, 97, 112, 125, 126, 132, 135 and 152.
The Hutchison Library for the photos on pp. 64 and 65 by Gérard.
Jerrican for the photos by Berenguier on p. 99, Chandelle on p. 67, Charron on p. 55, Daudier on p. 21, Dubuc on p. 85, Dufeu on p. 108 (bottom), Gaillard on p. 114, Gente on p. 35, Gordons on pp. 28 and 29, Lainé on pp. 19 and 20, Lerosey on p. 43, Le Scour on p. 124, Limier on pp. 117 and 119, Sittler on pp. 115 and 138, Wallet on p. 150.
Princess Hats for the letter on p. 88.
RATP for the photo on p. 106.
Sphere S.A. for the extract on p. 143.
Sport 2000 for the advertisement on p. 82.
Vidocq Photo Library/Graham Bishop for the photos on pp. 60, 79, 100, 102, 104, 105 and 108 (top).
Toby Hotels for the photo of The Embankment – Bedroom on p. 47 by Simon Harding.

UNIT **1**

Enchanté(e)

In this unit, you will learn how to …

- introduce yourself
- greet others
- say who you are
- give your nationality
- say what job you do
- say where you live.

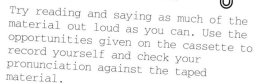

STUDY TIP

Try reading and saying as much of the material out loud as you can. Use the opportunities given on the cassette to record yourself and check your pronunciation against the taped material.

You will hear the dialogue printed below on tape: listen to it a couple of times first. Then listen again, this time looking at the English translation on p. 178. When it is beginning to make sense, read through the French version below and listen at the same time. You will have to do this several times until you feel comfortable with the material.

Dialogue 1: ## A la réception

Thompson Manufacturing is an English company (**une société anglaise**) which is setting up a new plant (**une nouvelle usine**) in France. They are sending two of their staff to spend six months in France to help get the new company established: Paul Smith, a sales engineer and Claire Stevenson from personnel.

The new director of Thompson France, Gérard Leclerc, is visiting Thompson Manufacturing to meet Paul Smith, Claire Stevenson and the general manager, John Davidson.

Monsieur Leclerc arrive à la réception.

M. Leclerc	Vous parlez français, Madame?
Réceptionniste	Oui, Monsieur.
M. Leclerc	Euh, bonjour, Madame. J'ai rendez-vous avec John Davidson.
Réceptionniste	C'est de la part de qui?
M. Leclerc	Je m'appelle Gérard Leclerc. Je suis directeur de Thompson France.

La dame à la réception téléphone à John Davidson.

Réceptionniste	Monsieur Davidson arrive.
M. Leclerc	Merci, Madame.
Mr Davidson	Bonjour, Monsieur. Je suis John Davidson. Heureux de faire votre connaissance.
M. Leclerc	Enchanté.

Vocabulary

arriver *to arrive*
à *at*
la réception *reception*
réceptionniste (*m/f*) *receptionist*
parler *to speak*
français *French*

oui *yes*
avoir *to have*
un rendez-vous *meeting*
avec *with*
s'appeler *to call oneself, be called*
être *to be*

le directeur *director*
la dame *woman*
téléphoner *to phone*

Notes

1 **Une société anglaise** *An English company.* All nouns are divided into two categories, masculine or feminine. **Société** is feminine, so the word for *a* is feminine, **une**. If the word were masculine (e.g. **rendez-vous**), then the word for *a* would be masculine, **un**. The adjective which accompanies the noun also has to be feminine or masculine as appropriate. **Société** is feminine so it takes the feminine form of the adjective **anglais**, **anglaise**. For a fuller explanation see Language structures on pp. 7–8.

2 **La nouvelle usine** *The new plant.* **Usine** is feminine, so the word for *the* is feminine, **la** (the masculine form is **le**). The adjective is the feminine form of **nouveau**, **nouvelle**.

3 **Monsieur, Madame, Mademoiselle** *Mr/sir, Mrs/madam, Miss.* In written French, **Monsieur** is abbreviated to **M.**, **Madame** to **Mme** and **Mademoiselle** to **Mlle**.

4 **Monsieur Leclerc arrive...** *Monsieur Leclerc arrives.* **Arrive** is the third person (*he/she*), present tense form of **arriver** *to arrive*. **Arriver** like **téléphoner** *to telephone* is a regular **er** verb. For more about these see p. 7.

5 **Vous parlez français** *Do you speak French?* **Parlez** is the formal second person (*you*), present tense form of

parler *to speak*. **Parler** is another regular **er** verb.

6 **Bonjour, Madame** *Good morning madam.* **Bonjour** also means *hello* and *good afternoon.* Use **bonsoir** for *good evening* and **bonne nuit** for *good night*.

7 **J'ai rendez-vous avec...** *I have a meeting with …* Note that the article **un** has been dropped in this phrase. **J'ai** is the first person (*I*), present tense form of **avoir** *to have*. For all the present tense forms of **avoir**, see p. 7.

8 **C'est de la part de qui?** Literally *on behalf of whom?* Also a useful phone expression.

9 **Je m'appelle** *My name is* (literally *I call myself*). This is an example of a reflexive verb – **s'appeler**. For more about reflexive verbs see p. 16.

10 **Je suis...** *I am …* This is the first person, present tense form of **être** *to be*. For all the present tense forms of **être**, see p. 7.

11 **Heureux de faire votre connaissance** *Pleased to meet you.* Literally (*I am*) *happy to make your acquaintance*. If you are a woman, change **heureux** to **heureuse**.

12 **Enchanté** Literally *enchanted, delighted*. If you are a woman, this is written **enchantée**, but the pronunciation does not change.

Key phrases

Bonjour, Madame (Leclerc)/**Monsieur**
  (Leclerc)/**Mademoiselle** (Davidson)
Je suis/je m'appelle Gérard Leclerc
Je suis directeur de Thompson France
Heureux de faire votre connaissance
Enchanté(e)
Merci

Good morning madam (Mrs Leclerc)/*Sir* (Mr
  Leclerc)/*Miss* (Davidson)
I am Gérard Leclerc
      the director of Thompson France
Pleased to meet you
Delighted (to meet you)
Thank you

Exercise 1

Listen to the cassette for a few moments. You will hear six people introducing themselves. They give their name, nationality and job. As you listen, check off each phrase you hear against the list below.

Note that when saying what job you do, you can omit **un** or **une**.

Je m'appelle...	*I am called …, my name is …*
Je suis...	*I am …*
Je suis américain	*I am (an) American (man)*
américaine	*(an) American (woman)*
anglais	*(an) English (man)*
anglaise	*(an) English (woman)*
écossais	*(a) Scottish (man)*
écossaise	*(a) Scottish (woman)*
gallois	*(a) Welsh (man)*
galloise	*(a) Welsh (woman)*
irlandais	*(an) Irish (man)*
irlandaise	*(an) Irish (woman)*
Je suis chef des achats	*I am purchasing manager*
chef du personnel	*personnel manager*
chef de production	*production manager*
chef de la publicité	*advertising manager*
chef des ventes	*sales manager*
comptable	*an accountant*
directeur (*m*)	*a director*
directrice (*f*)	*a director*
directeur-général	*general manager*
directrice de marketing	*marketing director (f)*
gérant(e)	*a manager(ess)*
homme/femme d'affaires	*a business man/woman*
ingénieur	*an engineer*
ingénieur commercial	*a sales engineer*
réceptionniste	*a receptionist*
secrétaire	*a secretary*
téléphoniste	*a telephonist*

| Exercise 2 | Now, introduce yourself out loud, in exactly the same way as the people you have heard. Give your name, job and nationality – use the check list in Exercise 1 to jog your memory. (If your job title is not given, choose the nearest approximation.) |

Exercise 3

Heureux de faire votre connaissance

Look at these pictures and match the English translation with its French equivalent. We haven't translated every word – just enough for you to be able to recognise which phrase goes with which. You will need to know the following expressions:

J'habite   *I live in*   **Je travaille à**   *I work at/for*

a) Bonjour. Je m'appelle Gérard Leclerc. Je suis français et j'habite Tours. Je suis directeur de Thompson France.

b) Bonjour. Je suis Claire Stevenson. Je suis anglaise et je travaille à Thompson Manufacturing. Je suis chef du personnel.

c) Je m'appelle John Davidson. Je suis anglais et j'habite Londres. Je suis directeur-général de Thompson Manufacturing.

d) Je suis Paul Smith. Je suis anglais. J'habite Milton Keynes. Je travaille à Thompson Manufacturing. Je suis ingénieur commercial.

1 Hello. I am English. I am a personnel manager.
2 I work at Thompson Manufacturing. I'm a sales engineer.
3 Good morning. I'm French – I live in Tours.
4 I am the general manager of Thompson and I'm English.

Exercise 4

1 How do you say:
   a) I live in Manchester
   b) I work for Twyford Chemicals?
2 Now say:
   a) Where *you* live
   b) Where *you* work.

(You can answer these questions out loud, write down the answers in your file or do both!)

Exercise 5

You are at the reception of the offices of a French client. You have a meeting with Madame Leblanc. Write in your part of the dialogue. Don't forget to give your job title (or the one you chose in Exercise 2).

Réceptionniste   Bonjour, Monsieur/Madame.

Vous   _____

Réceptionniste   C'est de la part de qui?

Vous   _____

Madame Leblanc arrives to meet you.

Mme Leblanc   Bonjour, Monsieur/Madame.

Vous   _____

Mme Leblanc   Je suis Monique Leblanc, chef des achats.

Vous   _____

Mme Leblanc   Heureuse de faire votre connaissance.

Vous   _____

Now read the dialogue out loud using **Monsieur** or **Madame** as appropriate. You may want to record yourself on cassette.

Listen to the model dialogue on tape. How did your version compare?

Comprehension 1

Now listen to four people telling you about themselves. When you have done so several times, fill in the grid below:

	Profession (*f*)	**Nationalité** (*f*)	**Ville** (*f*) (*town*)
Suzanne			
Paul			
Jean-Pierre			
Monique			

Pronunciation

Next time you meet a French person or see a French film, watch the way the French move their mouths as they speak. The mouth is more mobile, the lips more pursed than those of English speakers. You need to avoid the slack jaw of the Anglophone and to tighten the facial muscles as you speak French.

Listen to the tape to hear the pronunciation of the examples given below.

1 Depuis quand êtes-vous ici?
2 Qui êtes-vous?
3 Où est Liliane?
4 Il a six ans.

Language structures

You may feel inclined to skip this section if you don't like grammar, but we suggest you do read through it. Some knowledge of grammar is useful, if not essential, when learning a new language. A firm grasp of the concepts outlined below and in subsequent Language structures sections will prove invaluable.

Pronouns Personal pronouns

Je	*I*	
Tu	*You*	Use for children
		animals
		close friends
Il	*He*	
Elle	*She*	
Nous	*We*	
Vous	*You*	Use for more than one **tu**
		people you do not know well
Ils	*They*	Use for more than one male
		more than one masculine noun
		a mixture of males and females
		a mixture of masculine and
		feminine nouns
Elles	*They*	Use for more than one female
		more than one feminine noun

Verbs In French there are three sorts of verbs, those ending in **er, ir** and **re**. The verb endings change according to who does what (*person*), and when (*tense*).

Present tense of verbs that end in **er.**

Example: **téléphoner** *to telephone*
To form, start with the infinitive, take off the **er** and add the endings **e, es, e, ons, ez, ent.**

SINGULAR	
je téléphone	*I telephone*
tu téléphon**es**	*you telephone*
il téléphon**e**	*he telephones*
elle téléphon**e**	*she telephones*

PLURAL	
nous téléphon**ons**	*we telephone*
vous téléphon**ez**	*you telephone*
ils téléphon**ent**	*they telephone (m)*
elles téléphon**ent**	*they telephone (f)*

Some verbs don't follow the standard pattern:
avoir *to have* is one;

SINGULAR		PLURAL	
j'ai	*I have*	nous avons	*we have*
tu as	*you have*	vous avez	*you have*
il a	*he has*	ils ont	*they have (m)*
elle a	*she has*	elles ont	*they have (f)*

être *to be* is another.

SINGULAR		PLURAL	
je suis	*I am*	nous sommes	*we are*
tu es	*you are*	vous êtes	*you are*
il est	*he is*	ils sont	*they are (m)*
elle est	*she is*	elles sont	*they are (f)*

Nouns The definite article

Nouns in French are classed as either masculine or feminine. The words for *the* are:

le *(m sing)*	**le** directeur
la *(f sing)*	**la** société
These become **l'** before a vowel or **h**: **l'**homme d'affaires, **l'**usine	
les *(m/f pl)*	**les** directeurs, **les** sociétés

The indefinite article

The words for *a*, *an* are:

un *(m)*	**un** ingénieur
une *(f)*	**une** usine

Plurals

To make nouns plural (more than one), add an **s**:

le réceptionniste	**les** réceptionnistes

Some words ending in **al** form their plurals in **aux**:

le journal   *the newspaper*   les journ**aux**   *newspapers*

Adjectives

Adjectives are words that describe the nouns they appear with. They must 'agree' with their nouns, that is, if a noun is masculine singular, its adjective must also be masculine singular. In this unit you have met adjectives in the masculine singular and feminine singular forms.

Adjectives are dealt with more fully on pp. 59–60, but for now note that when you are introduced to an adjective in the vocabulary section, its feminine singular form will also be given. For example, **nouveau(elle)** tells you that the feminine singular form of **nouveau** is **nouvelle**. **Anglais(e)** tells you that the feminine singular form of **anglais** is **anglaise.**

Cultural briefing

When you are meeting people in France, whether they are friends or business colleagues, there are certain rules that must be followed. You must say **bonjour** or **bonsoir** and follow it with a name or **Monsieur/Madame/Mademoiselle** if you don't know them. Note that the difference between using **Madame** and **Mademoiselle** here is that the latter is used for a younger woman. If you know the woman is married, use **Madame**.

You also shake hands – not just the first time you meet, but on all subsequent occasions too. Remember to shake hands with everyone in the office when you leave (you may need to allocate extra time to do this!). It's also the custom to shake the workers' hands on the shop floor. It's a sign of **égalité**!

You will find that French business people are more formal than their English or American counterparts. You won't be on first name terms for a long time; be sure to use **vous** in addressing them. They are also much more aware of the pecking order than the British so it's worth your while finding out who is senior to whom. You can learn a lot about status within the company by simply observing who proffers their hand first (the more senior person).

Progress check

If you can complete the answers to these questions you have a good summary of what you should remember from this chapter. You can write down the answers if you prefer, but you may find it more useful and appropriate to give your answers orally.

How would you say the following?

1 Good morning, I am …

2 I am English and I'm a … with Marley Transport.
3 What is the meaning of:
   Je suis heureuse de faire votre connaissance?
   a) Who is speaking, a man or a woman?
   b) What is your reply?
4 You are asked 'Où habitez-vous?' What do you reply?
5 How do you say *I work for Agrichem*?

UNIT 2 Quel est votre nom?

In this unit, you will learn how to …

- give your full name
- fill in a simple form
- understand more about others' personal details
- talk in simple terms about your own family
- understand others talking about their families
- count from 0–30.

Dialogue 1: Au téléphone

The translation of this dialogue is on p. 179, but don't read it until you have listened once or twice to the passage on tape.

Brigitte Duclos is a secretary in the personnel department at Thompson France. She is receiving applications for jobs with the company from candidates Claire will interview later. An applicant (**un candidat**) telephones, seeking a job with Thompson France.

Brigitte	Allô, oui. Service du personnel.
Candidat	Bonjour, Madame. Je cherche un emploi dans votre société.
Brigitte	Quel est votre nom, Monsieur?
Candidat	Je m'appelle Dubois.
Brigitte	Et votre prénom?
Candidat	Pierre.
Brigitte	Quelle est votre profession?
Candidat	Je suis ingénieur.
Brigitte	Quelle est votre nationalité?
Candidat	Je suis français.
Brigitte	Où habitez-vous?
Candidat	J'habite Saumur.

Vocabulary

le service *department*	**votre** *your (formal)*	**quelle** *what, which (f sing)*
du *of, of the*	**quel** *what, which (m sing)*	**une profession** *profession*
chercher *to seek, to look for*	**le nom** *name*	**la nationalité** *nationality*
un emploi *job*	**et** *and*	**où** *where*
dans *in*	**le prénom** *first name*	**habiter** *to live, to live in*

Notes

1 **Allô** *Hallo.* This word is only used for telephone conversations.
2 **Service du personnel** Literally *department of personnel.* French does not have the *'s*, which allows English to say *John's wife* or *Mary's husband.* Say *the wife of John* or *the husband of Mary* instead.
3 **Je cherche un emploi** *I am looking for a job.* There is only one form of the present tense in French for our two forms in English. **Je cherche** means both *I look for* and *I am looking for.*
4 **Où habitez-vous?** *Where do you live?* More about asking questions on p. 17.
5 **J'habite Saumur** *I live in Saumur.* Note that in French you don't need to translate the preposition *in.*

Key phrases

Allô	*Hello (on the phone)*
Je cherche un emploi avec votre société Thompson France	*I am looking for a job with your company* Thompson France
Je suis anglais(e)/américain(e)	*I am English/American*
J'habite Milton Keynes/Paris	*I live in Milton Keynes/Paris*

Exercise 1

Now it's your turn to give some details about yourself. Look at this form and fill it in. The new word **domicile** (*m*) means where you live.

```
Nom:            _____

Prénom:         _____

Profession:     _____

Nationalité:    _____

Domicile:       _____

_____
```

Now copy the form and complete it for three of your colleagues at work. Look at the list on p. 3 to find their job titles or the nearest approximation.

| **Exercise 2** | Imagine you are now phoning France. Out loud give as much information as you can about yourself. It is only through rehearsing language in this way that you will be prepared for the real thing! |

| **Exercise 3** | Listen to the cassette. You will hear the numbers in French from 0–30. We have left a gap after each number for you to repeat. Check the spellings on p. 18 or look at the page numbers in this book. |

| **Exercise 4** | Brigitte has received several applications already. Look at the two below and try to work out what they mean. You should be able to understand even those words you haven't met before because they are similar to the English. You will find both applications on tape. Listen carefully to how each word is pronounced and then read them out loud yourself. |

Nom:	García
Prénom:	Dominique
Nationalité:	Espagnole
Age:	Vingt-deux (22) ans
Profession:	Téléphoniste
Domicile:	San Sebastián

Elle s'appelle Dominique García. Elle est espagnole. Elle a vingt-deux ans. Elle est téléphoniste et elle habite San Sebastián.

Nom:	Tissérand
Prénom:	Jean-Louis
Nationalité:	Belge
Age:	Trente-trois (33) ans
Profession:	Chef des ventes
Domicile:	Compiègne

Il s'appelle Jean-Louis Tissérand. Il est belge. Il a trente-trois ans. Il est chef des ventes et il habite Compiègne.

You may have noticed that the French say *I* **have** *33 years* (**J'ai trente-trois ans**) instead of *I* **am** *33 years old*. There are more examples of this in the following exercise.

Comprehension 1

Listen to Brigitte talking about the other candidates over the phone, then complete the table. You may need to listen several times:

Here are some words to help you: **canadien** (*m*), **canadienne** (*f*) *Canadian*; **suisse** *Swiss* (this form does not change).

Nom	Prénom	Nationalité	Age	Profession
Voisine	Frédéric			
Leclerc	Geneviève			
Berrogain	Daniel			
Bérous	Martine			

Exercise 5

Now, imagine *you* are a **chef du personnel**. You're telling a colleague about the candidates for a job in your company. Choose four of the six people you have met in this exercise and record your description of them. Rewind, then listen to your recording. Don't forget to mention:

1 their name **2** their age **3** their nationality **4** their profession.

Comprehension 2

Here we have a couple of reading passages for you in which two French people tell you about themselves and their family. You don't have to understand every word, just the general gist. Some vocabulary is included here to help you; if you're really stuck there are translations on p. 179.

1 Je m'appelle Dominique Dupont. Je suis française et je viens de Fontainebleau. je suis mariée et j'ai une fille. Elle s'appelle Claudine. Mon mari s'appelle Yves. Il est ingénieur. Il est chef de production chez un fabricant de voitures. Moi, je travaille dans un restaurant.

Vocabulary

je viens de *I come from*   **un fabricant** *manufacturer*   **une voiture** *car*

2 Je m'appelle Patrick Joubert. Mon entreprise s'appelle Créations Joubert. C'est une petite entreprise familiale, une petite fabrique de chapeaux. Je suis marié. Ma femme s'appelle Chloé. Elle travaille avec moi. Ma soeur aussi travaille avec moi. Elle s'appelle Martine et elle est célibataire.

Vocabulary

une entreprise *firm*   **une soeur** *sister*   **célibataire** *unmarried*
un chapeau *hat*   **aussi** *also*

Now read these statements and decide if they are true (**vrai**) or false (**faux**). A word of warning: Dominique is usually a girl's name in France.

		Vrai	Faux
1	**a)** Dominique is a Frenchman.	☐	☐
	b) Yves is married with one child.	☐	☐
	c) Yves is married to an engineer.	☐	☐
	d) Dominique works for a car manufacturer.	☐	☐
	e) Dominique is married to Yves.	☐	☐
2	**a)** Patrick's company manufactures hats.	☐	☐
	b) Créations Joubert is a large company.	☐	☐
	c) Patrick is not married.	☐	☐
	d) Chloé works at the same company as Patrick.	☐	☐
	e) Martine is Patrick's unmarried sister.	☐	☐

La famille (the family)

Vocabulary

les enfants (m) *children*   **le mari** *husband*
la femme *wife*   **la mère** *mother*
la fille *daughter*   **le père** *father*
le fils *son*   **la soeur** *sister*
le frère *brother*

Exercise 6

Here is the family tree of John Davidson, the general manager of Thompson Manufacturing.

John Davidson   Monique Davidson

Stephen   Ruth

Can you work out their relationships in French?

Example: Monique est **la femme** de John.   *Monique is John's wife.*

Remember to get the gender right, that is, **le** for a masculine word, **la** for a feminine one.

1 Stephen est _____ _____ de Ruth.
2 Ruth est _____ _____ de Monique et de John.
3 John est _____ _____ de Monique.
4 Stephen est _____ _____ de Monique et de John.
5 Monique est _____ _____ de Stephen.
6 Ruth est _____ _____ de Stephen.

Exercise 7

Qui sont-ils? (*Who are they?*)
Let's turn that activity on its head. Can you work out who is speaking in the following exercise?

1 Ma femme s'appelle Monique.
2 Ma soeur s'appelle Ruth.
3 Ma fille s'appelle Ruth.
4 Mon fils s'appelle Stephen.
5 Mon mari s'appelle John.

Exercise 8

How many of those job titles do you remember? Match the French with its English equivalent. We've done the first one for you.

1 chef de production   **a)** production manager
2 chef des ventes   **b)** purchasing manager
3 secrétaire   **c)** manager(ess)
4 chef des achats   **d)** accountant
5 gérant(e)   **e)** engineer
6 comptable   **f)** sales manager
7 chef de la publicité **g)** personnel manager
8 ingénieur   **h)** secretary
9 chef du personnel   **i)** telephonist
10 téléphoniste   **j)** advertising manager

Exercise 9

Say which nationality these people are.

Example: Mademoiselle Dubois est canadienne.

Don't forget to make the nationality agree with the person.

1 M. Leclerc (*French*).
2 Mme Vandenberghe (*Belgian*).
3 Mlle Dubois (*Canadian*).
4 Mme Vasquez (*Spanish*).
5 M. O'Donnell (*Irish*).
6 Mlle Kohl (*Swiss*).

Pronunciation

 The **r** in French is one of the more difficult sounds to pronounce. Place your tongue against the bottom front teeth and make it into a convex shape. Then place it on the hard palate and make a sort of gargling noise. You'll need to practise!

Listen to the tape to hear the pronunciation of the examples given below.

1 Richard est arrivé hier.
2 Marianne a un rendez-vous avec le directeur.
3 Je suis heureux de vous revoir.
4 Merci et au revoir.

Language structures

Verbs   Reflexive verbs

 These are verbs which refer back to themselves as in *I wash myself, I shave myself.* They have two parts, the verb itself and the pronoun (*myself, yourself,* etc.) The pronoun also changes according to who is doing the action. Look at the table below to see how it works.

Example: **S'appeler** *to be called* (literally *to call oneself*)

SINGULAR	
je m'appelle	*I am called*
tu t'appelles	*you are called*
il s'appelle	*he is called*
elle s'appelle	*she is called*
PLURAL	
nous nous appelons	*we are called*
vous vous appelez	*you are called*
ils s'appellent	*they are called (m)*
elles s'appellent	*they are called (f)*

Adjectives

Possessive adjectives

To indicate possession (*my, your*, etc.) you need to use adjectives which agree with the word they refer to.

> **Mon** (*m*) *my*   **Ma** (*f*) *my*
> **mon** mari   **ma** femme
>   **mes** (*m/f pl*)
>   **mes** enfants

NB If a noun begins with a vowel or **h**, the possessive adjective will be **mon** in the singular, whether the noun is masculine or feminine.

Example: **mon** entreprise

As you see from these examples, the adjective does *not* agree with the person talking, but with the person or thing they are talking about.

> **Notre** (invariable) *our*   **notre** famille
> **Votre** (invariable) *your*   **votre** fils
>   **votre** soeur

Notre and **votre** are used for both masculine and feminine nouns in the singular. Their plural forms and more about other possessive adjectives can be found in Units 8 and 13.

Questions

You can ask questions by using words like **qui** (*who*) **quand** (*when*) **où** (*where*).

> **Qui êtes-vous?**   *Who are you?*
> **Quand travaillez-vous?**   *When do you work?*
> **Où êtes-vous?**   *Where are you?*

When asking questions in this way, you usually turn the verb around or *invert* it. Compare:

1 **La fabrique où vous travaillez.**   *The factory where you work.*

2 **Où travaillez-vous?**   *Where do you work?*

Exercise 10

A French colleague is asking you about yourself in a fairly informal way. You want to ask a more senior colleague the same questions but in a less colloquial way. How do you do it? Remember to invert the verb.

1 Et vous habitez où?
2 Vous travaillez où?
3 Vous êtes marié(e)?
4 Vous êtes chef de production?
5 Vous cherchez un emploi ici en France?

Numbers   0–30

0	zéro	11	onze	22	vingt-deux
1	un	12	douze	23	vingt-trois
2	deux	13	treize	24	vingt-quatre
3	trois	14	quatorze	25	vingt-cinq
4	quatre	15	quinze	26	vingt-six
5	cinq	16	seize	27	vingt-sept
6	six	17	dix-sept	28	vingt-huit
7	sept	18	dix-huit	29	vingt-neuf
8	huit	19	dix-neuf	30	trente
9	neuf	20	vingt		
10	dix	21	vingt et un		

Cultural briefing

Don't be surprised if you hear the words **directeur** (*m*) or **directrice** (*f*) used in a variety of different contexts in a French company. Starting at the top, they can mean the *directors* on the Board of Directors or **Conseil d'Administration**. (These are also called **administrateurs**.) They do *not* mean the *Managing Director*. This person is known as the **P.-D.G** or **Président-Directeur Général**. Otherwise, **directeur/directrice** means the *head of a department*. We have already met the following:

- **le directeur** (or **chef**) **du personnel**
- **le directeur de marketing**
- **le directeur commercial**
- **le directeur-général.**

Progress check

1 Give a French person the following information:
   a) whether you are married or single
   b) the name of your partner.
2 Say at least two sentences about your family.
3 Name three nationalities which are French speaking.
4 Give the name, job title and nationality of your boss. Where does s/he live?
5 Give the nationalities of the following personalities:
   a) Queen Sofia

   b) President Mitterand
   c) King Baudouin
   d) José Carreras
   e) Terry Wogan
   f) Brigitte Bardot
   g) Queen Elizabeth II.
6 What relation is:
   a) Prince Charles to Queen Elizabeth II
   b) Liza Minnelli to Judy Garland
   c) Dennis Thatcher to Carole Thatcher
   d) Princess Diana to Prince Charles
   e) Lenny Henry to Dawn French?

UNIT **3** Je voudrais réserver...

In this unit, you will learn how to …

- book a hotel room
- count from 31–60
- give and understand phone numbers
- start using dates.

Dialogue 1a: Faire une réservation

Paul Smith and Claire Stevenson are going to spend six months working at Thompson France to help get the new plant established. They are going to make a preliminary visit to find accomodation and meet their future colleagues. They are to travel on 16 December by plane (**en avion**) from Heathrow to Paris and then by train to Angers. Debbie, one of the secretaries, is arranging hotel accommodation for them.

The first time Debbie calls the hotel, she is unlucky. It is full (**complet**).

Réceptionniste	Allô, oui?
Debbie	C'est bien l'Hôtel Anjou?
Réceptionniste	Oui, j'écoute.
Debbie	Je voudrais réserver deux chambres, s'il vous plaît.
Réceptionniste	Je suis désolée, Madame. L'hôtel est complet.
Debbie	Merci bien, Madame. Au revoir.

Vocabulary

un avion *plane*
complet(ète) *full*

écouter *to listen*
réserver *to reserve*

une chambre *room*

Notes

1 **Faire une réservation** *To make a reservation.*
2 **C'est bien l'Hôtel Anjou?** *Is that the Hotel Anjou?* Debbie checks she has the right number by adding **bien** (*really*).
3 **J'écoute** *I am listening.* Over the phone it means *go ahead.*
4 **Je voudrais réserver deux chambres** *I'd like to book two rooms.* **Je voudrais** from **vouloir** *to wish* or *to want*. When you have two verbs together like this, the second is always an infinitive.

5 **S'il vous plaît** *Please.* Literally *if it pleases you*. If you address someone as *tu*, it will change to **s'il te plaît**. And you may see it shortened sometimes, in notes or memoranda, as **S.V.P.**
6 **Je suis désolée** *I'm sorry.*
7 **Au revoir** *Goodbye* (from **revoir**, *to see again*). It is rather formal and final, so you may wish to say **à demain** (*see you tomorrow*) or **à tout à l'heure** (*see you soon*).

Key phrases

C'est l'Hôtel Anjou/Concorde**?**	*Is that the Hotel* Anjou/Concorde*?*
J'écoute	*Go ahead*
Je voudrais réserver une chambre/deux chambres	*I would like to reserve* one room/two rooms
S'il vous plaît	*Please*
Je suis désolé(e)	*I am sorry*
Au revoir	*Good bye*

Dialogue 1b: ## Faire une réservation

This time Debbie has more luck.

Réceptionniste	Allô, oui?
Debbie	C'est bien l'Hôtel Concorde?
Réceptionniste	Oui, Madame.
Debbie	Je voudrais réserver deux chambres, s'il vous plaît.
Réceptionniste	Oui, Madame. Pour combien de personnes?
Debbie	Deux chambres pour une personne.
Réceptionniste	Oui. Pour combien de nuits?
Debbie	Une chambre pour deux nuits et l'autre pour quatre nuits à partir du 16 (seize) décembre.

Vocabulary

une personne *person*   **la nuit** *night*   **l'autre** (*m/f*) *the other (one)*

Notes

1 **Pour combien de personnes?** *For how many people?* Use **combien** on its own to mean *how much?* (money) and with **de** to mean *how many?* (e.g. people, nights).

2 **A partir du 16 décembre?** *From 16 December?* Although **partir** means to leave, **à partir de...** means *with effect from.* More about months on p. 31.

Key phrases

Une nuit/deux nuits/trois nuits à partir du 16 décembre	*One night/two nights/three nights from 16 December*

Dialogue 1c: Faire une réservation

The receptionist checks his bookings …

Réceptionniste	Ah, je suis désolé. Je n'ai plus qu'une seule chambre.
Debbie	Bon. Je la prends.
Réceptionniste	Pour deux nuits ou quatre nuits, alors?
Debbie	Pour deux nuits seulement.
Réceptionniste	Oui. C'est à quel nom?
Debbie	Au nom de Mademoiselle Claire Stevenson, de la société Thompson Manufacturing en Angleterre.
Réceptionniste	Et votre numéro de téléphone?
Debbie	C'est le 081 228 1918.
Réceptionniste	Très bien. Donc une chambre pour une personne pour deux nuits au nom de Stevenson.
Debbie	C'est une chambre avec salle de bains?
Réceptionniste	Oui, Madame.
Debbie	Merci. Au revoir, Monsieur.

Vocabulary

ou *or*
alors *then*
seulement *only*

le numéro de téléphone
telephone number
très *very*

donc *therefore*
une salle de bains *bathroom*

Notes

1 **Je n'ai plus que...** *I only have … left.*
2 **D'accord** *OK.* Use this often and you will sound very French!
3 **Je la prends** *I'll take it.* **Prends** is the first person present tense of **prendre**, *to take*. The full form is on p. 26. Notice also that in English we use the future (*I will take*) where French prefers the present (*I take*). **La** is a pronoun replacing **une chambre**. There is more about pronouns on p. 70.
4 **C'est à quel nom?** *It's in whose name?* Although the receptionist is referring to a third person (Miss Stevenson), she could

have asked Debbie the same question. It's an indirect way of asking somebody their name.
5 **C'est le 081 228 1918.** Did you notice how French telephone numbers are said in pairs? We'll practise this later in the unit.
6 **Une chambre pour une personne** *A single room* (literally *a room for one person*).
7 **C'est une chambre avec salle de bains?** *Is it a room with a bath(room)?* If you want a shower, say **avec douche**.

Key phrases

D'accord
Au nom de Claire Stevenson
De la société Thompson Manufacturing/ICI
Très bien
Une chambre pour une personne/deux personnes
C'est une chambre avec salle de bains/ douche/WC?

OK
In the name of Claire Stevenson
From Thompson Manufacturing/ICI
Fine
A single/double room

Is it a room with a bathroom/shower/toilet?

| **Exercise 1** | Debbie has to find another hotel for Paul Smith. She telephones the Hôtel France. Play Debbie's part in the conversation. Remember to use the phrase **à partir du...** |

Practise the dialogue out loud until you are satisfied with your fluency and pronunciation. You can then write in Debbie's part.

Réceptionniste   Allô, oui.

Debbie   (*Ask if that's the Hôtel France.*)

_____

Réceptionniste   Oui, j'écoute.

Debbie   (*Say that you would like to reserve a room.*)

_____

Réceptionniste   Oui, Madame. Pour combien de personnes?

Debbie	_____
Réceptionniste	Pour combien de nuits?
Debbie	(*Say it's for four nights from 16 December.*)
	_____
Réceptionniste	C'est à quel nom?
Debbie	_____
Réceptionniste	Et votre numéro de téléphone?
Debbie	(**le 081 228 1918**).
Réceptionniste	Parfait. Merci, Madame.
Debbie	_____

Now check that you were right by listening to the dialogue on tape.

Exercise 2

1 Now imagine that *you* are going to Paris for four nights from 16 December and arrange the booking at the Hôtel France for yourself. Speak the whole conversation out loud.

2 Your husband/wife/friend has just announced that he or she is free to go with you but only for the weekend (**le weekend**). Book a double room from Friday evening to Sunday morning (**du vendredi soir au dimanche matin**), 19–21 December.

Exercise 3

Debbie sends a fax to confirm Claire's booking. This is what she writes:

THOMPSON
MANUFACTURING

Fax Message

Date: 5/12

To: Hôtel Concorde

From: Debbie Clark

Je confirme notre réservation d'une chambre pour une personne avec salle de bains pour les nuits du 16 et 17 décembre, au nom de Mlle Stevenson.

Debbie Clark

Now write a similar fax to confirm your own booking: either version 1 or version 2.

Exercise 4

Listen to the cassette. You will hear the numbers in French from 31–60. We have left a gap after each number for you to repeat. Check the spellings on pp. 26–7 or look at the page numbers in this book.

Exercise 5

On tape you will hear the telephone numbers of Debbie, Claire Stevenson and Paul Smith. Jot them down, then check the answers on p. 180. Remember that in France, telephone numbers are given in pairs.

Exercise 6

Can you answer these brain-teasers? They're all based on the preceding dialogues.

1 The receptionist in Dialogue 1 says '**Je suis désolée**'. How do you know from the transcript whether it is a man or woman speaking?

2 If we say **une chambre pour une personne**, how do we say *a double room?*

3 **Bien** is used twice in Dialogue 1, but with different meanings. Can you say what they are?

Comprehension 1

Alison Steward works for a travel agency in the UK. She receives a number of enquiries from French clients. What kind of accommodation does each ask for? Listen to the information and fill in the details on the grid.

Clients	How many nights?	How many people?	Facilities	How many rooms?
1				
2				
3				
4				

Vocabulary

la télévision *television* **le parking** *car park*

Comprehension 2

Alison has received a letter from a French client. Read it through with her, then answer the true/false questions which follow. Remember that you don't have to understand it all. There is a translation of the passage on p. 181.

> Monsieur
>
> Je viens à Londres au mois d'août. Je voudrais réserver une chambre d'hôtel pour ma famille. Nous sommes quatre personnes: ma femme, moi et nos deux enfants, un garçon et une fille.
>
> Nous cherchons un petit hôtel avec parking. Nous voudrions une chambre pour deux personnes avec salle de bains et deux chambres pour une personne pour les enfants.
>
> Voulez-vous nous envoyer une liste d'hôtels et le prix?
>
> En vous remerciant d'avance, je vous prie d'agréer l'expression de mes sentiments les meilleurs.
>
> *Guillaume Lenoir*

Vrai ou faux?

		Vrai	Faux
1	Guillaume is coming to London with his family.	☐	☐
2	They are bringing their car.	☐	☐
3	He wants rooms with bathrooms for the children.	☐	☐
4	He wants to book two rooms.	☐	☐
5	The family wants a large hotel.	☐	☐
6	Guillaume asks for a price list.	☐	☐

You'll find the answers on p. 181.

Pronunciation

The **u** in words like **tu**, **publicité** and names like **Dubois** is another difficult sound for non-French speakers to pronounce. Try these hints to help you achieve the correct sound. Place the tip of the tongue against the bottom teeth, then purse your lips as though you were going to whistle and say *u*. Scottish speakers should have no trouble pronouncing this sound as their *u* is similar. Listen to the Scottish football reporters saying the word *football* – you'll find the oo in foot sounds remarkably similar to a French **u**!

Listen to the tape to hear the pronunciation of the examples given below.

1 Une nuit à partir du vingt.

2 Pour une personne.

3 Quel numéro?

4 Tu es venu quand?

Language structures

Verbs   Present tense of **re** verbs

Example: **Attendre** *to wait*

To form, take off the **re** from the infinitive and add the endings: **s, s,** – (no ending), **ons, ez, ent**.

SINGULAR	PLURAL
j'attends	nous attend**ons**
tu attend**s**	vous attend**ez**
il attend	ils attend**ent**
elle attend	elles attend**ent**

Prendre *to take* is an irregular verb ending in **re**. Look at the forms:

SINGULAR	PLURAL
je prends	nous prenons
tu prends	vous prenez
il prend	ils prennent
elle prend	elles prennent

Now listen to the pronunciation of **attendre** and **prendre** on the tape.

Numbers   31–60

31	trente et un	34	trente-quatre
32	trente-deux	35	trente-cinq
33	trente-trois	36	trente-six

37	trente-sept	49	quarante-neuf
38	trente-huit	50	cinquante
39	trente-neuf	51	cinquante et un
40	quarante	52	cinquante-deux
41	quarante et un	53	cinquante-trois
42	quarante-deux	54	cinquante-quatre
43	quarante-trois	55	cinquante-cinq
44	quarante-quatre	56	cinquante-six
45	quarante-cinq	57	cinquante-sept
46	quarante-six	58	cinquante-huit
47	quarante-sept	59	cinquante-neuf
48	quarante-huit	60	soixante

Exercise 7

Look at these telephone numbers and say them out loud. Practise till you can say them clearly and confidently. Then check with the cassette to see if you are right.

1 32-41-12-35
2 49-33-26-22
3 37-60-44-27
4 56-13-14-24
5 55-19-42-36

Cultural briefing

Using the telephone in France is not difficult. When you arrive in France it is wise to buy a telephone card because most phones these days are no longer coin operated. You can buy a card at a post office or the ubiquitous **bureau de tabac** (where you can also buy stamps and tobacco). As in the United Kingdom, put the card in first, then dial the number (**composer le numéro**). If you wish to ring home or the office, dial 19, the UK code (44) and then the subscriber's number, minus the initial zero of the local code. If you want to ring within France and don't know the number, ring **Renseignements** *Directory Enquiries* by dialling 12.

If you're ringing a French or Belgian office, the best time to do so is 9–11 a.m. or 3–5 p.m.

Progress check

1 On the phone, ask for the Hôtel du Cerf.
2 Ask for two rooms, one with a shower and one with a bath.
3 You are told 'Je suis désolé'. What does that mean?
4 Ask for a double room with bathroom.
5 Say you wish to stay for three nights.
6 Give your office phone number – 42 57 31.
7 Give your home phone number – 12 55 40.

UNIT 4 J'arrive le 16 à 21 heures

In this unit you will learn how to …

- discuss simple travel arrangements
- express more dates
- start using times.

Dialogue 1: Le programme de la visite

Debbie telephones Gérard's secretary in France to explain the arrangements for Claire and Paul's visit. Listen to her at least twice before you look at the French transcript.

Debbie	Bonjour, Monsieur. Ici Debbie Clark. Je suis secrétaire chez Thompson Manufacturing. Je téléphone d'Angleterre.
Secrétaire	Bonjour Mademoiselle. Qu'est-ce que je peux faire pour vous?
Debbie	C'est pour confirmer la date d'arrivée de Monsieur Smith et Mademoiselle Stevenson. Ils arrivent le 16 décembre. Ils prennent le vol Heathrow–Paris. Ils prennent le train jusqu'à Angers. Ils arrivent vers 21 (*vingt et une*) heures.
Secrétaire	Est-ce qu'ils ont une chambre d'hôtel?
Debbie	Oui. Mademoiselle Stevenson à l'Hôtel Concorde pour deux nuits et Monsieur Smith à l'Hôtel France pour quatre nuits. Pour le retour, Mademoiselle Stevenson prend l'avion le 18 (*dix-huit*) et Monsieur Smith le 20 (*vingt*) décembre.

Vocabulary

ici *here*
chez *at*
de *from, of*
pour *for*

l'arrivée (*f*) *arrival*
le vol *flight*
le train *train*
jusqu'à *until*

vers *towards, about*
le retour *return*

Notes

1 **Ici Debbie Clark** *This is Debbie Clark* (literally *here is Debbie Clark*). This expression should only be used on the phone.

2 **Je téléphone d'Angleterre** *I'm phoning from England.* This dialogue has lots of examples of present tense **er** verbs. If you need to recap, look at p. 7.

3 **Qu'est-ce que je peux faire pour vous?** *What can I do for you?* Another way of forming a question. More about this in Language structures on p. 34. **Je peux** *I can* is from **pouvoir** and is irregular. You will find the full forms on p. 34.

4 **C'est pour confirmer la date** *It is to confirm the date.* **C'est** (*it is*) is a key phrase: learn it well!

5 **Le 16 décembre** *The sixteenth of December.* Note the differences between expressing the date in French and in English.

6 **Ils prennent le vol** *They are taking the flight.* **Prendre** means *to take* (food and drink, as well as trains and planes). The full form was given in Unit 3: Language structures.

7 **Vers 21 heures** Literally *towards 21.00 hours.* Here the time is given using the international 24-hour clock: for more details see p. 30.

8 **Est-ce qu'ils ont une chambre d'hôtel?** *Have they got a hotel room?* Another way of asking a question. We deal with this on p. 34.

Key phrases

Ici Debbie Clark	*This is Debbie Clark*
Je téléphone d'Angleterre	*I am phoning from England*
Qu'est-ce que je peux faire pour vous?	*What can I do for you?*

Exercise 1

Can you answer these brain-teasers? They're based on the preceding dialogue.

1 How do the French and English ways of expressing the date differ? There are at least three ways.
2 Why do the French say **vingt et une heures**?
3 All the verbs in the dialogue are in the present tense, but they can be translated in several different tenses in English. Jot down some possible translations.

Exercise 2

Listen to the cassette. You will hear the days of the week beginning with Monday (**lundi**). Repeat them after the presenter. Then write down the answers to the questions below. Don't worry about the spelling at this stage: you can look that up later on p. 34.

1 What day is it today?
2 What day was it yesterday?
3 And in two days time?

The 24-hour clock

The 24-hour system is used in France, as in the United Kingdom, for stating the times of trains, planes, formal meetings and so on. Instead of *half past*, *a quarter to* and so on, the time is expressed purely in terms of numbers. Look at how it is done:

huit heures dix	*8:10*	**dix-huit heures**	*18:00*
neuf heures quarante	*9:40*	**seize heures vingt**	*16:20*

Exercise 3

Now you'll hear the times of arrival of various colleagues going to France, according to the international clock (08.00 hours, etc.). The first one is: **dimanche, à quinze heures trente** (*Sunday, at 15.30*). Listen to the tape and jot them down.

To do the next exercise you will need to use the verb **prendre** *to take* (see p. 26). You will also need to know **partir** *to leave* which is pronounced for you now on tape.

Exercise 4

Gérard Leclerc has stayed longer than planned in England. This is his new schedule:

> **Vendredi**
>
> départ : 08·00
> avion : 11· 00
> arrivée à Paris : 13·00 [treize heures]
> train [Montparnasse] : 14·50 [quatorze heures cinquante]
> arrivée à Angers : 16·21
>   [seize heures vingt et un]

1 If you were telephoning Gérard's secretary in France to let her
   know the new arrangements and had to leave an answer-
   phone message in French, what would you say? (You will
   need to know **il part** *he is leaving* from **partir** *to leave*.) Try
   recording yourself on cassette then listening back to the
   message!

2 Gérard telephones his wife to tell her of the new
   arrangements. What does he say? (You will need to know **je
   pars** *I leave*.)

3 Now imagine you are going on a business trip tomorrow. Here
   are the details:

> départ   Manchester: 07.30
> arrivée Glasgow: 11.50
> rendez-vous   Mc Laren Associates: 12.30
> départ Glasgow: 16.15
> arrivée Manchester: 20.30

Tell your colleague about your schedule. Record yourself if
you wish to.

Exercise 5

Study this diagram of the months and seasons then listen to the
tape to hear the correct pronunciation.

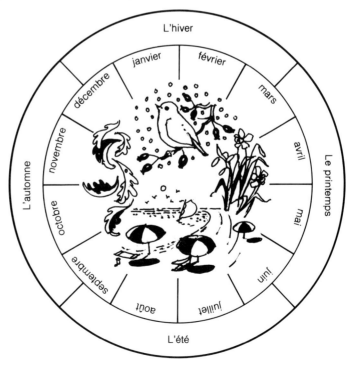

Exercise 6

Now listen to the cassette again. You will hear a number of dates being mentioned, but not in the order your see them below. Jot them down so you have the French and English equivalents. The first one has been done for you.

1 *15 April*   **le quinze avril**

2 *6 January*   _____

3 *21 May*   _____

4 *30 September*   _____

5 *5 November*   _____

6 *18 August*   _____

7 *8 February*   _____

8 *11 June*   _____

Exercise 7

C'est quand votre anniversaire? *When is your birthday?*

Out loud, tell us the important dates in your life: You need to start '**Mon anniversaire, c'est le...**', or '**L'anniversaire de ma femme, c'est le...**'

1 When is your birthday?
2 Your wife's or husband's?
3 Your boyfriend's (**mon copain**)?
4 Your girlfriend's (**ma copine**)?
5 Your children's?
6 Your parents'?

Comprehension 1

Your secretary is checking your appointments for the week. Write the days and times next to the names of the people as you hear them.

Mme Pinot   _____

M. Michel   _____

Chef des achats chez Leroy   _____

Chef de production   _____

Chef de production et chef des ventes   _____

Comprehension 2

This is a transcript of a call made by an English secretary to a company in France.

Allô, bonjour... Oui?...Euh, je m'appelle Louise Hetherington, je suis la secrétaire de John Baker de Permatour à Brighton. Je vous téléphone pour vous dire que tout est arrangé pour la visite de Monsieur Baker chez vous la semaine prochaine. Je vais vous écrire aujourd'hui avec tous les détails mais je veux juste vous confirmer par téléphone que Monsieur Baker arrive en France lundi le treize avril à 13 h 40. Son numéro de vol c'est le BA 657 qui part de Heathrow à 12 h 45 et qui arrive à Orly à 13 h 40. Après il prend le TGV directement à Lyons pour arriver à Lyons vers 19 h 00 – l'heure exacte de son arrivée est 19 h 05. J'ai réservé une chambre pour lui à l'Hôtel Biarritz, rue Pont Lévy – c'est pour deux nuits. Il revient en Angleterre mercredi, le quinze avril, dans l'après-midi. J'espère que ça vous convient. Ça vous va...? Excellent. Je lui dirai que tout va bien pour sa visite alors. Merci bien et au revoir.

Now jot down the following details, so that the French secretary can inform her boss of Mr. Baker's plans:

1 date of arrival
2 time of arrival
3 flight number
4 type of train he will catch
5 name and address of hotel
6 length of stay
7 date of return journey
8 approximate time of return journey.

Vocabulary

midi (*m*) *midday, noon*

Pronunciation

Vowels in French are 'pure' (in other words, they are a single sound). To make a French **i** for example, do the following:
a) almost close your lips b) draw them to the side (as though you were saying *cheese*!) c) put the tip of the tongue against your bottom teeth d) say *ee*. Remember that, although this sort of explanation is a help, it is vital for you to listen to the tape and imitate the sounds as closely as you can.

Listen to the tape to hear the pronunciation of the examples given below.

1 Allô? Ici Martine Mitterand.
2 Il arrive lundi.
3 Je vais partir mardi.
4 Qui est le directeur?

Language structures

Questions In Unit 2 (p. 17) we learned how to ask questions with words like **qui, quand, où**. We also learned that you often reverse the word order – **où êtes-vous** instead of **où vous êtes**. An easier way of asking questions is to keep the same order but to raise your voice at the end of the sentence. **C'est une chambre avec salle de bains** can mean a) *It's a room with a bathroom;* or b) *Is it a room with a bathroom?*

Exercise 8

Listen to the cassette and say whether the six sentences you hear are statements or questions.

Three more ways of asking questions to note down in your file:

1 **Combien?**   *How much?*
   Combien de?   *How many?*
   C'est combien?   *How much is it?*
   Combien de nuits?   *How many nights?*

2 **Est-ce que?**
   Place this phrase in front of any statement to make a question
   Vous avez une chambre   *You have a room*
   Est-ce que vous avez une chambre? *Have you got a room?*

3 **Qu'est-ce que?**
   This complicated phrase simply means *what*.
   Qu'est-ce que vous voulez?   *What do you want?*

Listen to the cassette to hear the correct pronunciation of these three phrases.

Days of the week

lundi	Monday
mardi	Tuesday
mercredi	Wednesday
jeudi	Thursday
vendredi	Friday
samedi	Saturday
dimanche	Sunday

Verbs In an earlier dialogue we met the phrase **je peux** *I can*. It comes from **pouvoir** *to be able to*. Look at the forms:

SINGULAR	PLURAL
je peux	nous pouvons
tu peux	vous pouvez
il peut	ils peuvent
elle peut	elles peuvent

An important verb we met in this unit is **venir** *to come:*

SINGULAR	PLURAL
je viens	nous venons
tu viens	vous venez
il vient	ils viennent
elle vient	elles viennent

And **partir** *to leave* is another:

SINGULAR	PLURAL
je pars	nous partons
tu pars	vous partez
il part	ils partent
elle part	elles partent

Cultural briefing

French business people work hard, but they have many more holidays than their British counterparts. France has a great number of national holidays, which are usually religious festivals. This means that in some months, there are many four-day weeks. What is more, if the holiday falls on a Thursday or Tuesday, the French usually **font le pont** *make a bridge*, that is, they take Friday or Monday off as well.

The month of August is of course 'sacred'. Everyone flees Paris and the big cities to holiday homes at the seaside or in the country. Beware of travelling on French roads on the nearest weekend to July and the last weekend in August. You will find the rest of the French population on the road as well. Have a look at this list below; you will know which days to avoid when going on a business trip to France.

1er janvier	*Nouvel An*
1er mai	*Fête du Travail*
8 mai	*Fête de la Libération*
14 juillet	*Fête Nationale*
15 août	*Assomption*
1er novembre	*Toussaint*
11 novembre	*Anniversaire de l'Armistice*
25 décembre	*Noël*
Fêtes mobiles	*Lundi de Pâques (Easter Monday)*
(festivals with no	*Ascension*
fixed dates)	*Lundi de Pentecôte (Whit Monday)*

Progress check

1 You're phoning France:
  a) say who you are
  b) say where you are calling from.
2 Confirm
  a) your arrival in Paris on Thursday, 13 February
  b) you are taking the train from Paris to Saumur
  c) your arrival time at 6.00 in the evening
  d) you have a room booked at the Hôtel du Cerf for two nights.
3 Say you will return to England on Saturday, 15 February at 8.00 in the morning.

4 Confirm
  a) that two colleagues will fly out on 2 March
  b) their arrival in Saumur at 15.00 on Tuesday 4 March.
5 Say
  a) you have a meeting with M. Paul Roger on Friday, 14 February at 14.00
  b) you have a meeting with Sandrine Bernard on Saturday at 9.30 a.m.
6 Give
  a) your birthday
  b) the birthday of your partner.

UNIT **5** Aller et retour

In this unit you will learn how to …

- buy your railway tickets
- find out about train times
- know where your train leaves from
- understand and give simple directions
- make small talk to acquaintances
- count from 61–100+.

> ### STUDY TIP
>
> In this unit you have a couple of short reading passages to look at. Don't think you need to understand every word, or even most of the text. You can practise 'skimming' (reading to get the general idea) or 'scanning' (looking for the answers to specific information). Both are useful reading techniques.

Dialogue 1:   Au guichet

Listen to the dialogue straight through a couple of times. Then read the notes and work out exactly what it means. Once you feel happy with the meaning, listen again without looking at your book. Finally, look at the transcript below.

Paul and Claire are on their way to visit Thompson France. They arrive at Charles de Gaulle airport where they have to take a train to Paris.

Paul	Deux allers simples pour la Gare du Nord s'il vous plaît, Monsieur. Ça fait combien?
Employé	Ça fait 60F (soixante francs), Monsieur.
Paul	Voilà un billet de 500F (cinq cents francs). Je suis désolé, je n'ai pas de monnaie.
Employé	Voilà, Monsieur.
Paul	Merci. Le train est à quelle heure?
Employé	Il y en a un toutes les quinze minutes, Monsieur.
Paul	Quel quai, s'il vous plaît?
Employé	Quai numéro un.

Vocabulary

le guichet *ticket office*
la gare *station*
l'employé *clerk*

voilà *here (it) is*
le billet *ticket*
la monnaie *change*

le quai *platform*

Notes

1 **Au guichet** *At the ticket office.*
2 **Deux allers simples** *Two single tickets.*
3 **Un aller-retour** *A return ticket.*
4 **La Gare du Nord** One of the famous Paris railway stations for trains to and from the north.
5 **Voilà un billet de 500F** *Here's a 500 franc note.* More about numbers on pp. 45–6. Note the abbreviation **F** for francs. Here **billet** means *a bank note*; it can also mean *a train or cinema ticket.* You will

need to use it like that in Exercise 1.
6 **Ça fait combien?** *How much is that?* (Literally *that makes how much?*) One of the many ways of asking for the price.
7 **Je n'ai pas de monnaie** *I haven't any change.* More about this on p. 44.
8 **Le train est à quelle heure?** *What time is the train?* Notice the word order.
9 **Il y en a un** *There is one.*
10 **Toutes les quinze minutes** *Every fifteen minutes.*

Key phrases

Un aller simple/deux allers simples/un
  aller-retour pour la Gare du
  Nord/Angers
Voilà un billet de...
Le train est à quelle heure?
Quel quai?

One single/two singles/one return to the Gare
  du Nord/Angers

Here's a ... note
What time is the train?
Which platform?

Exercise 1   You are buying a ticket from Paris to Nice. Rehearse your part out loud and then write it in the blanks.

Vous   (*Ask for a ticket to Nice*)

_____

Employé   Aller simple ou aller-retour?

Vous   (*Ask for a return ticket and how much it costs*)

_____

Employé   140F (*cent quarante francs*), Monsieur.

Vous   (*Say you are sorry, you have no change*)

_____

              (*Ask when the train is*)

_____

Employé   A quinze heures, Monsieur.

Vous   (*Ask which platform it is*)

_____

Employé   Quai numéro 17 (*dix-sept*).

Now listen to the full dialogue on tape.

| Exercise 2 | Claire has the leaflet you see below: it explains how to get from the airport (**l'aérogare** (*f*)) to Paris. A confused fellow traveller asks Claire for help. Can you answer his questions? Remember that you don't have to understand all the leaflet. Simply read for the specific information your require. |

1 How long does it take to get into Paris?
2 How often do the trains leave?
3 Where do I buy a ticket?
4 Where can I get off?

PARIS ◀▶ AÉROGARES CDG (ROISSY)

ROISSY RAIL

un train pour être à l'heure

■ 35 minutes de trajet.

■ 1 départ toutes les 15 minutes (voir horaire ci-contre).

■ Des dessertes directes au cœur de Paris.

■ De nombreuses correspondances avec le métro et le RER.

DE PARIS AUX AÉROGARES CDG (ROISSY)

• **Vente des billets :** dans toutes les gares RER (lignes A, B, C).
• **Points de départ :** toutes les gares de la ligne B du RER entre Cité Universitaire et Gare du Nord.
— Monter à bord des trains affichés dont le code commence par E :ECHO, EDEN, ELAN, ERIC, ETAL ou ETEL : départ toutes les 15 minutes de 5 h 30 à 23 h 30 (voir horaire ci-contre).
• **Arrivée :** gare de Roissy-Aéroport Ch.-de-Gaulle.
— A la sortie de la gare, emprunter : soit la navette aérogare 1, soit la navette aérogare 2 (ces navettes desservent aussi le parc B).

DES AÉROGARES CDG (ROISSY) A PARIS

• **Points de départ :** prendre la navette aéroport :
— Aérogare 1 : Porte 30, niveau Arrivée.
— Aérogare 2 : Portes A5 et B6.
— Descendre à la gare SNCF Roissy-Aéroport CDG.
• **Vente des billets :** dans la gare RER de Roissy-Aéroport CDG.
— Prendre le train en correspondance vers Paris (voir horaire ci-contre).
• **Arrivée :** dans toutes les gares de la ligne B du RER situées dans Paris (correspondance métro dans 3 gares).

• **Tarifs au 1-1-85** (en 2ᵉ classe) :
— Aérogares CDG- Roissy ◀▶PARIS (métro et RER inclus) : 23,50 F.
— Aérogares CDG- Roissy ◀▶ PARIS Gare du Nord : 21 F.
— Carte Orange 5 zones.

Horaire valable jusqu'au samedi 28 septembre 1985, au-delà l'aéroport Ch.-de-Gaulle devrait être desservi par un train toutes les 7 minutes.

Exercise 3

Demandez les titres de transport RATP.

Paris sur le bout des doigts

Pour un nombre limité de voyages: le ticket. Il s'achète à l'unité ou par carnet de 10, il est valable pour un seul trajet. Seuls les tickets à l'unité sont en vente dans les bus. Dans le métro et le RER Paris, la tarification est indépendante du parcours; dans les bus, elle varie en fonction de la distance (1 à 2 tickets dans Paris, 2 à 6 tickets en banlieue). ***Pour circuler librement pendant 1 journée entière: Formule 1.*** La meilleure formule pour effectuer un nombre illimité de voyages pendant 1 journée, dans Paris et sa banlieue. Renseignez-vous aux guichets du métro et du RER. ***Et pour vos enfants: des tarifs réduits... voire très réduits:*** Tickets demi-tarif pour les enfants de moins de 10 ans, et voyage gratuit pour les moins de 4 ans!

Ask for all the RATP travel formulas.

Paris in the palm of your hand. Besides Paris Visite (see p. 8) the RATP offers you various possibilities: ***For a limited number of trips: the ticket***. Tickets can be bought singly or by 10 (ask for a "carnet") and are valid for one trip. Only single tickets are sold on buses. The fare on the metro and the RER within Paris city limits is fixed, on buses it varies according to the distance covered (1 or 2 tickets within Paris, 2 to 6 in the suburbs.) ***For unlimited transportation during one day: Formule 1.*** It allows you to take an unlimited number of trips during one day, in Paris and the suburbs. Inquire at metro and RER ticket offices. ***And for your children:*** Reduced rates... even very reduced rates. Half-price for children under 10, free travel for those under 4!

Paul and Claire arrive at the Gare du Nord. They have to make their way by métro to Montparnasse station. They have an information leaflet in both French and English. Read it through and search for the French equivalent of the following words. We have left space for you to write in the answer.

valid	_____	the suburbs	_____
singly	_____	unlimited	_____
sold	_____	inquire	_____
a trip	_____	reduced rate	_____

Exercise 4	At the Gare du Nord, Paul asks a passenger (**un passager**) how to get to Montparnasse. Listen to the way he does it and then read the French transcript. **Pour aller à...** means *to get to ...* or *how do I get to ...?*

Paul	Excusez-moi, pour aller à la gare Montparnasse, s'il vous plaît?
Passager	Vous prenez la direction Porte d'Orléans, jusqu'à la gare Montparnasse.
Paul	Merci, Monsieur.
Passager	Je vous en prie (*you're welcome*).

Now on the tape you will hear the same conversation, but this time *you* have to ask the questions. Before you start each conversation you will be given a different station to ask for. Practise the conversation until there are no hesitations! Note how the person you speak to says '**vous prenez la direction...**' (*you take the direction of ...*).

Comprehension 1

Listen to the train announcements on the tape and look out for the following information concerning Jane and Paul's train to Angers:

1 time of departure
2 platform
3 time of arrival.

Exercise 5	Now for some numbers. Listen to the tape where you will hear the numbers from 61–100 and the numbers 200, 500 and 1000. There is a gap for you to repeat them. Listen again and this time jot the numerals down. The numbers from 70 upwards become complicated, so try and work out the pattern. If you're not sure, look at the end of the unit for a list of numbers and how they operate.

Exercise 6	How well have you learned those numbers? Write down the numbers that your hear.

Exercise 7	This time, circle the numbers which are not the same as the ones you hear.

75   79   81   85   99   77   63   83   96   80

Exercise 8	Now listen to the second list of numbers again and make a note of the numbers you *did* hear. Check your answers with ours on p. 183.

Exercise 9	In the first dialogue you met **toutes les quinze minutes** *every fifteen minutes*. Have a look at the phrases over the page and try

translating them. This way you will work out that **tout** has more than one meaning and that its form changes according to its context. The answers are on p. 183.

1 Tout le monde.
2 Toute entreprise.
3 Tous les garçons et les filles.

Dialogue 2: Dans le train

Paul and Jane are now safely installed on their train. A fellow passenger starts talking to Paul. Listen to their conversation.

Passager	Vous êtes anglais?
Paul	Oui, je viens de Milton Keynes en Angleterre.
Passager	Et c'est votre première visite en France?
Paul	Oui, c'est ma première visite.
Passager	C'est un voyage d'affaires?
Paul	Oui. Je suis ingénieur commercial chez Thompson Manufacturing. Ma collègue et moi allons à Angers. Notre société a une nouvelle usine là-bas.
Passager	Vous avez appris le français en Angleterre? Vous parlez très bien.
Paul	Merci. Oui, j'ai appris le français au collège et nous suivons des cours de français depuis six mois chez Thompson Manufacturing.

Vocabulary

en *in*	**là-bas** *over there*	**depuis** *since*
premier(ère) *first*	**apprendre** *to learn*	**un mois** *month*
la visite *visit*	**le collège** *college*	
un voyage d'affaires *business trip*	**suivre** *to follow*	
	les cours (*m pl*) *courses*	

Notes

1 C'est votre première visite en France? *Is it your first visit to France?* **Premier** is the masculine form of the adjective. Note also that preposition **en** – we use it for *in* (**je suis en Angleterre**) and for *to* (**je vais en France**).

2 C'est un voyage d'affaires? *Is it a business trip?* It's good to know **Vous êtes en vacances?** *Are you on holiday?*

3 Ma collègue et moi *My colleague and I.* **Moi** means *me/I.*

4 Vous avez appris le français en Angleterre? *Have you learned French in England?* This phrase uses the past tense; we will learn more about it in due

course. For the moment, just note that it resembles the English structure *you have* plus the part of another verb we call the *past participle.* In this case, **appris** is the past participle of **apprendre** *to learn.*

5 J'ai appris le français au collège *I learnt French at school.* Look at the Language structures on p. 44 to see why we say **au collège**.

6 Nous suivons des cours de français depuis six mois *We've been following French courses for six months.* (Literally *we follow French courses since six months.*) See Language structures on p. 44 for a full discussion of **depuis**.

Key phrases

Je viens de... en...	*I come from ... in ...*
C'est un voyage d'affaires	*It is a business trip*
Je suis en vacances	*I am on holiday*
C'est ma première/seconde/troisième/ quatrième visite en France	*It's my first/second/third/fourth visit to France*
Ma collègue/mon ami et moi allons à...	*My colleague/my friend and I are going to ...*
J'ai appris le français au collège/chez Thompson	*I learnt French at school/at Thompson's*
Nous suivons des cours depuis six mois	*We've been following courses for six months*
Je travaille en France depuis trois mois	*I've been working in France for three months*

Exercise 10

At Angers, Paul and Claire take a taxi. On the way to their hotel, they have a short conversation with the driver. Below, you will see the transcript of the driver's part in the conversation. Read through it first and make sure you understand it (**montez** means *get in* from **monter** *to climb* or *go up*, and **bon séjour** means *have a good time* or *enjoy your stay*).

Now listen to the driver on tape and reply to his questions following the prompts. Repeat the exercise until you feel happy with your accent, intonation and speed of delivery, then write in your part if you wish. When you're ready, listen to a second recording of the dialogue, this time with your part included. Reply in the first person (**je**):

Vous	(*Hôtel Concorde, please.*)
Chauffeur de taxi	Très bien. Montez. Vous êtes anglais?
Vous	(*Yes, I'm English.*)
Chauffeur de taxi	Vous êtes en vacances?
Vous	(*No, it's a business trip.*)
Chauffeur de taxi	Vous parlez très bien français.
Vous	(*Thank you. I've been following a French course for six months.*)
Chauffeur de taxi	Voilà votre hôtel. Ça fait 40F (quarante francs). Bon séjour.

Exercise 11

Francine Deschamps works in a travel agency dealing with enquiries about transport. She receives a number of queries from customers. What do they want to know? (**Au Mans** means *to Le Mans*; you will find out why in Language structures.)

Pronunciation

En fait je suis anglaise.

You will have noticed many 'nasal' sounds in French: that is, sounds produced through the nose, such as **on** in words like **réception**, **ance** in words like **connaissance** and **en** in words like **ventes**. To help you hear the correct sound, hold your nose and say *on*. The result will be a little exaggerated, but it will allow you to feel and hear what the correct pronunciation is like.

Listen to the tape to hear the pronunciation of the examples given below.

1 Bonjour, je suis Monique Leblanc.
2 Je vous téléphone demain.
3 Mon prénom? C'est Jean.
4 Combien de personnes?

Language structures

Prepositions **à**

In French we need to say *at the school*, rather than *at school*. This means we combine **à** *at* and **le** *the*. That combination becomes **au**. Look what happens to **à** in combination with **la**, **les** and before words beginning with a vowel.

> à + le = **au** parc, **au** Mans, **au** Canada
> à + la = **à la** société
> à + l' = **à l'**entreprise
> à + les = **aux** compagnies

depuis

To say you have been doing something for a certain length of time, use the formula *present tense + depuis...*

> **Vous suivez des cours de français depuis combien de temps?**
> *How long have you been taking French lessons?*
> Literally
> *You follow*   *French lessons*   *since*   *how long?*

Negatives To make a positive sentence (**J'ai de la monnaie** *I have got some change*) into a negative one (**Je n'ai pas de monnaie**) place **ne... pas** round the verb:

POSITIVE	NEGATIVE
Je suis en vacances	Je **ne** suis **pas** en vacances
C'est un voyage d'affaires	Ce **n'**est **pas** un voyage d'affaires

Of the two parts, **pas** is the more important and in spoken French you often find that the **ne** disappears completely.

| Exercise 12 |

Now try out some of those new structures.

1 You are talking to a Frenchman in the train. Somehow he has got the wrong idea about you! Contradict him by saying you are not what he says you are.

Example: **Vous allez à Nantes? Non, je ne vais pas à Nantes.**

  a) Ah, vous êtes américain!
  b) Et vous êtes de York?
  c) Vous êtes avec votre femme?
  d) Vous êtes chef des achats?
  e) Vous parlez bien français!

2 You've put him right on those points. Now tell him you have been working for Thompson's for six years, you've been living in London for ten, you've been learning French for nine months and coming to France for the past six.

Verbs Present tense of verbs that end in **ir**

Example: **finir** *to finish*

The last sort of verbs is those ending in **ir**. To form, take the infinitive, remove the **ir** and add the following endings: **is, is, it, issons, issez, issent.**

SINGULAR	PLURAL
je fin**is**	nous fin**issons**
tu fin**is**	vous fin**issez**
il fin**it**	ils fin**issent**
elle fin**it**	elles fin**issent**

Numbers 61–100+

61	soixante et un	79	soixante-dix-neuf
62	soixante-deux	80	quatre-vingts
63	soixante-trois	81	quatre-vingt-un
64	soixante-quatre	82	quatre-vingt-deux
65	soixante-cinq	83	quatre-vingt-trois
66	soixante-six	84	quatre-vingt-quatre
67	soixante-sept	85	quatre-vingt-cinq
68	soixante-huit	86	quatre-vingt-six
69	soixante-neuf	87	quatre-vingt-sept
70	soixante-dix	88	quatre-vingt-huit
71	soixante et onze	89	quatre-vingt-neuf
72	soixante-douze	90	quatre-vingt-dix
73	soixante-treize	91	quatre-vingt-onze
74	soixante-quatorze	92	quatre-vingt-douze
75	soixante-quinze	93	quatre-vingt-treize
76	soixante-seize	94	quatre-vingt-quatorze
77	soixante-dix-sept	95	quatre-vingt-quinze
78	soixante-dix-huit	96	quatre-vingt-seize

97	quatre-vingt-dix-sept	200	deux cent
98	quatre-vingt-dix-huit	500	cinq cent
99	quatre-vingt-dix-neuf	1000	mille
100	cent		

70 in French is **soixante-dix** (60 + 10), 71 is **soixante et onze** (60 + 11), 72 is **soixante-douze** (60 + 12) and so on up to 80. 80 is **quatre vingts** (4 × 20), 81 is **quatre-vingt-un** (4 × 20 + 1) and so on up to 90. 90 is **quatre-vingt-dix** (4 × 20 + 10), 91 is **quatre-vingt-onze** (4 × 20 + 11) and so on up to 100.

For numbers over 100, you say **cent...** 101 is **cent et un**, 102 is **cent-deux**, 110 is **cent-dix** and so on. For numbers over 200, 300, etc. you say **deux cent...**, **trois cent...** and so on up to 1000 **mille**.

Cultural briefing

The Gare du Nord is just one of the six major railway stations in Paris. Trains for the South-West go from Austerlitz and if you are going to Nancy or Strasbourg you go to the Gare de l'Est. You will need to punch your ticket before getting on the train: look out for orange machines marked **Compostez votre billet**. You can buy tickets beforehand in England at France Railways Ltd., 179 Picadilly, London W1V 0BA.

It's good to be aware of the fact that the French Railway system is much more efficient and sophisticated than British Rail: you may wish not only to travel by rail in France rather than by plane, but also to effect deliveries in France by the *SNCF* network. The *TGV* (train de grande vitesse) network will be expanding throughout the 1990s, with the Pas de Calais, Lille and Brussels axis next in line for development. Currently you can go down south as far as Lyon and west to Bordeaux.

Progress check

1 You wish to buy a return ticket to Saumur. What do you say?
2 You have no change. What do you say?
3 You have missed the train you intended to catch. Ask for the time of the next train.
4 Ask where the platform is.
5 Tell the taxi driver
   a) it's your third time in France
   b) you're on a business trip
   c) you learnt French at school
   d) you have been taking lessons in your company for three months

   e) you are lost – ask the way to the rue Jean-Jacques Rousseau.
6 At the hotel, give your phone number (82-92-75).
7 You overhear the following. What do they mean?
   a) Bon séjour!
   b) Je vous en prie!
   c) Je ne suis pas en vacances.

UNIT 6 Chambre numéro 200

In this unit you will learn how to …

- check in at a hotel
- talk a little about hotel facilities
- give the time with more confidence
- find more permanent accommodation in France
- express likes and dislikes.

Dialogue 1a: **Arrivée à l'hôtel**

Claire arrives at her hotel and goes to check in. Listen to the dialogue a couple of times before you work through the notes.

Claire	Bonsoir, Monsieur. J'ai une chambre réservée au nom de Stevenson.
Réceptionniste	Ah, oui, Mademoiselle Stevenson. Vous êtes en déplacement pour la société Thompson, n'est-ce pas?
Claire	Oui, je suis responsable du personnel.
Réceptionniste	Vous avez une pièce d'identité?
Claire	Voilà mon passeport.
Réceptionniste	Merci, Mademoiselle. Voulez-vous bien remplir cette fiche?
Claire	Oui, bien sûr.

Vocabulary

en déplacement *on a (business) trip*
responsable *responsible*

une pièce d'identité *means of identification*
le passeport *passport*

remplir *to fill in*
la fiche *form*
bien sûr *of course*

Notes

1 **Vous êtes en déplacement pour la société Thompson** *You're on a (business) trip from Thompson's.*

2 **N'est-ce pas?** *Aren't you?, Don't you?, Can't you?*, etc. depending on context.

3 **Je suis responsable du personnel** *I am responsible for personnel.*

4 **Voulez-vous remplir la fiche?** *Do you want to fill in the form?* Think of the microfiche in the library and you will remember the French for *form*.

Key phrases

J'ai une chambre réservée au nom de...	*I have a room reserved in the name of ...*
Voilà mon passeport	*Here's my passport*
Voilà la fiche	*Here's my form*
Oui, bien sûr	*Yes, of course/sure*

Dialogue 1b: Arrivée à l'hôtel

The receptionist gives Claire the key and she asks whether the hotel has a restaurant.

Réceptionniste Voilà votre clef. C'est la chambre numéro deux cent, avec salle de bains.

Claire Est-ce qu'il y a un restaurant?

Réceptionniste Oui, il est ouvert de 19 h 30 (dix-neuf heures trente) à 22 h 00 (vingt-deux heures).

Claire A quelle heure est le petit déjeuner?

Réceptionniste A partir de 7 h 00, Mademoiselle.

Claire Merci, Monsieur.

Réceptionniste Je vous en prie. Bonne soirée, Mademoiselle.

Vocabulary

la clef *key*　　　　　　　　　**ouvert(e)** *open*
un restaurant *restaurant*　　　**le petit déjeuner** *breakfast*

Notes

1 **Est-ce qu'il y a un restaurant?** *Is there a restaurant?* **Il y a** *there is* or *there are* is a key phrase.
2 **Il est ouvert** *It is open.* The opposite of this phrase is **il est fermé**.

3 **A quelle heure est le petit déjeuner?** *What time is breakfast?* More about telling the time on p. 51.
4 **Je vous en prie** *You're welcome.*
5 **Bonne soirée** *Have a good evening.*

Key phrases

Il y a
Est ce qu'il y a un restaurant/un bar/un ascenseur?
A quelle heure est le petit déjeuner/le déjeuner/le dîner?
Bonne soirée!
Bonne journée!
(Il est) ouvert/fermé

There is
Is there a restaurant/bar/lift?

What time is breakfast/lunch/dinner?

Have a good evening!
Have a good day!
(It is) open/closed

| **Exercise 1** |

On tape you will hear one side of a dialogue between Paul and the receptionist at the Hôtel Concorde. You have to answer for Paul. When you are happy with your performance, look at the printed version below and fill in Paul's part. Paul starts the conversation. Your questions will be prompted by the presenter.

Paul　　　　　　——————————————

Réceptionniste　Ah oui, Monsieur Smith. Vous êtes en déplacement pour la société Thompson, n'est-ce pas?

Paul　　　　　　——————————————

Réceptionniste　Vous avez une pièce d'identité?

Paul　　　　　　——————————————

Réceptionniste　Merci, Monsieur. Voulez-vous bien remplir cette fiche?

Paul　　　　　　——————————————

Réceptionniste　Voilà votre clef. C'est la chambre numéro trois cent deux, avec douche.

Paul　　　　　　(*Is there a bar?*)

| Réceptionniste | Là-bas, Monsieur. |
| Paul | (*What time is dinner?*) |

| Réceptionniste | A vingt heures, Monsieur. |
| Paul | (*Thank you. Good evening.*) |

<table>
</table>

Exercise 2

How is your hotel vocabulary? Match these symbols with the French names or phrases.

1 le parking
2 l'ascenseur (*m*)
3 le téléphone
4 le téléviseur
5 les cartes de crédit (*f pl*) acceptées

6 la boutique
7 le gymnase
8 le sauna
9 la piscine
10 la navette aéroport

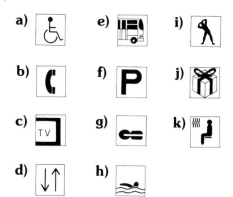

Exercise 3

Imagine you're staying at the Hôtel Concorde. Tell a French colleague all about the facilities it offers. Have a look at the symbols below and start off with the following phrases:

- **A l'hôtel, il y a...**
- **Dans la chambre, il y a...**
- **Ils acceptent...**

Don't forget to do this exercise out loud and to record yourself if you have that facility.

HÔTELS – ADRESSE	TÉLÉPHONE (TÉLEX)	FERMETURE		NOMBRE DE CHAMBRES			PRIX			RESTAURANT		Salon pour séminaire (capacité)	Langues étrangères parlées
		Hebdomadaire	Annuelle	Total	Bain ou douche, w.c.	Cabinet de toilette, w.c.	Chambre	Petit déjeuner	Demi pension	Prix	Capacité		
***Concorde 18 boulevard Foch	41.87.37.20 (720.923)			73	73		330-380	38		C	90	180	GB D-1

CONFORT

L'heure

Unit 3 introduced the 24-hour clock, with its simple translation from English to French: *14.25 quatorze (heures) vingt-cinq*. Telling the time in the ordinary way is not so simple. Look at the clocks below and work out the French system. Remember that here **moins** means *minus*, **demi(e)** means *half* and **le quart** means *quarter*.

- une heure

- deux heures

- deux heures et quart

- deux heures et demie

- trois heures moins le quart

- minuit/midi

- deux heures vingt

- trois heures moins vingt-cinq

- trois heures moins dix

Look at the section Language structures on p. 59 if you need more help.

Exercise 4

Now listen to the tape. You will hear the talking clock telling the time. Jot down the times you are given.

Exercise 5

Paul is waiting to check into his hotel. He overhears the receptionist giving information to guests about the hotel's services. Note down the times she gives in response to these enquiries:

1 A quelle heure est le petit déjeuner?
2 A quelle heure est le déjeuner?
3 A quelle heure est le dîner?
4 A quelle heure est-ce que le bar est ouvert?

Exercise 6

Paul is telephoning Thompson France to tell them his schedule for the coming four days. Look at his diary below and speak for him. Remember to use the first person (**je**). You may need the following vocabulary:

visiter l'usine   to visit the factory
déjeuner avec   to have lunch with
dîner avec   to have dinner with
quitter l'hôtel   to leave the hotel.

Monday

9.00.p.m. Arrive Angers

Tuesday
9.00 a.m Meeting with sales manager at Thompson France
12:00 p.m. Lunch with Claire & Marianne
1.00 p.m. Visit the factory

Wednesday
9.30.a.m. Meeting with production manager at Silex
2.30.p.m. Tour of Silex's factory with Gérard Leclerc

Thursday
8.00 a.m Breakfast with P. D-G of Lumarche et Cie
3.00.p.m. Visit to the building site [le chantier] with Robert Bernier

Friday
8.00.a.m. Leave hotel for Paris
10.45 a.m. Arrive Paris
1.00.p.m. Plane to London

Saturday

Sunday

Comprehension 1

John Davidson is coming out to France after Christmas and has asked Paul to book a hotel for him. He wants the following facilities:

a) a bath or shower
b) a radio, television and telephone in his room
c) a swimming pool and gym
d) round-the-clock room service.

Look at the brochures and decide which hotel would be the most appropriate.

180 CHAMBRES
dont 4 appartements et
1 appartement présidentiel.
Salle de bains (20 chambres avec douche), radio, TV, téléphone, mini-bar.
La plupart des chambres sont climatisées et insonorisées.

RESTAURANT ET BAR
"Le Chateaubriand": restaurant traditionnel.
"Le Thomann": bar d'ambiance.

4 SALONS RÉUNIONS
ET RÉCEPTIONS
de 20 à 120 m², tous insonorisés et climatisés.

AUTRES SERVICES
Salon de coiffure. Galerie marchande.

255 CHAMBRES
et suites.
Salle de bains, radio, TV couleurs, avec circuit vidéo, téléphone direct.
Service en chambre 24 h sur 24.

RESTAURANTS
"Le Faucon": restaurant de tradition française et internationale.
"Le Shalimar": coffee-shop, ouvert 24 h sur 24.

SALONS RÉUNIONS
ET RÉCEPTIONS
jusqu'à 200 personnes.
Équipement complet.

HÔTEL CLIMATISÉ
ET INSONORISÉ

LOISIRS ET SERVICES
Piscine. Gymnase. Sauna.
2 squash.
Centre d'affaires.

100 CHAMBRES
dont 2 suites et 1 chambre pour handicapé.
Salle de bains, radio, TV, téléphone, mini-bar.

RESTAURANT ET BAR
"Le Majoral": spécialités régionales.
Bar "Le Fustier".

4 SALONS DE RÉUNIONS
ET RÉCEPTIONS
de 60 à 240 m² et 2 bureaux clients.
Salons pour repas d'affaires (10 à 240 personnes).

HÔTEL CLIMATISÉ
ET INSONORISÉ

LOISIRS
Piscine avec terrasse aménagée et bar. 2 courts de tennis.

Dialogue 2a: A l'agence immobilière

Claire arrives with a colleague, Marianne, at a flat agency (**une agence immobilière**) to look for a flat for her stay in France. She explains what she needs to the agent.

Agent	Mesdames, bonjour.
Claire	Bonjour. Je cherche un logement. Je vais passer six mois ici à partir du mois de janvier. Je cherche un appartement à louer.
Agent	Un petit studio?
Claire	Oui. Pas trop grand, et pas trop cher..., mais pas trop petit, quand même, et assez confortable. Et je voudrais une salle de bains, pas une douche. Meublé, bien sûr.

Vocabulary

un logement *flat*
passer *to spend (time)*
un appartement *apartment*
louer *to rent, to hire*
petit(e) *small*

un studio *studio apartment*
trop *too*
grand(e) *big*
cher(ère) *expensive*
quand même *all the same*

assez *quite*
confortable *comfortable*
meublé(e) *furnished*

Notes

1 **Mesdames**   This is the plural form of **Madame**. **Messieurs** is the plural of **Monsieur**; **Mesdemoiselles** is the plural of **Mademoiselle**.

2 **Je vais passer six mois ici** *I am going to spend six months here.*   **Je vais** is from **aller** *to go*. The full forms of **aller** and a

discussion of how it can be used to express the future tense can be found in Unit 8 on p. 78.

3 **Pas trop grand** *Not too big.*   You can work out **pas trop cher** and **pas trop petit** by checking the vocabulary list above.

Key phrases

Je cherche un logement/appartement à louer	*I am looking for a flat/an apartment to rent*
Je vais passer six mois ici/une année	*I am going to spend six months here/a year*
Un studio pas trop grand/petit/cher	*A studio appartment that's not too big/small/expensive*
Un appartement assez confortable/ meublé/charmant	*Quite a comfortable flat/furnished/charming*

Dialogue 2b: A l'agence immobilière

The agent shows them some details of various apartments.

Agent   Eh bien, voici un charmant petit appartement au premier étage avec balcon. Celui-ci donne sur un beau parc. Voici un petit appartement avec un garage à côté. Et puis il y a ce studio avec une petite salle de bains; il y a un parking à côté.

Claire   Le studio, ça fait combien par mois?

Agent   Le loyer est de 2.500F par mois, charges comprises. Bien meublé: table, chaises, canapé, lit, télévision même. Regardez. Prenez votre temps.

Vocabulary

eh bien *well*
voici *here is*
charmant(e) *charming*
un étage *floor/storey*
un balcon *balcony*
donner (sur) *to give (on to)*
beau (belle) *beautiful*

un parc *park*
un garage *garage*
à côté *at the side, beside*
le loyer *rent*
par *per*
les charges *(f)* *bills*
compris(e) *included*

la chaise *chair*
le canapé *sofa*
le lit *bed*
même *even*
regarder *to look*

Notes

1 **Eh bien, voici un charmant petit appartement** *Well, here's a charming little apartment.*

2 **Au premier étage avec balcon** *On the first floor with a balcony.*

3 **Celui-ci donne sur un beau parc** *This one looks onto a beautiful park* (literally *gives on to*). More about **celui-ci** and **celui-là** *that one* on p. 59.

4 **Ce studio** *This studio apartment.* See p. 59 for all the forms of **ce**.

5 **Charges comprises** *Bills included.*

6 **Regardez. Prenez votre temps** *Look around. Take your time.* For giving orders/commands use the **vous** form of the verb. More about this on p. 90.

Key phrases

Voici un/une	*Here is a …/Here you have a …*
Il y a un parking à côté/un parc en face	*There is a car park next door/park opposite*
Le loyer est 2.500F par mois	*The rent is 2500 francs per month*
Regardez	*Have a look*
Prenez votre temps	*Take your time*

Exercise 7

Look at these rooms in flats that Claire and Marianne saw in the **agence immobilière**. What comments do you think they made? Use the phrases **celui-ci est...** *this one is ...* or **celui-là est...** *that one is ...* You may need to use these adjectives:

- petit
- cher
- grand
- beau
- spacieux(euse)
- confortable
- charmant.

Try and make as many phrases as you can and say them out loud.

Exercise 8

Expressing likes and dislikes

Read through this list of expressions, listen to their pronunciation on tape and decide what they mean (if you're stuck look up the words you don't know in the Vocabulary list at the back of the book):

- C'est bien
- C'est horrible
- J'aime assez
- J'adore
- Je déteste.

Now list them in order of intensity, from liking most (**1**) to liking least (**5**). Look back at the photos in the previous exercise and use these new expressions about the flats. You could say **celui-ci est horrible** or **j'adore celui-là**. Use your imagination!

Comprehension 2

Listen to Paul, Claire and Marianne going to see the flat that Paul has found. When you have listened to their conversation a couple of times, jot down the answers to the following questions:

1 Is the flat large or small?
2 Is it comfortable?
3 What does Claire like about it?
4 What furniture does it have?
5 Where will Paul leave his car?

Comprehension 3

Read these two information sheets for new houses in different parts of France. Look at the translation on p. 185 if you're stuck.

En Charente

Construction aux formes anciennes, matériaux traditionnels, murs blancs, tuiles roses. Elle comprend un rez-de-chaussée, un étage et un garage.

La salle à manger est à côté de la cuisine. L'entrée, l'escalier et le cellier sont à l'arrière de la maison. A l'étage, il y a trois chambres, une salle de bains, et une galerie.

En Haute Provence

Une maison adaptée au style régional avec un jardin et un balcon à l'étage des chambres.

Le rez-de-chaussée comporte un vaste séjour avec salle à manger et cuisine bien séparée. La salle à manger, la salle d'eau, la lingerie et le cabinet de toilette donnent sur le hall d'entrée. Un passage permet l'accès au garage.

A l'étage, il y a deux chambres, avec salle de bains et cabinet de toilette indépendant. La chambre ouvre sur le balcon.

1 Now, find the French for:
   a) entrance hall   e) walls
   b) stairs   f) dining room
   c) garden   g) kitchen
   d) opens on to   h) toilet.

2 Look at the plan and decide which of the descriptions belongs with it.

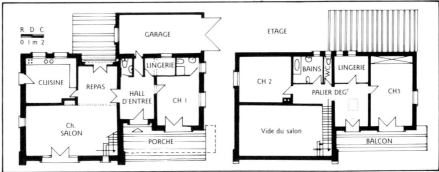

Pronunciation

The French **e** can appear in four guises: **e** on its own, **ê** with a circumflex, **è** with an accent grave and **é** with an accent aigu (sometimes called *e acute*). Take care with the pronunciation. The plain **e** is hardly pronounced at all (**je parle français**). The **ê** is pronounced like the *e* in *fed, red*; **è** is similar but has a shorter and more closed sound.

1 Ils sont en grève.
2 Accès interdit.
3 Restaurant Calèche, bonjour.

The **é** is pronounced rather like the *a* in *pay* – but don't add the *y* sound!

1 Mettez le canapé ici.
2 J'ai bien regardé.
3 C'est au rez de chaussée.

The French **c** is pronounced hard before the vowels **a**, **o** and **u**, sounding like the English *k*, as in **café**, **couleur**. Before the vowels **i** and **e**, the **c** has a soft sound like the English *s*, as in **cinéma**, **cinq**. The cedilla accent is added to the **c** to give it a soft sound before the vowels **a**, **o** and **u**, as in **ça**, **garçon**.

1 Le café.
2 Le cinéma.
3 Le garçon.

Language structures

Prepositions   **de**   *of, from*

The form of **de** changes, according to whether it is followed by **le**, **la** or **les**.

de + le	=	**du**	**du** seize décembre
de + la	=	**de la**	**de la** société Thompson
de + les	=	**des**	le bout **des** doigts

You can use these combinations to mean *some*: **du vin** *some wine*, **de la viande** *some meat*, **des crevettes** *some prawns* (you meet some of these words in Unit 7).

De remains unchanged before an adjective whether masculine, feminine or plural:

de bons vins
de nouvelle marchandise
de nouveaux modèles

Expressing time For times leading up to half past the hour, add the minutes to the hour.
Il est deux heures dix. *It's ten past two.*

For times from half past onwards, subtract the minutes from the next hour.
Il est deux heures moins vingt. *It's twenty to two.*

Exercise 9 Look at these signs which hang in several French shops. Out loud, practise this sentence pattern: **il est fermé/ouvert de... heures à... heures**.

Le matin
Ouvert de 8.30 à 12.00
L'après-midi
Ouvert de 14.00 à 18.00

	Ouvert de	à
Le matin	9 h	1 h
L'après-midi	2 h	5 h 30

Pronouns **celui-ci** and **celui-là**

MASCULINE SINGULAR	FEMININE SINGULAR	
celui-ci	**celle-ci**	*This one*
celui-là	**celle-là**	*That one*
MASCULINE PLURAL	FEMININE PLURAL	
ceux-ci	**celles-ci**	*These ones*
ceux-là	**celles-là**	*Those ones*

Example: **Je préfère celui-ci à celui-là.** *I prefer this one to that one.*

Adjectives **ce, cette, ces** *this, these*

ce (*m*)	**ce** studio
cette (*f*)	**cette** maison

Before a word beginning with a vowel or **h** use **cet**:
cet appartement
ces (*m/f pl*) **ces** logements

Agreement
In Unit 1 we learnt that adjectives must agree with their nouns, that is, if a noun is masculine singular, its adjective must also be masculine singular. Look at the following examples:

MASCULINE SINGULAR le restaurant est **ouvert**
le **petit** déjeuner

FEMININE SINGULAR une **petite** salle de bains
une maison **adaptée** au style

MASCULINE PLURAL	materiaux **traditionnels** murs **blancs**
FEMININE PLURAL	cartes de crédit **acceptées** aux formes **anciennes.**

Add an **e** to make a masculine singular adjective feminine.
Add an **s** to make a singular adjective (masculine or feminine) plural.

There are exceptions. Look at the following adjectives and try to spot the pattern:

cher (*m*), chère (*f*)   particulier (*m*), particulière (*f*)
spacieux (*m*), spacieuse (*f*)   précieux (*m*), précieuse (*f*).

Adjectives ending in **er** in the masculine form, take the feminine ending **ère**.
Adjectives ending in **eux** in the masculine form, take the feminine ending **euse**.

Beau is very irregular. Look at these examples:

SINGULAR	PLURAL
Le **beau** garçon	Les **beaux** garçons
Le **bel** homme	Les **beaux** hommes
(**bel** before a vowel or h)	
La **belle** femme	Les **belles** femmes

Position of adjectives

Most adjectives go after the noun they refer to (**un appartement** *spacieux*, **un studio** *moderne*); some very common adjectives, however, precede their noun. Examples are:

beau (*handsome*), **bon** (*good*), **grand** (*big*), **jeune** (*young*), **joli** (*pretty*), **petit** (*small*), and **vieux** (*old*).

With a noun they look like this: **un** *grand* **appartement**; **un** *petit* **studio**.

Cultural briefing

Chambres de Commerce
These are literally Chambers of Commerce, but they play a much more considerable role in French life than their British equivalents. It is compulsory for French companies to belong to **Chambres de commerce** which means that they hold records on who is doing what in the business world in their region. They receive monies from local businesses in the form of the **taxe d'apprentissage** which they spend on vocational training. Much of the language training, for instance, takes place through the local **Chambre de Commerce**. Because they have their finger on

the local pulse, it is well worth approaching the **Chambre de Commerce** in the region in which you are interested for help on local companies, agents or training opportunities.

Progress check

1 At the hotel, complete the following tasks:
   a) say you have a room reserved
   b) give your name and company
   c) hand over your passport
   d) ask if there is a bar and restaurant in the hotel
   e) ask if there is a television in your room
   f) ask at what time breakfast is served
   g) ask whether the restaurant is open.
2 On the phone to a colleague, give the following details about the hotel:
   a) it has a sauna and swimming pool
   b) it has a large gymnasium
   c) it has a small boutique.
3 Give the following details about your programme for the next day. You will be:

   a) meeting the sales manager at 9.30 a.m. at Tratex in Angers
   b) visiting the Purchasing Manager at 11.00
   c) dining with the managing director at 1.00.
4 Describe your colleague's apartment, mentioning:
   a) price
   b) size
   c) comfort
   d) number of rooms
   e) view
   f) location
   g) furniture.

UNIT 7 Qu'est-ce que vous prenez?

In this unit you will learn how to …

- reserve a table at a restaurant
- order a full meal at a restaurant
- order a snack meal at a cafeteria
- express more likes and dislikes.

Dialogue 1: Réserver une table

Gérard Leclerc has invited Paul and Claire (**il a invité Paul et Claire**) to dinner along with Marianne. His secretary phones the restaurant *Le Toussaint* to book a table (**elle réserve une table**). Listen to the conversation several times before reading the transcript and then the notes.

Employé	Restaurant Le Toussaint. J'écoute.
Secrétaire	Bonsoir, Monsieur. Je voudrais réserver une table pour ce soir.
Employé	Bien sûr, Madame. Pour combien de personnes?
Secrétaire	Quatre personnes.
Employé	A quelle heure?
Secrétaire	A huit heures.
Employé	D'accord. Une table pour quatre personnes à huit heures. A quel nom?
Secrétaire	Au nom de Leclerc.
Employé	C'est noté, Madame. Au revoir.

Vocabulary

inviter *to invite*

Notes

1 **Pour ce soir** *For this evening.*
2 **C'est noté** *I've made a note* (literally *it is noted*).

Key phrases

Je voudrais réserver une table pour ce soir/pour cet après-midi/pour ce matin	*I would like to reserve a table for this evening/for this afternoon/for this morning*

Exercise 1

On tape you hear the receptionist at the restaurant *La Calèche*. You are phoning to book a table for two at 7.30 this evening. Answer the receptionist's questions. When you can do this as fluently as possible, write in your answers in the space provided below.

Employé Restaurant La Calèche. J'écoute.

Vous _____

Employé Bien sûr, Monsieur. Pour combien de personnes?

Vous _____

Employé A quelle heure?

Vous _____

Employé D'accord. A quel nom?

Vous _____

Employé C'est noté, Monsieur. Au revoir.

Now listen to the model dialogue on tape – this time your part has been played. Check that what you said was correct.

Exercise 2

Your meal at *La Calèche* was so enjoyable that you decide to visit the restaurant again. You reserve a table for lunch there this afternoon at 1.00 p.m. for yourself and two friends. Rewind your tape and substitute the new details.

Exercise 3

On your tape you will hear the manager of *Chez Henri* taking bookings over the phone: fill in his diary with the correct details.

	Société Leroy	M. Legrand	Mme Dufour
Combien de personnes			
Jour			
Heure			

Dialogue 2a: **Au restaurant**

Gérard Leclerc, Claire, Paul and Marianne arrive at *Le Toussaint*.
Listen to part of their conversation.

Serveuse	Messieurs-Dames, bonsoir.
Gérard	Bonsoir. J'ai réservé une table pour quatre personnes.
Serveuse	A quel nom Monsieur?
Gérard	Au nom de Leclerc.
Serveuse	Oui. Voilà votre table, là-bas dans le coin. Je vous apporte la carte.
Gérard	Vous avez choisi?... Mademoiselle, s'il vous plaît.

Vocabulary

le coin *corner*　　　　　　**la carte** *menu*
apporter *to bring*　　　　**choisir** *to choose*

Notes

1　**J'ai réservé** *I have reserved.*　Look further down the dialogue to **Vous avez choisi?** *Have you chosen?* for another example of the perfect tense.

2　**Là-bas dans le coin** *Over there in the corner.*
3　**Je vous apporte la carte** *I'll bring you the menu.*　Notice that the **vous** (*you*) is placed before the verb.

Key phrases

J'ai réservé une table pour... personnes　　*I've reserved a table for … people*
Garçon/Mademoiselle, s'il vous plaît　　*Waiter/waitress (over here please)!*

Dialogue 2b: **Au restaurant**

The waitress comes over and takes Marianne's order.

Serveuse	Alors, qu'est-ce que vous prenez?
Marianne	Moi, je prends le poulet. J'aime beaucoup.
Serveuse	Vous ne prenez pas d'entrée, Madame? Cocktail de crevettes ou melon?
Marianne	D'accord. Je préfère le melon.

Vocabulary

le poulet *chicken*
aimer *to like*
une entrée *starter*

le cocktail de crevettes *prawn cocktail*
le melon *melon*

Key phrases

Moi, je prends le poulet — *I'll have the chicken*
J'aime (beaucoup) le melon — *I like melon (a lot)*
Je préfère le cocktail des crevettes — *I prefer prawn cocktail*

Dialogue 2c: Au restaurant

The waitress then takes Gérard's order.

Gérard	Pour moi, un cocktail de crevettes et un steak au poivre.
Serveuse	Comment voulez-vous votre steak, Monsieur? Bien cuit, saignant, à point?
Gérard	Je le veux à point, s'il vous plaît. Je n'aime pas le steak saignant.
Serveuse	Et comme boisson? Vin rouge? Vin blanc?
Gérard	Apportez une carafe de rouge et un pichet d'eau.
Serveuse	D'accord.

Vocabulary

un steak *steak*
le poivre *pepper*
vouloir *to want/wish*
bien cuit(e) *well-cooked*
saignant(e) *rare*

à point *medium*
la boisson *drink*
le vin *wine*
rouge *red*
blanc(he) *white*

une carafe *carafe*
un pichet *jug*
l'eau (*f*) *water*

Notes

1 **Comment voulez-vous votre steak?** *How do you like your steak?* Literally *how do you want your steak?* (from **vouloir** *to want* or *to wish*).
2 **Comme boisson?** *What would you like as a drink?* Literally *as a drink?*
3 **Apportez une carafe de rouge** *Bring a carafe of red (wine).* Use the **vous** form for giving orders or commands (see p. 90).

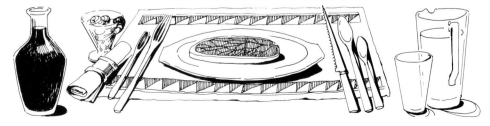

Key phrases

Pour moi un steak au poivre   *A peppered steak for me*
Un steak bien cuit/saignant/à point   *A well-cooked/rare/medium steak*
Apportez la carte/une carafe de rouge/   *Bring the menu/a carafe of red/a jug of water*
    un pichet d'eau

Exercise 4

How do you say:

1 I like melon
2 I like melon a lot
3 I prefer steak
4 I don't like prawn cocktail?

Exercise 5

1 Look at the menu at *L'Idée Hippo*. Decide on a menu for yourself (wine, entrée, main course and dessert) and order it (out loud). Remember to start with **pour moi** or **je prends**.

2 Order for your husband (**pour mon mari**) or for your wife (**pour ma femme**). You can be as extravagant as you like!

CARTE

Entrées

Melon nature	40 F
Cocktail d'avocat	45 F
Crudités	30 F
Terrine du chef	40 F

Plats

Escalope de veau	70 F
Ris de veau	80 F
Côte d'agneau	65 F
Entrecôte	75 F

Desserts

Mousse au chocolat	20 F
Crème caramel	20 F
Glaces	28 F
Sorbets	28 F
Fruits de saison	29 F

Exercise 6

Now listen to another short conversation which takes place next day when Claire and Paul are having a snack lunch in a café. **Manger** means *to eat*.

Garçon	Qu'est-ce que vous prendrez?
Paul	Un sandwich au jambon
Claire	Et moi, je prends une tarte aux pommes.
Garçon	Et qu'est-ce que vous allez boire?
Claire	Un thé au lait, s'il vous plaît.
Paul	Moi, je prends un café.
Garçon	Café noir ou café crème?
Paul	Un café noir.

Some of those words are new to you; match up the French with the English translation. If you're stuck, look up the words you don't know in the Vocabulary list at the back of the book.

1 tea with milk   **a)** un café
2 apple pie   **b)** un crème
3 black coffee   **c)** une tarte aux pommes
4 white coffee   **d)** un sandwich au jambon
5 ham sandwich   **e)** un thé au lait

Exercise 7

SALON DE THÉ

Café	1	6.80
Thé	2	10.00
Jus de Fruits		9.00
		11.30
Pâtisserie		10.60
		11.70
		59.40

Here is the bill (**l'addition** (*f*)) for four friends in a tea shop (**un salon de thé**). Study it first so that you know the price of each item.

We will be using the past tense in this exercise. You may wish to look at p. 70 for a full explanation of how it works. For the moment you need to know:

j'ai pris *I had, took*   **elle/il a pris** *she/he took*
j'ai bu *I drank*   **elle/il a bu** *she/he drank*

● Martine a pris un jus d'orange et une tarte aux pommes à 10F60.
● Jean-Luc a bu un café – il n'a pas pris de gâteau.
● Bernard a pris un thé et une tarte aux cerises (*cherry pie*) à 11F10.
● Nicole a pris un thé et un baba au rhum à 11F30.

We want you to calculate how much each person paid and to say out loud what each person said. You will need to say **je dois payer...** *I must pay* ... Complete the conversation first, then say out loud what each of the four friends said.

Martine   J'ai pris un jus d'orange et une tarte aux pommes. Je dois payer 19F60.

Jean-Luc _____

Bernard _____

Nicole _____

Now listen to the full conversation on tape; you may wish to press the pause button and repeat each sentence separately.

Comprehension 1

Listen to the conversation over dinner at *Le Toussaint*. Match up which person orders what:

1	Mme Dufour	**a)**	steak au poivre
2	Anne-Marie	**b)**	poulet flambé à l'Armagnac
3	L'homme	**c)**	sole à la Normande.

How was the steak to be cooked?

Comprehension 2

Read the following passage about cooking (**la cuisine**) in France. We have given you a limited vocabulary to help you understand.

Découvrir la France c'est aussi découvrir sa cuisine

La cuisine est très importante pour les Français et la cuisine française est connue partout dans le monde. Dans toutes les villes le voyageur peut bien manger sans payer très cher.

Dans les auberges, le propriétaire ou la propriétaire fait la cuisine. Ils ont appris les recettes de leurs parents ou grands-parents dans leur jeunesse. Ils les connaissent bien. Ils les aiment comme ils aiment leur pays, leur région et leur métier. Dans leur menu, ou à leur carte à un prix modique, vous trouvez des produits amoureusement cuisinés pour vous.

A Angers, Eric, propriétaire du Saint Gourmand, a 25 ans. Sa femme, Carole, a 22 ans. Eric a pour la cuisine la passion que d'autres ont pour la musique. Il n'a pas de spécialités. Tous ses plats sonts des spécialités. Le midi, le repas d'affaires, 59 francs, vous est servi en trois quarts d'heure.

Vocabulary

connu(e) *known*
partout *everywhere*
le voyageur *traveller*

une auberge *inn*
ils ont appris *they have learned*
la jeunesse *youth*

d'autres *others*
le plat *dish*

We have translated four of the more important phrases or sentences. Match them up with their French equivalent in the space provided for you.

1 They have learnt the recipes from their parents.

2 At lunch time, the business lunch is served to you in three-quarters of an hour.

---

3 They love them as they love their country, region and job.

---

4 In all towns, the traveller can eat well without paying too much.

Now note down and learn any words *you* feel are especially important; if you do not know what they mean, look at the translation on p. 187. To find out whether a noun is masculine or feminine, or what the feminine form of an adjective is look up the word in the vocabulary list at the back of the book.

Pronunciation

Listen to how the French slide one word into another, especially when the following one starts with a vowel. This is called making the *liaison*. Sometimes grammatical conventions help you to do this, for example, **ce** becomes **cet** in front of nouns beginning with a vowel or silent **h.**

Listen to the tape to hear the pronunciation of the examples given below.

1 Je vais   Je vais à Londres.
2 Nous   Nous allons à Paris.
3 Où allez-vous?   Vous allez-où?
4 Cet après-midi.
5 Cet enfant.

Language structures

Verbs   Perfect tense (or **passé composé**)

Use this tense for talking about the past, where in English you might use *I did* or *I have done*.

Use the present tense of **avoir** and add a past participle (equivalent to *done, said,* etc.). To form the past participle start with the infinitive, remove the **er**, **ir**, or **re** endings then add:

é	for *er* verbs
i	for *ir* verbs
u	for *re* verbs

Some verbs have irregular past participles. You will see some examples of both regular and irregular past participles below.

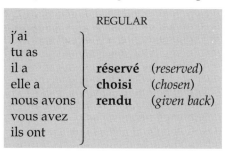

	REGULAR	
j'ai		
tu as		
il a	**réservé**	*(reserved)*
elle a	**choisi**	*(chosen)*
nous avons	**rendu**	*(given back)*
vous avez		
ils ont		

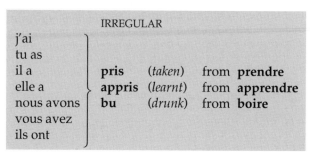

	IRREGULAR		
j'ai			
tu as			
il a	**pris**	*(taken)*	from **prendre**
elle a	**appris**	*(learnt)*	from **apprendre**
nous avons	**bu**	*(drunk)*	from **boire**
vous avez			
ils ont			

Exercise 8

The day after the dinner with Gérard, Paul told a colleague about the meal. Try as many sentences out as you can: you need to use phrases like **J'ai pris**, **j'ai bu**, **il a mangé**, **nous avons payé**.

Pronouns   Object pronouns

To say *it*, use **le** for a masculine word and **la** for a feminine word. Place it between the subject pronoun (**je**, **tu**, etc.) and the verb.

To say *them*, use **les** for both feminine and masculine.

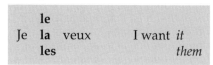

	le		
Je	**la**	veux	I want *it*
	les		*them*

Cultural briefing

Meals still play an important part in French life and you will certainly be expected to have a decent lunch with your French colleagues, either in the works canteen or at a local restaurant. Gone, however, are the days of the three-hour lunch session, certainly in Paris. You may be invited to a breakfast meeting: most French **cadres** or middle managers start the day from between 8 and 9 a.m. They continue working through until 7 or 8 in the evening and then face a long metro ride into the suburbs – hence the saying **métro**, **boulot**, **dodo** (*the metro, the daily grind, then sleep*).

Signing the contract often happens over a protracted lunch and in a highly convivial atmosphere. This is why being able to hold your own in the social sphere is very important. Detailed negotiations, however, will have taken place beforehand, so don't be fooled into thinking that making business decisions is taken lightly.

Progress check

1 Order a table for four at 7.30 p.m. on Saturday, 14 March.
2 At a restaurant, order the following items:
   a) chicken for yourself, melon for your wife, prawn cocktail for your colleague
   b) steak for all three (two well-cooked and one underdone) and red wine to drink
   c) black coffee for yourself and two white coffees for your companions.
3 At a cafeteria order the following items:
   a) tea with milk
   b) orange juice

   c) a ham sandwich
   d) one rum baba
   e) one apple pie.
4 Say you prefer:
   a) a medium cooked steak
   b) white wine.
5 Say you like:
   a) ham
   b) peppered steak.
6 Say you owe 96 francs.
7 Now say what you and your friends ate and drank at the cafeteria. Use the past tense.

8 Questions d'argent

In this unit you will learn how to …

- cash a cheque
- find out the exchange rate
- understand something about the French banking system
- open a bank account in France.

STUDY TIP

You don't need to understand every word of a reading passage in order to follow the general drift. Remember this when you reach the reading comprehension part of this unit. However, at this stage you may wish to invest in a good dictionary. The size depends on how comprehensive you want it to be and how portable. Try it out in the shop by looking up a couple of words that have puzzled you then compare the entries with those on the French side. Don't economise – a good dictionary is a wonderful investment. There is more about dictionary skills on p. 112.

Dialogue 1: **Changer des chèques**

Claire goes to the bank to cash some travellers' cheques.

Claire	Je voudrais changer cent livres en francs, s'il vous plaît. Quel est le taux de change aujourd'hui?
Employé	Vous changez des espèces ou des travellers?
Claire	Je veux changer des chèques de voyage.
Employé	Alors, c'est à 9,78 francs. Vous avez une pièce d'identité s'il vous plaît?
Claire	Oui. J'ai un passeport.
Employé	Voilà, Madame. Passez à la caisse.

A la caisse

Employé	Voilà, Madame. Cinq cents, sept cents, neuf cents, neuf cent cinquante, soixante, soixante-dix, soixante-dix-huit.

Vocabulary

changer *to change*
une livre *one pound*
le taux de change *rate of exchange*
aujourd'hui *today*

les espèces (*f*) *cash*
les travellers (*m*) ⎫
les chèques (*m*) ⎬ *travellers' cheques*
de voyage ⎭
la caisse *cashier's desk*

Notes

1 **Je voudrais changer** *I would like to change.* **Je veux toucher** *I want to cash.* **Voudrais** and **veux** are from **vouloir** and must be followed by an infinitive.

2 **Passez à la caisse** *Go to the cashier's desk.* Use the **vous** form to tell someone what to do. See p. 90.

Key phrases

Je voudrais changer... livres en francs
Quel est le taux de change?
Je veux changer des chèques de voyage/ des travellers/cent livres

I would like to change ... pounds into francs
What is the rate of exchange?
I want to cash travellers cheques/one hundred pounds

Exercise 1	What would you say if you wanted to:

a) cash a cheque
b) exchange cash
c) find out the exchange rate?

Say each sentence out loud. Then rewind your cassette and check the dialogue to see if you were right.

Exercise 2	Christian works for a bank in France. Listen to his conversation with a customer telephoning to order travellers cheques. Find out:

a) how much he wants to change
b) what denominations he asks for
c) what documentation he will have to produce
d) what time he will call in at the bank to collect the cheques.

Comprehension 1   Before he went to France, Paul wrote to several banks asking about banking services and information on opening an account. The leaflet over the page was amongst the information he received from the Crédit Lyonnais.

Avoir un compte au Crédit Lyonnais...

- Pouvoir retirer de l'argent un dimanche, ou un soir à minuit, quand les banques sont fermées...
- Être sûr de trouver l'argent partout, en voyage...
- Ne plus être obligé de penser à payer le téléphone, l'eau, le gaz, l'électricité...
- Disposer d'un moyen commode pour toucher votre salaire et toutes vos rentrées d'argent régulières...
- Payer vos achats en signant simplement la facture, en France comme à l'étranger...
- Faire plus pour la sécurité des vôtres, avec une cotisation modique...
- Placer vos papiers et vos objets de valeur dans un abri inviolable...

Voici quelques-uns des services dont vous pouvez bénéficier au Crédit Lyonnais grâce à votre Compte-Chèques et à votre Carte Bleue. Ces services ont été conçus pour vous simplifier la vie, vous aider à mieux gérer votre budget et vous garantir une meilleure sécurité.

Find the French for:

1 an account
2 to withdraw money
3 when the banks are shut
4 to pay the telephone and water bill
5 by simply signing the bill
6 a modest payment
7 to manage your budget.

If you're having trouble, the translation on p. 188 should help you. When you've finished look at the answers on p. 187.

Dialogue 2: Ouvrir un compte

Paul decides to open a bank account (**ouvrir un compte**). This is his conversation with the bank clerk.

Employé	Vous désirez, Monsieur?
Paul	Je vais travailler ici pendant six mois à partir de janvier et je voudrais ouvrir un compte courant.
Employé	Oui. Vous avez une pièce d'identité, Monsieur?
Paul	Oui. Tenez, voilà mon passeport.
Employé	Monsieur Smith? Vous êtes anglais?
Paul	Oui, Monsieur.
Employé	Il faut un compte étranger en francs. Vous avez une adresse en France?
Paul	Oui. C'est le numéro 6, rue St Etienne.

Employé	Bien, vous déposez de l'argent sur le compte aujourd'hui?
Paul	Oui. Je voudrais déposer cinq cents francs aujourd'hui. A partir du mois de janvier, mon salaire va être viré directement sur mon compte.
Employé	J'ai besoin d'une signature. Voulez-vous signer ici, Monsieur?... Merci.

Vocabulary

désirer *to want, wish*
pendant *during, for*
ouvrir *to open*
un compte courant *current account*

étranger(ère) *foreign*
déposer *to deposit*
l'argent *(m) money*
le salaire *salary*
virer (sur) *to transfer (to)*

avoir besoin de *to need*

Notes

1 **Je vais travailler ici** *I am going to work here.* Use **je vais** plus the infinitive of another verb to talk about what you will be doing in the future. You'll find another example with **va être viré**, below.

2 **Je voudrais ouvrir un compte courant** *I would like to open a current account.*

3 **Il faut un compte étranger en francs** *You need a foreigners' account in francs.* **Il faut** *it is necessary* is followed by a noun,

as here, or infinitive. It's an alternative to **je dois** (p. 67 Unit 7).

4 **Vous déposez de l'argent sur le compte aujourd'hui?** *Are you depositing money in the account today?*

5 **Mon salaire va être viré directement au compte** *My salary is going to be transferred directly to my account.*

6 **J'ai besoin de...** *I need ...*

Key phrases

Je vais travailler/habiter ici pendant six mois

I am going to work/live here for six months

Je voudrais ouvrir un compte courant/un compte-joint

I would like to open a current account/a joint account

Tenez, voilà mon passeport/ma pièce d'identité

Here, this is my passport/my identification

Je voudrais déposer...

I would like to deposit ...

Exercise 3

Imagine you are going to France for a year. Following the details below, answer the questions that the cashier asks you on tape:

- en France pendant une année
- à partir du mois, de septembre
- pièce d'identité – un permis de conduire (*driving licence*)
- addresse – 49, rue Aristide Briand
- mille francs à déposer sur le compte.

Can you remember Paul's details in the original dialogue? Rewind your cassette and answer the questions for Paul.

Comprehension 2

Look at the information on the Diners Club card then answer these questions:

1 What will the card allow you to do?

2 What is the advantage of the second card?

En France comme à l'étranger, DINERS CLUB votre passeport financier.

Une carte de crédit internationale : vous réglez d'une simple signature dans plus d'un million et demi d'établissements : boutiques, restaurants, hôtels, compagnies aériennes, et ce dans le monde entier.

Des distributeurs et des points de retrait dans le monde entier : Vous pouvez retirer avec votre carte jusqu'à 4000 F en France par période de 7 jours dans les agences de la BNP, de la BARCLAYS, de la BANQUE WORMS et de CHEQUE POINT. Et à l'étranger, l'équivalent de 1000 $ US en devises locales dans plus de 27,000 distributeurs automatiques au Canada, au Japon, en Angleterre et aux U.S.A. ainsi que dans tous les bureaux Diners Club dans le monde.

Une protection en cas de perte ou de vol : Il vous suffit de nous téléphoner au (1) 47.62.75 75, vous êtes entièrement protégé contre toute utilisation frauduleuse de votre carte Diners Club.

Une réserve d'argent grâce au crédit permanent : Diners Club vous offre un crédit de 3.000 à 140.000 F, que vous pourrez utiliser en toute sécurité. Ainsi, vous aurez le choix, chaque mois de régler vos achats en France et dans le monde entier au comptant, en trois versements (avec 45 F de frais forfaitaires) ou à crédit. Si vous souhaitez bénéficier de ce service, il vous suffit de le mentionner sur votre demande de carte.

Votre deuxième carte Diners Club : pour 285 F/an, vous pouvez la faire établir au nom de votre conjoint ou au nom d'un autre membre de votre famille.

Exercise 4

On tape you will hear four customers asking Christian questions about bank facilities. What do they ask?

Vocabulary

les quittances (*f*) *bills*   **le chéquier** (*m*) *cheque book*   **les impôts** (*m*) *taxes*

Pronunciation

You will have noticed that many letters in French words are not pronounced at all – especially final consonants. The **s** at the end of many words is silent (**je vais, tu vas**), unless it is followed by a vowel (**nous allons, vous allez**). This is important for words like **anglais** (with the silent s) and **anglaise**, where the **s** is pronounced.

Listen to the tape to hear the pronunciation of the examples given below.

1 Je prends celui-ci.
2 Tu t'en vas maintenant?
3 Ils arrivent jeudi.
4 Ils partent demain.

Language structures

Verbs   The infinitive

In this unit you have met a number of verbs with all types of ending. Look at this table with some of the more important ones.

er	ir	er
payer *to pay* **changer** *to change* **retirer** *to withdraw* **gérer** *to manage* **trouver** *to find*	**garantir** *to guarantee*	**remettre** *to pay in*

Some verbs are always followed by the infinitive of another verb. Look at these examples:

vouloir *to want*
je voudrais changer *I would like to change*

pouvoir *to be able to*
vous pouvez retirer *you can withdraw*

> **il faut** *it is necessary*
> **il faut passer à la caisse** *you need to go to the till*

The infinitive can also be used, where English would use the present participle.

Example: **Voir, c'est croire**   *Seeing is believing!*

There are more examples of this on p. 74.

Future with **aller**

You can easily talk about the future by using the present tense of **aller** *to go* + an infinitive:

Je vais	
tu vas	
il va	changer un chèque
elle va	
nous allons	
vous allez	retirer de l'argent
ils vont	
elles vont	

Adjectives   Possessive adjectives

Use	**votre**	with a	singular	noun to mean *your*
	vos		plural	
	notre		singular	*our*
	nos		plural	

SINGULAR	PLURAL
votre salaire	vos collègues
votre banque	vos rentrées d'argent
notre entreprise	nos passeports
notre pays	nos pièces d'identité

| **Exercise 5** |

You're in the bank. How do you say:

1 I am going to change a travellers' cheque
2 I am going to withdraw some money
3 I am going to open an account
4 I am going to cash a cheque
5 I am going to pay the electricity bill?

Cultural briefing

You should know enough now to understand the following passage about French currency.

L'argent français.

En France, l'unité monétaire est le franc. Cent centimes font un franc. Il y a des pièces d'un franc, deux francs, cinq francs et dix francs. Il y a aussi des pièces de cinq, dix, vingt, et cinquante centimes. Il y a des billets de vingt francs, cinquante francs, cent francs, deux cents francs, cinq cents francs et mille francs.

As in the United Kingdom, France has a number of financial institutions which specialise in different areas. There are a number of 'mutual banks' such as the *Crédit Agricole, Crédit Coopératif* and *Crédit Mutuel,* all of which have grown out of the co-operative movement and have members. These banks are expanding and moving out of their traditional sectors towards national and international banking.

You will certainly see many branches of the *Caisse d'Épargne* (or Savings Bank). This is the traditional type of Savings Bank with tax-free accounts for investors.

BNP (la Banque Nationale Populaire) and *Crédit Lyonnais* are High Street Banks. These institutions are nationalised: they also hold seats on a number of boards of private companies.

How do the French spend their money? Traditionally, food has always been an important element in the monthly budget – now it is housing. Mortgages and housing saving schemes (**plans d'épargne logement**) were introduced in the 1960s with the result that 55 per cent of the French now own their own home. They can find it difficult to pay back these loans due to variable interest rates and unemployment; a new law was introduced in 1990 to enable people to reschedule or even wipe out such debts entirely. Life insurance and other saving schemes are also important in the French person's budget. As in other countries in Europe, people are worried about their pension now that the retirement age is 60 for men and women and state pensions do not keep up with inflation.

Progress check

1 At the bank, carry out the following transactions:
   a) ask what the exchange rate is today
   b) ask to change £200 into francs
   c) say you wish to cash ten travellers cheques
   d) hand over your passport
   e) ask if you can open a bank account
   f) give your address in France
   g) say you wish to deposit 700 francs
   h) say your salary will be paid directly into your account.

2 Explain the following advantages of your French credit card:
   a) you can (**vous pouvez**) withdraw money when the banks are closed
   b) you can pay your telephone, water and electricity bill
   c) you can pay for your purchases by signing the bill.

UNIT **9** Achats et ventes

In this unit you will learn how to …

- buy presents
- buy clothes
- ask the way
- talk about the future.

Dialogue 1: Dans la rue

Claire and Paul meet up (**ils se retrouvent**) in town. They ask a passer-by the way to the shops (**ils demandent le chemin**).

Paul	Pardon, Madame. Pouvez-vous nous dire où nous trouverons des magasins pour acheter des cadeaux?
Passante	Qu'est-ce que vous cherchez comme cadeaux?
Paul	Eh bien, des parfums, des vins de la région, des cassettes, des vêtements...
Passante	Eh bien, allez au bout de cette rue, tournez à droite, puis prenez la première rue à gauche. Là vous trouverez les magasins. Pour les parfums et les vêtements, il faut aller aux Nouvelles Galeries. Si vous voulez moins cher, il y a Euromarché. Les vins, vous les trouverez partout.
Paul	Merci bien, Madame.
Passante	Je vous en prie, Monsieur.

Vocabulary

se retrouver *to meet (one another)*
demander *to ask*
le chemin *way*
trouver *to find*
le magasin *shop*
acheter *to buy*

le cadeau(x) *present*
comme *as, in the way of*
le parfum *perfume*
la région *area*
une cassette *tape*
les vêtements (*m*) *clothes*
le bout *end*

la rue *street*
tourner *to turn*
à droite *(on the) right*
à gauche *(on the) left*
moins *less*
partout *everywhere*

Notes

1 **Ils se retrouvent** *They meet each other* The **se** here means *one another.*
2 **Pouvez-vous nous dire...** *Could you tell us ...*
3 **... où nous trouverons des magasins** *... where we will find some shops.* This is the future tense: for more about this construction see p. 91.
4 **Allez..., tournez..., prenez...** *Go ..., turn ..., take ...* These are all commands; look at p. 90 to see how they are used.
5 **Là vous trouverez...** *There you will find ...* This is the future tense again.

Key phrases

Pouvez-vous nous/me dire où nous trouverons/je trouverai des magasins/Euromarché?	*Can you tell us/me where we will find/I will find some shops/Euromarché?*
Allez au bout de cette rue	*Go to the end of this road*
Tournez à droite/à gauche	*Turn right/left*
Prenez la première rue à droite/à gauche	*Take the first road on the right/left*

Exercise 1	John Davidson is visiting Saumur during a visit to the French **usine**. He wants to buy some presents for his family. Using the information below, say what a French colleague might reply to his questions.

Example: Je voudrais des cigares pour mon père.
Il faut aller à *La Civette*, Place Bilange.

1 Je voudrais quelque chose (*something*) pour mon fils. Il est très sportif.
2 Je voudrais un beau cadeau pour ma fille.
3 Je voudrais un jouet (*a toy*) pour mon autre fils.
4 Je voudrais de bons vins.

Maison LELOGEAIS
Jouets: Jeux de Société, Peluches ...
6 Avenue du Général de Gaulle – SAUMUR
41 67 78 33

BEAUTÉ-SERVICE
Yvonne FREDET
Parfumerie
ESTEE LAUDER – SHISEIDO – YVES SAINT-LAURENT – DIOR etc
40, rue D'Orléans – SAUMUR – ☎ 41 51 06 39

SPORT 2000
TECHNIQUE & TEXTILE SPORT-LOISIRS LACOSTE
tennis, golf, ski, natation, danse, musculation, running, sports d'équipe
Votre magasin SPORT 2000
GT Sport, 11 rue St Jean – 49400 SAUMUR   *Tél. 41 51 28 35*

CADEAUX – SOUVENIRS   VITRINES A CIGARES CLIMATISÉES
La Civette TABAC
3, Place Bilange (prés du Théâtre) **49400 SAUMUR Tél. 41 51 14 55**
Ouvert tous les jours de 7 H 30 à 19 H 30

Prêt à Porter Féminin   *Madeleine* **Lambert**
Rayon Spécial Grandes Tailles
29, Place Bilange – SAUMUR   ☎ **41 51 07 86**

CAVES DE GRENELLE

Méthode Champenoise – Méthode traditionnelle

SAUMUR BRUT – MÉTHODE AROMATISÉE:
Pêche Impériale – Poire Impériale – Orange Impériale – Myrtille Impériale

Caves de Grenelle   20 rue Marceau   49400 SAUMUR
Tél. : 41.50.17.63 — Fax: 41.50.83.65

| **Exercise 2** | Now listen to the receptionist telling John Davidson how to get to all these shops. He is staying at the Hôtel Anne d'Anjou, quai Mayaud.

Listen to the tape first, then read the transcript. Follow the directions with your finger on the map and work out what each direction means. (For a fuller explanation, see p. 90.) |
| --- | --- |

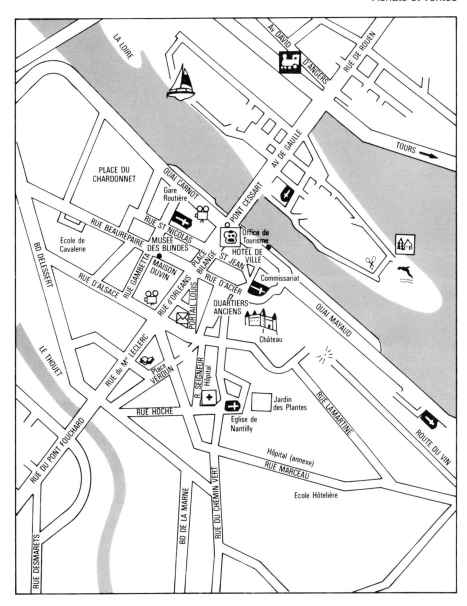

1 La Place Bilange? Bon, vous prenez la direction centre-ville (*town centre*) jusqu'à l'office du tourisme. Puis, vous tournez à gauche.

2 Avenue du Général de Gaulle? Vous prenez la direction centre-ville jusqu'à l'office du tourisme. Puis, vous tournez à droite.

3 Rue St Jean... Bon, vous continuez tout droit jusqu'à l'office du tourisme. Vous tournez à gauche et puis vous prenez la première rue à gauche. Ça, c'est la rue St Jean.

4 Rue d'Orléans? Bon alors vous allez jusqu'au centre-ville. Vous tournez à gauche et vous traversez la Place Bilange. Vous continuez tout droit et c'est la rue d'Orléans.

Exercise 3   **Où suis-je?**

Listen to the tape, then follow the directions on the map and say where each person is.

Vocabulary

devant *in front of*
le batîment *building*
une église *church*

traverser *to cross (over)*
un pont *bridge*
la gare routière *bus station*

un peu plus loin *a bit further*

Dialogue 2a: **Dans un grand magasin**

Paul and Claire go shopping in a department store (**un grand magasin**).

Paul	Excusez-moi, je cherche des disques compacts.
Vendeur	Le rayon musique est au rez-de-chaussée. Là-bas, juste après l'escalier roulant.
Paul	Et les livres?
Vendeur	Au sous-sol. Vous prenez l'escalier roulant, ou l'ascenseur, qui est en face de l'escalier.

Vocabulary

un disque compact *compact disc*
le rez-de-chaussée *ground floor*

l'escalier roulant (*m*) *escalator*
un livre *book*
le sous-sol *basement*

l'ascenseur (*m*) *lift*
qui *who, which*
en face de *opposite*

Notes

1 **Le rayon musique** *The music department.*
Le rayon livres *The book department.*

2 **Là-bas, juste après l'escalier roulant**
Over there, just beyond the escalator.

Key phrases

Je cherche des disques compacts
Et les livres?

I am looking for some compact discs
And (where are) the books?

Dialogue 2b: Dans un grand magasin

Claire buys a blouse (**un chemisier**).

Vendeuse	Bonjour, Madame. Est-ce que je peux vous aider?
Claire	Je cherche un chemisier.
Vendeuse	C'est pour vous, Madame? Vous faites du combien?
Claire	En Angleterre je fais du trente-six. Je pense que c'est quarante-deux.
Vendeuse	Qu'est ce que vous préférez comme couleur? J'ai ce modèle en bleu, blanc, ou rose.
Claire	Le rose me plaît beaucoup. Je peux l'essayer?
Vendeuse	Bien sûr. Le salon d'essayage est en face... Cela vous va très bien, Madame.
Claire	Vous pensez que c'est la bonne couleur?
Vendeuse	Certainement.
Claire	Vous avez une jolie jupe bleu marine en vitrine.
Vendeuse	Vous voulez l'essayer? C'est votre taille.

Vocabulary

aider *to help*
penser *to think*
la couleur *colour*
bleu *blue*
rose *pink*

essayer *to try (on)*
le salon d'essayage *fitting room*
joli(e) *pretty, nice*
une jupe *a skirt*

bleu marine *navy blue*
la vitrine *window*
la taille *size*

Notes

1 **Vous faites du combien?** *What size are you?* Literally *how much do you make?* Use the same verb, **faire**, to reply: see p. 90 for all the forms.

2 **Je fais du trente-six** *I am a 36* French sizes are different to British ones. A conversion chart is included overleaf.

3 **Le rose me plaît beaucoup** *I like the pink one a lot* (literally *the pink one pleases me*). The verb is **plaire**.

4 **Cela vous va très bien** *That suits you very well.* Notice the use of **aller** *to go* in this phrase.

5 **C'est la bonne couleur?** *Is it the right colour?* **Bonne** is the feminine form of **bon** *good.*

Key phrases

Je fais du 36	*I am a 36*
Le rose/bleu/bleu marine/blanc/me plaît beaucoup	*I like the pink/blue/navy blue/white a lot*
Je peux l'essayer?	*Can I try it on?*
Vous avez une jolie jupe/un joli chemisier en vitrine	*You have a nice skirt/pretty blouse in the window*

Exercise 4

Look at the pictures below. Go into the same shop as Claire and ask for what you would like. The **vendeuse** on tape will ask you the same questions that she asked Claire. When you have done the exercise once, you can rewind and buy something else!

un pantalon

une chemise

une robe

une veste

un collant

Collar sizes (men's shirts):

English	14	$14\frac{1}{2}$	15	$15\frac{1}{2}$	16	$16\frac{1}{2}$	17
French	36	37	38	39/40	41	42	43

Shoes (women):

English	$4\frac{1}{2}$	5	$5\frac{1}{2}$	6	$6\frac{1}{2}$	7
French	38	38	39	39	40	41

Shoes (men):

English	7	8	9	10	11	12	13
French	41	42	43	$44\frac{1}{2}$	$45\frac{1}{2}$	47	48

Suits (men):

English	36	38	40	42	44	46
French	46	48	50	52	54	56

Dresses:

English	10	12	14	16	18
French	38	40	42	44	46

Exercise 5

Look at this plan of a large department store. Match up the question and its answer.

1 Pardon, Monsieur. Pouvez-vous me dire où je trouverai le restaurant?

2 Pardon, Madame. Il y a un téléphone ici?

3 Le rayon vêtements femmes, s'il vous plaît.

4 Excusez-moi, je cherche la papeterie (*stationery*).

5 S'il vous plaît Madame, où se trouve (*where is*) le rayon musique?

a) Les disques, et cetera? Au rez-de-chaussée à côté des vêtements hommes.

b) Au premier étage, juste en face de l'escalier roulant.

c) C'est ici, au rez-de-chaussée, au fond.

d) Oui, Mademoiselle, au deuxième étage à côté des toilettes.

e) Au deuxième étage, près de l'escalier roulant.

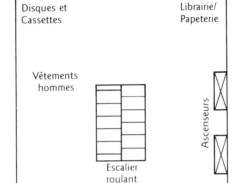

REZ-DE-CHAUSSEE

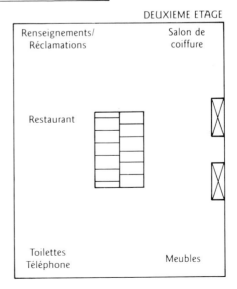

Comprehension 1

Rather than pay cash, you may prefer to use plastic. Read through the description of the carte Pass:

La carte Pass

La carte Pass a deux fonctions. C'est une carte de paiement. Vous n'avez besoin ni d'argent liquide ni de chéquier. Vous présentez tout simplement la carte et en utilisant votre code secret vous pouvez faire jusqu'à 3000F d'achats par semaine. Elle est aussi une carte de crédit permanent. Contre un remboursement de 150 à 450F par mois, vous disposez d'un prêt de 3000F à 9000F.

Now find the French for the following words:

a) cheque book
b) cash
c) credit card
d) repayment
e) loan.

Can you explain how the card works? You can either jot down some notes in English or try to paraphrase the passage, out loud, in French.

Comprehension 2

Philip Johnson is the owner of a hat factory in England. He has received the letter below from a French firm.

Saint-Avertin
le 15 mars 199-

Messieurs

Nous sommes importateur direct en chapeaux (cérémonie et mariée...). Nous visitons et sommes implantés sur toute la France. Pour compléter notre gamme de produits, nous cherchons de nouveaux fabricants.

Pourriez-vous nous envoyer une brochure ou des photos de vos produits avec un tarif, afin de connaître vos articles et envisager un rendez-vous lors de notre prochain voyage en Grande-Bretagne.

Dans l'attente de vous lire,
Veuillez agréer, Messieurs, nos salutations distinguées.

Henri Yves

Henri Yves

Vocabulary

la gamme *range*
pourriez-vous? *could you?*
envoyer *send*
afin de connaître *so that we
    can find out about …*

envisager *consider*
lors de *at the time of*
prochain *next*
l'attente *(f) expectation*

**veuillez agréer Messieurs,
    nos salutations
    distinguées** *yours
    faithfully*

Try to understand as much of this letter as possible. (If you have difficulties, there is a translation at the back of the book.) Then answer the following questions:

1 What is M. Yves's line of business?
2 Why does he write to Philip Johnson?
3 What does he ask Philip Johnson to do?

‖ Colours

blanc(he)	*white*	**noir(e)**	*black*
bleu(e)	*blue*	**orange**	*orange*
bleu marine	*navy blue*	**pourpre**	*purple*
brun(e)	*brown*	**rose**	*pink*
écru(e)	*cream*	**rouge**	*red*
gris(e)	*grey*	**vert(e)**	*green*
jaune	*yellow*		

Comprehension 3

Monsieur Yves' visit to Philip Johnson's firm was a success and he later telephoned to place an order for some goods. For each item, write down the colour, product number and price.

	Couleur	Numéro	Prix
a			
b			
c			
d			
e			
f			

‖ Pronunciation

No word in French ever sounds like an English one – even those which are straight borrowings from English such as many sporting terms (**le cricket, le rugby, le penalty**, etc.). Always attempt to pronounce such words **à la française** – otherwise you will be completely misunderstood! Take care too with brand or company names like ICI or Lucky Strike. You may find the spoken version utterly incomprehensible!

Listen to the tape to hear the pronunciation of the examples given below.

1 J'adore manger au McDo!   *I love eating at McDonald's!*
2 Il a acheté un T-shirt.   *He bought a T-shirt.*
3 Il porte des baskets.   *He's wearing trainers.*
4 Un pull en coton.   *A cotton pullover.*

Language structures

Verbs   Commands

Notice how we use the second person plural (the **vous** form) to tell people what to do or give them commands:

Tournez à droite	*Turn right*
Tournez à gauche	*Turn left*
Continuez tout droit	*Go straight ahead*
C'est tout droit/le premier tournant	*It's straight ahead/the first turning*
Prenez la première rue/la deuxième rue/la troisième rue à droite/gauche	*Take the first road/the second road/the third road on the right/left*
Traversez la place/la Place Bilange.	*Cross the square/Bilange square.*

(For more about asking the way, look back at Unit 4.)

faire *to do*, or *to make*

This is a useful verb in French – and it is irregular:

je fais	nous faisons
tu fait	vous faites
il/elle fait	ils/elles font

You need to use **il fait** when talking about the weather

il fait beau	*it is a nice day*
il fait mauvais	*it is a horrible day*
il fait du vent	*it is windy*
il fait du soleil	*it is sunny*
but	
il pleut	*it is raining*
il neige	*it is snowing*

Future tense

In Unit 6 we learnt how to talk about the future using **je vais** + the infinitive. In this unit we have met the true future tense – *I will …*

To form, add the endings **ai**, **as**, **a**, **ons**, **ez**, **ont** to the infinitive of the verb.

Example: **trouver**

SINGULAR
je trouver**ai**	*I will find*
tu trouver**as**	*you will find*
il trouver**a**	*he will find*
elle trouver**a**	*she will find*

PLURAL
nous trouver**ons**	*we will find*
vous trouver**ez**	*you will find*
ils trouver**ont**	*they will find*
elles trouver**ont**	*they will find*

ir and **er** verbs work in the same way:

je choisirai	*I will choose*
je prendrai	*I will take*

Some verbs are irregular:

venir	**je viendrai**	*I will come*
être	**je serai**	*I will be*
pouvoir	**je pourrai**	*I will be able to*
vouloir	**je voudrai**	*I will like*
avoir	**j'aurai**	*I will have*

Negatives In Unit 5 you learned how to make a sentence negative by using **ne... pas**. Now meet **ne... plus** *no longer* and **ne... ni... ni** *neither ... nor* ... Look at these examples:

Il ne vient plus	*He doesn't come any more*
Je n'aime ni Jean ni Luc	*I like neither Jean nor Luc*

In the next unit, you will see examples of **ne... rien** *nothing*.

Je n'ai rien à déclarer	*I have nothing to declare*

Cultural briefing

If you are in the retailing sector, you need to be quite sure who is in charge of buying in the stores which you are targeting. Some stores have a central buying system with all operations proceeding from Head Office. Other chains may give their local managers more opportunities to use their own initiative in selecting products to be sold, discounted or promoted. You need to check which system your store operates before entering into agreements with local managers. Be sure to have a clear idea of what is being offered and for how much; retailing in France is a tough business.

If you are simply doing personal shopping in France, shops will be open in the mornings from 9 till 12 and then again from 2 or 3 in the afternoon to 7 in the evening. The situation on Sundays is more complicated. Most shops are closed but there will always be a **boulangerie** (*f*) *baker's*, or **pâtisserie** (*f*) *cake shop* open in the morning. In smaller centres you will find the **boucherie** (*f*) *butcher's* and **épicerie** (*f*) *grocer's* open also.

Progress check

1 Ask a passer-by where the following are:
   a) Place Bilange
   b) Avenue Charles de Gaulle
   c) Rue St. Jean.
2 Say you are looking for the following items:
   a) clothes
   b) wine
   c) records
   d) books
   e) toys.
3 What do the following mean?
   a) Il faut aller à Prisunic.
   b) Prenez l'escalier roulant au rez-de-chaussée.

   c) Prenez la direction centre-ville jusqu'à Place Bilange et puis tournez à gauche.
4 You decide to buy a blouse (or shirt). Tell the assistant:
   a) what size you are
   b) which colour you prefer
   c) there are some blue trousers in the window …
   d) and ask if you may try them on.
5 Say:
   a) you will visit Tours tomorrow
   b) you will find perfume at Euromarché
   c) you will ask the receptionist.

10 Bonne route!

In this unit you will learn how to …

- ask for petrol at a service station
- obtain other services at a garage
- understand road signs
- deal with customs.

> ### STUDY TIP
>
> There are several ways you can improve your fluency when you speak. Of course, it is early days yet in your study of French and you will still have to concentrate on accuracy in structure and vocabulary, but there will come a time when you wish to speak faster and with less hesitancy. The more repetition you do, the better. At first you may simply want to get your tongue round the French: when you can do this, try to speed up your delivery until the point when you don't have to think about what you are going to say next. It's a good idea to go back to earlier chapters and do the oral exercises again – you will be surprised how easy they now seem, which will give you the confidence to work on accent, intonation and fluency.

Dialogue 1: ### A la station-service

Claire has arrived (**Claire est arrivée**) in France in January with her car. She has stopped (**elle s'est arrêtée**) at a garage to fill up with petrol.

Claire   Le plein, s'il vous plaît.
Pompiste   Normal, super ou sans plomb?
Claire   Super, s'il vous plaît.
Pompiste   Vous voulez que je vérifie l'huile et l'eau?
Claire   Oui, s'il vous plaît.
Pompiste   … Vous n'avez besoin ni d'huile ni d'eau.
Claire   Bon. Je vous dois combien, alors?
Pompiste   Alors, l'essence, ça fait 163 francs.
Claire   Voilà un billet de 500 francs. Je suis désolée. Je n'ai pas de monnaie. Vous me donnez un reçu, s'il vous plaît?
Pompiste   Bien sûr. Voilà, Madame. Au revoir et bonne route.

Vocabulary

s'arrêter *to stop*
plein *full*
sans plomb *lead-free*

vérifier *to check*
l'huile *oil*
l'essence *petrol (f)*

un reçu *receipt*

Notes

1 **Vous voulez que je vérifie l'huile et l'eau?** *Do you want me to check the oil and water?* (Literally *do you want that I check ...*)

2 **Vous n'avez besoin ni d'huile ni d'eau** *You don't need either oil or water.*

3 **Je vous dois combien, alors?** *How much do I owe you then?*

4 **Ça fait...** *That costs ... or that comes to ...* You can also use **ça fait** to ask how much something costs: **ça fait combien?**

Key phrases

Le plein, s'il vous plaît
Voilà un billet de...
Je vous dois combien?
Ça fait... francs
Je n'ai pas de monnaie
Vous me donnez un reçu?
Bonne route!

Fill her up please
Here's a ... note
How much do I owe you?
That comes to ... francs
I haven't any change
Can you give me a receipt?
Safe journey!

Exercise 1

These are some other reasons for stopping at a petrol station. Match the French phrases, pronounced for you on tape, with the English translation.

1 to wash the car
2 to check the brakes
3 to check the water
4 to check the oil
5 to carry out a service
6 to carry out repairs
7 to wipe the windscreen

a) faire une révision
b) laver la voiture
c) essuyer le pare-brise
d) faire des réparations
e) vérifier les freins
f) vérifier l'huile
g) vérifier l'eau

Exercise 2

Paul stops at a garage too. Complete his conversation with the attendant. Speak your part out loud and then complete the blanks in the written dialogue.

Then listen to the cassette to hear the full version.

Paul   (*Ask for a full tank.*)

_____

Pompiste   Normal, super ou sans plomb?

_____

Paul	(*Ask for unleaded.*)
	_____
Pompiste	Vous voulez que je vérifie l'huile et l'eau?
	_____
Paul	(*Ask him to check the oil and water and clean the windscreen.*)
	_____
Pompiste	Voilà. C'est fait. Ça fait 100 francs pour l'essence.

CARAVANING LOISIRS SAUMUROIS
MAGASIN PIÈCES DÉTACHÉES
TOUTES MARQUES
ATELIER RÉPARATIONS
"Le Fleuret"   49400 SAUMUR NORD   Tél. 41 67 83 73

POLE POSITION

41.43..48.00
**DES PIÈCES DÉTACHÉES
NEUVES A PRIX DISCOUNT**
221, Route d'Angers (face Leroy Merlin) ANGERS

**Centre de Contrôle
et d'expertise automobile**
Contrôle véhicules + 5ans • Contrôle sécurité
Contrôle partiel • Marquage ANTIVOL (agréé par les assurances)
CCEAA – Z.I. Beaucouzé – Tél. 41.73.25.50

Ets FOURNIER Fils
RADIATEUR AUTOMOBILE
NEUF – ÉCHANGE – RÉPARATION
TATOUAGE SÉCURITÉ AUTO
176, rue Bellevue – 49400 SAUMUR   Tél 41 67 31 31

Comprehension 1   Look at these garage advertisements. Where would you go if you wanted:

a) a car service

b) spare parts at a discount

c) caravan repairs?

| **Exercise 3** | Look at these pictures of road signs. See if you can link them up with their meaning according to the French Highway Code (**le Code de la Route**). Some of the words are rather difficult, so we have given you some clues: |

Vocabulary

interdit *forbidden*   **les marchandises** (*f pl*) *goods*   **rétréci(e)** *narrow*
la chaussée *road surface*   **le sens** *direction*   **l'endroit** (*m*) *place*

a) virage à droite
b) chaussée glissante
c) circulation dans les deux sens
d) endroit fréquenté par les enfants
e) sens interdit
f) interdiction de tourner à droite à la prochaine intersection
g) accès interdit aux véhicules affectés au transport de marchandises
h) arrêt et stationnement interdits
i) chaussée rétrécie.

Comprehension 2   **Location de voitures** (*car hire*)

Les nombreuses agences parisiennes proposent des voitures de marques françaises et étrangères. Les agences locales offrent des tarifs plus avantageux que les agences internationales, mais vous devrez généralement rendre la voiture là òu vous l'avez louée, et non dans une autre ville.

Vous devrez présenter un permis de conduire valable et une pièce d'identité. L'âge minimum peut être fixé à vingt et un ou à vingt-cinq ans. On vous demandera une caution substantielle, formalité dont vous serez normalement exempté si vous êtes détenteur d'une carte de crédit reconnue.

Vocabulary

étranger (ère) *foreign*
mais *but*
rendre *to return*
louer *to rent, hire*

la ville *town*
valable *current*
une caution *deposit, guarantee*

dont *of which, from which*
un détenteur *holder*
reconnu(e) *recognised*

Now can you answer these true/false questions?

	Vrai	Faux
1 In Paris you can only hire French cars.	☐	☐
2 Local firms are cheaper than international ones.	☐	☐
3 You can always take the car back to another town if it is more convenient.	☐	☐
4 You need to produce a current driving licence.	☐	☐
5 The minimum age for hiring a car is variable.	☐	☐
6 You have to pay a substantial deposit unless you hold a recognised credit card.	☐	☐

Dialogue 2: A la douane

Derek, a lorry driver with Thompson Manufacturing, is coming over to France from England with parts for the factory. Listen to his conversation with the customs official (**le douanier**).

Douanier Bonjour, Monsieur. Vos papiers, s'il vous plaît.
Derek Oui, les voilà. Permis de conduire, carte grise et certificat d'assurance.
Douanier Oui. C'est correct. Vous avez votre passeport? ...Bon. Vous allez où?
Derek A Angers. Je livre des marchandises pour l'entrepôt.
Douanier Vous n'avez rien à déclarer?
Derek Rien du tout.
Douanier Il faut que je fouille votre chargement. Voulez-vous garer votre camion là-bas, s'il vous plaît.
Derek Mais, c'est pas vrai! Vous en avez pour longtemps?
Douanier Quinze minutes, maximum.

Vocabulary

le papier *paper*
le permis de conduire *driving licence*
la carte *card*
le certificat d'assurance *insurance certificate*

livrer *to deliver*
l'entrepôt *warehouse*
fouiller *to search*
le chargement *load, freight*
garer *to park*
le camion *lorry*

maximum *at most*

Notes

1 **La carte grise** Literally *the grey card.* This is documentation for commercial traffic.
2 **Je livre des marchandises pour l'entrepôt** *I am delivering some goods for the warehouse.*
3 **Vous n'avez rien à déclarer?** *You have nothing to declare?*
4 **Vous en avez pour longtemps?** *Will it take you a long time?* (Literally *you have of it for a long time?*)

Key phrases

Les voilà. Permis de conduire, certificat d'assurance...	*Here you are. Driving licence, insurance ...*
Vous n'avez rien à déclarer?	*Anything to declare?*
Rien	*Nothing*
Rien du tout	*Nothing at all*
C(e n') est pas vrai!	*It's not true! You're kidding!*

Exercise 4

You and a colleague arrive at customs in your car. Answer the questions out loud and then complete the written dialogue.

Douanier Bonjour! Vos passeports, s'il vous plaît.

Vous (*You hand over your passports.*)

_____

Douanier Vous allez où?

Vous (*You're going to Paris. It's a business trip.*)

_____

Douanier Vous n'avez rien à déclarer?

Vous (*Yes some cigars.*)

_____

Douanier Il faut fouiller votre voiture. Garez-vous là-bas s'il vous plaît.

Vous (*You have a meeting at two o'clock. Ask if it will take long.*)

_____

Douanier Non. Dix minutes, maximum.

Comprehension 3

Paul has stopped to ask for directions. A motorist has broken down nearby. He is talking to the breakdown mechanic (**dépanneur**).

Listen to their conversation.

1 What has happened to the motorist?
2 What is going to happen?

Vocabulary

Qu'est-ce qui s'est passé?   **remorquer** *to tow*
  What's happened?

‖

Pronunciation

There are many regional differences between accents in France, just as there are in the United Kingdom. French Canadians and French speakers in Africa sound even more different – so be prepared to hear accents you may not be accustomed to. In France, the main difference in accent is that between the South and the North. Southerners tend to speak more slowly, with a more nasal pronunciation and a more noticeable final **e**. The **accent pointu** of the North is more akin to British received pronunciation, or standard *BBC* English.

Listen to the tape to hear the pronunciation of the examples given below.

1 J'adore la campagne.
2 Je n'aime pas les fraises.
3 J'arrive tous les matins à onze heures.
4 Toulouse est une ville très sympathique.

Language structures

Verbs The past tense using **être**

In Unit 7 we saw that in French we talk about past events using the verb **avoir** as in **j'ai téléphoné**. However, some verbs need to use **être** instead. We have seen two examples in the introduction to the first dialogue: **Claire est arrivée** *Claire has arrived*, and **elle s'est arrêtée** *she has stopped*.

Verbs which take **être**:

- Verbs which involve motion (**arriver**, **monter**, **descendre** *to go down*, **aller**, **venir**).
- Reflexive verbs (verbs which reflect back on themselves and need an extra pronoun) – **s'arrêter**, **se lever**, **s'appeler**, etc.

You may have noticed that with these sorts of verbs the past participle (**arrivé**, **levé**, etc.) must agree with the subject and take an **e** (*f*), **es** (*f pl*) or **s** (*m pl*) ending where appropriate. Look at these examples:

je suis allé**(e)**	nous sommes allé**(e)s**
tu es allé**(e)**	vous êtes allé**(e)(s)**
il est allé	ils sont allé**(s)**
elle est allé**e**	elles sont allé**es**
je me suis levé**(e)**	nous nous sommes levé**(e)s**
tu t'es levé**(e)**	vous vous êtes levé**(e)(s)**
il s'est levé	ils se sont levé**s**
elle s'est levé**e**	elles se sont levé**es**

Cultural briefing

‖ You should be able to understand some of this passage which concerns driving regulations in France. We have given you help on the more difficult sections.

Pour entrer en France avec une voiture immatriculée à l'étranger, il vous faut:

- un permis de conduire valable
- un certificat d'immatriculation   *a tax certificate*
- un indicateur de nationalité autocollant   *a car sticker showing nationality*
- un triangle de panne   *a warning triangle*
- des ampoules de rechange   *replacement bulbs.*

La carte verte n'est pas obligatoire (*essential*). Une assurance tous risques (*all risks insurance*) est recommandée.
Le port de la ceinture de sécurité (*wearing of seat belts*) est obligatoire.
Les enfants de moins de dix ans (*less than ten years old*) doivent voyager à l'arrière (*in the back*).

En ville la vitesse est limitée à 50 km/h (*in town, the speed limit is ...*).
A Paris, la vitesse est limitée à 80 km/h sur le périphérique (*on the ring road*).
Ailleurs (*elsewhere*), la limite de vitesse est 90 km/h sur route, 110 km/h sur piste à double voie (*on dual carriageway*) et 130 km/h sur autoroute.

Progress check

1 At the service station ask:
   a) for the tank to be filled up ...
   b) ...with lead-free petrol
   c) how much you owe
   d) for a receipt.
2 At Customs:
   a) hand over your driving licence, green card and insurance certificate
   b) say you have nothing to declare.
3 What do the following mean?
   a) sens interdit

   b) arrêt et stationnement interdits
   c) virage à droite.
4 And the following?
   a) Il faut fouiller votre voiture.
   b) Garez-vous là-bas.
   c) Vous en avez pour longtemps?
5 How do you say:
   a) I went to Lille last week
   b) I got up at 8.00 a.m. this morning?

11 Si on allait à Paris?

In this unit you will learn how to …

- make small talk
- find your way around Paris
- understand some tourist literature
- understand something about French transport.

Dialogue 1: Faire des projets

One weekend, Guy Lamarque, a colleague, suggested going for a trip to Paris. They decided to go there by train. First of all they discussed places to visit (*des endroits (m) à visiter*) and their programme for the day.

Guy	C'est la première fois que vous venez en France? Vous connaissez Paris?
Paul	Non, je n'y suis jamais allé.
Guy	Si on y allait un samedi? On peut faire les coins touristiques: l'Arc de Triomphe, les Champs Elysées, la Place de la Concorde. Ça vous dit?
Paul	Ce sera très intéressant.
Guy	Vous aimez les musées? Ils sont fermés le mardi, mais ils sont ouverts le week-end.
Paul	Ça coûte cher la visite?
Guy	Ça dépend. Entre 15 et 30 francs. Le soir, on pourra aller au cinéma et manger au restaurant.
Paul	Ça me plairait énormément.

Vocabulary

un endroit *place*	**le musée** *museum*	**le soir** *(in the) evening*
la fois *time/occasion*	**coûter** *to cost*	**le cinéma** *cinema*
les coins (*m*) **touristiques** *tourist spots*	**la visite** *visit*	**énormément** *enormously*
	entre *between*	

Notes

1 **Vous connaissez Paris?** *Do you know Paris?* Use **connaître** *to know* for places and peoples and **savoir** also *to know* for things. See p. 109.

2 **Je n'y suis jamais allé** *I've never been there.* **Y** is another word for *there* and precedes the verb. There's another example in the next line.

3 **Si on y allait un samedi?** *Should we go on Saturday?* (Literally *if one went there on Saturday?*) French likes to use **on** *one* a great deal; it takes the same verbal form as **il** and **elle**.

4 **Ça vous dit?** *Does that appeal to you?* Literally *does that say to you?* From **dire** *to say.*

5 **Ça coûte cher la visite?** *Is the visit expensive?* Note the word order.

Key phrases

Si on allait...	*How about going ...*
Ça vous dit?	*Does that appeal?*
Ce sera très intéressant	*That will be very interesting*
Ça coûte cher?	*Is that expensive?*
Ça dépend	*That depends*
Ça me plairait beaucoup	*I would enjoy that a lot*

Exercise 1

This time Guy and Paul are in Angers. Listen to the tape and answer Guy's prompts out loud. When you are happy with your answers fill in the transcript below.

Guy C'est votre première visite en France? Vous connaissez Angers?

Paul (*No, I've never been.*)

_____

Guy Si on y allait un dimanche? On peut faire les coins touristiques – le musée, le château, le jardin public... Ça vous dit?

Paul (*That will be very interesting.*)

_____

Guy Vous aimez les musées? Ils sont fermés le mardi mais ils sont ouverts le week-end.

Paul (*Is it expensive to go in?*)

_____

Guy Ça dépend. Entre 20 et 25 francs. Le soir, on pourra aller au théâtre et manger au restaurant après...

Paul (*That would be really nice.*)

_____

| Exercise 2 | Look at these advertisements. Decide on at least three places to go and suggest to an (imaginary) friend that you go together. Don't forget to do the exercise out loud. |

Use the following expressions (see p. 34 if you have forgotten the days of the week):

- Si on allait à... un samedi?
- On peut visiter...
- Ça vous dit d'aller à...?

COMMENT FAIRE?	QUE VOIR?
BASTILLE • Prendre le bateau CANAUXRAMA au port de l'Arsenal (départ 10 h).* • Vous êtes pressés : au M° Jaurès, prendre la navette (1/2 h). Départ toutes les heures quai de la Loire sur le Bassin de la Villette.	**BASTILLE** Place de la Bastille Opéra de la Bastille Promenade de 3 h sur le canal St-Martin jusqu'au Parc de la Villette. Voûtes de la Bastille Ponts tournants et écluses Bicyclub Canal de l'Ourcq
CH. DE GAULLE-ETOILE • Prendre la ligne 6, direction Nation par Denfert. • Descendre à Trocadéro.	**CH. DE GAULLE-ETOILE** *Arc de Triomphe △ Champs Elysées
TOUR EIFFEL • Prendre le 69 à Champ de Mars-Suffren. Descendre à Solférino-Bellechasse.	**TOUR EIFFEL** Champ de Mars
PONT NEUF • Descendre à Pont Neuf.	**PONT NEUF** Pont Neuf-Croisière sur la Seine
QUARTIER LATIN ou St-Michel ou Eglise St-Sulpice ou Place du 18 Juin 1940.	**QUARTIER LATIN** Ile de la Cité. Marché aux fleurs. *Conciergerie △ *Ste-Chapelle *Notre-Dame Bd St-Michel *Musée Delacroix Couvent des Cordeliers △ Bd St-Germain

Comprehension 1

Read this passage about the Paris museums. Then fill in the grid to show when they are open or closed.

Le Louvre, ancien palais royal, est le musée le plus célèbre du monde. Vous y trouverez la Joconde de Léonard de Vinci, la Vénus de Milo et des antiquités égyptiennes et orientales. Il est ouvert le jeudi, samedi et dimanche de 9 h à 18 h, le lundi et mercredi de 9 h à 21 h 45, et fermé le mardi.

Beaubourg – le Centre national d'Art et de Culture Georges Pompidou – est ouvert de 12 h à 22 h en semaine et de 10 h à 22 h week-end et les jours fériés. Il est connu à cause de son architecture moderne. A l'intérieur, vous trouverez une bibliothèque d'information, un laboratoire de recherche musicale et le musée national d'art moderne.

Le Louvre

	lundi	mardi	mercredi	jeudi	vendredi	samedi	dimanche
9 h–12 h							
12 h–18 h							
18 h–21 h 45							

Beaubourg

	lundi	mardi	mercredi	jeudi	vendredi	samedi	dimanche
10 h–12 h							
12 h–22 h							

Dialogue 2: Voyager en métro

Paul and Guy discuss the Paris Métro system.

Paul J'ai pris le métro seulement une fois, en décembre, le jour de mon arrivée en France. C'est le même système que le métro de Londres?

Guy Ça marche comment à Londres?

Paul Eh bien, on trouve la ligne et on prend la direction: est–ouest, ou nord–sud. Pour les correspondances, il faut suivre les panneaux qui indiquent le nom de la ligne.

Guy A Paris ce n'est pas tout à fait pareil. On suit la direction de la station au bout de la ligne. Par exemple: nous sommes à Montparnasse; nous allons d'abord au Louvre; la station s'appelle justement Musée du Louvre – c'est très pratique – donc il faut prendre la direction Porte de Clignancourt jusqu'à Châtelet, puis la direction Pont de Neuilly jusqu'au Louvre. On y va?

Vocabulary

le métro *Underground*
seulement *only*
est *east*
ouest *west*
nord *north*
sud *south*

les correspondances (*f pl*) *connections*
le panneau(x) *sign*
indiquer *to show, indicate*
tout à fait *entirely*
pareil *similar, the same*

par exemple *for example*
d'abord *first of all*
donc *therefore*

Notes

1 **C'est le même système que...?** *Is it the same system as ...?* Use **...que** to compare one thing with another. **Même** is one word for *the same*, **pareil** is another later in the dialogue.

2 **Ça marche comment?** *How does it work?* Notice the word order.

3 **On y va?** *Shall we go?* (Literally *one goes there?*)

Key phrases

C'est le même système que...?
Ça marche comment?
On prend la direction: est–ouest, ou nord–sud
Ce n'est pas pareil
Il faut suivre les panneaux
Il faut prendre la direction...
On y va?

Is it the same system as ...?
How does it/that work?
You take either east–west or north–south.

It's not the same
You have to follow the signs
You have to take the direction...
Shall we go?

Exercise 3	Paul and Guy have chosen their programme for the day. Here is what they are going to do:

1 Visite au musée du Louvre.
2 Déjeuner sur les Champs Elysées.
3 Visite à la cathédrale de Notre Dame (métro: Cité).
4 Dîner à un restaurant sur le boulevard Saint-Michel.
5 Retour.

Using this information and the métro plan below work out the journeys that Paul and Guy would have to make if they went everywhere by métro starting from **Étoile**.

Example: **Pour aller à... il faut prendre la direction... jusqu'à...**
Don't forget to say each sentence out loud.

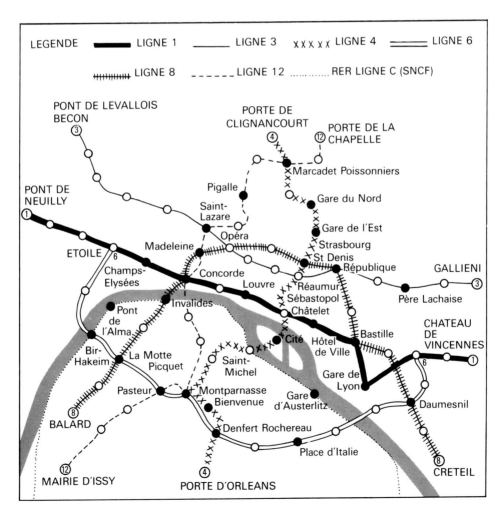

Comprehension 2

Paul and Guy heard a commentary during their trip on the **bateau-mouche**. Jot down the order in which you hear the following phrases:

1 Maintenant, nous passons sous le Pont Neuf.
2 Et maintenant nous arrivons à la cathédrale de Notre Dame.
3 Vous avez les Invalides sur votre droite.
4 Le Châtelet et un peu plus loin, l'Hôtel de Ville, sont à gauche.
5 Le musée du Louvre est sur votre gauche.
6 A droite, le musée d'Orsay.
7 Sur votre gauche vous voyez le Jardin des Tuileries.

Comprehension 3

Transports à Paris

Autobus

Le service d'autobus de la RATP est efficace et très étendu, mais pas toujours rapide à cause de la circulation. Il est particulièrement pratique pour la banlieue. Les arrêts sont signalés par des panneaux rouges et jaunes avec le numéro de la ligne. La plupart des bus circulent de 7 h du matin à 20 h 30: certains roulent jusqu'à minuit et demi. Selon le trajet, vous payerez 1, 2 ou 3 tickets, que vous pouvez acheter dans le bus.

Métro

Le métro parisien est l'un des plus efficaces et des plus propres du monde. C'est aussi l'un des meilleurs marché. Les lignes de RER (Réseau Express Régional) relient les banlieues au centre de la ville en un temps record. Vous pouvez acheter des tickets de métro à l'unité (5 francs) ou par carnets de dix (31,20 francs). Les billets pour le RER sont un peu plus chers. Le premier train de métro part a 5 h 30, le dernier vers une heure du matin.

Taxi

Vous pouvez héler un taxi, ou le prendre à une station. Vous payerez non seulement le prix indiqué par le taximètre, mais aussi un tarif qui est affiché sur la fenêtre du taxi, par exemple, un supplément pour les bagages. En moyenne, vous payerez 25,80 francs le kilomètre.

Vocabulary

étendu extensive	**bon marché** cheap	**affiché(e)** posted
à cause de because of	**meilleur marché** cheaper	**la fenêtre** window
circuler/rouler to run	**relier** to link	**en moyenne** on average
selon depending on	**un carnet** book (of tickets)	
propre clean	**héler** to hail	

Look down the following list of English translations and match each one up with its French equivalent. Then list the words you consider important and learn them.

1 The Paris métro is one of the most efficient and clean in the world.
2 On average, you will pay 25,80 francs per kilometre.
3 It is particularly practical in the suburbs.
4 Certain (buses) run till 12.30 a.m.
5 The RER lines link the suburbs to the town centre in record time.

Pronunciation

When pronouncing a French word you need to give equal weight to each syllable, unlike in English where one particular syllable is stressed and the others are glided over. Think of a word which exists in both languages (such as *imagination*): in French each syllable is pronounced separately and equally. In English the stress falls on the second *a*. The only example where this does not hold true is in the unaccented **e** (**je travaille**, **je mange**).

Listen to the tape to hear the pronunciation of the examples given below.

1 Imagination   Quelle imagination!
2 Compétence   Ça ressort de sa compétence.
3 Spécialiste   Il est spécialiste en droit.
4 Préjudice   L'entreprise a subi un préjudice.

Language structures

Verbs   **connaître** and **savoir**

Both verbs mean to know but are used in quite different ways.

Use **connaître** if you know a person or country.
Example: **Vous connaissez Paris?** *Do you know Paris?*

Use **savoir** if you know a fact.
Example: **Oui, je sais.** *Yes, I know.*

Here are the full forms:

je sais	nous savons
tu sais	vous savez
il/elle/on sait	ils/elles savent
je connais	nous connaissons
tu connais	vous connaissez
il/elle/on connaît	ils/elles connaissent

Prepositions

Many verbs are followed by particular prepositions – usually **à** or **de**. You need to be on the look out for them and to jot them down as they crop up. Look at the following examples:

> **Décider de**   Ils ont décidé d'y aller en train
> **Proposer de**   Il a proposé à Paul d'aller faire un tour

Pronouns   **cela**

Cela means *that*, **ceci** means *this*. **Cela** is used a great deal in everyday conversation and is shortened to **ça** when speaking informally. Look back at the first dialogue and count how many times it was used.

Expressing place   **y**

This is another little word meaning *there* (among other things!) and is neater to use than **là**. Place it before the verb as in:

> **On y va?**   *Shall we go (there)?*
> **Je n'y suis jamais allé**   *I've never been (there)*

Adjectives   Comparatives and Superlatives

To say something is *more* (beautiful) *than* use the formula:

> **plus** (beau) **que**
>   (joli)

Example: **Il est plus intelligent que moi.** *He is cleverer than me.*

To say something is *the most* (beautiful) use the formula:

> **le plus** (beau)/**la plus** (belle)/**les plus** (beaux/belles)

Example: **La femme la plus célèbre du monde.** *The most famous woman in the world.*

Exercise 4

Look at these sentences. Decide whether you would use the word **connaître** or **savoir**.

1 I know a nice little restaurant.
2 Do you know if Paul has left yet?
3 He knows how to swim now.
4 I know him quite well.
5 I know Italy quite well.
6 One never knows.

Comprehension 4

Listen to the tape. You will hear someone discussing her colleagues. Write down what you hear; then compare it with the transcript on p. 192.

Cultural briefing

If, like Paul, you have made arrangements to meet a French person at a particular time, you may find that you have to **patienter un peu** (*wait a while*). Many French people are not particularly punctual and don't take time so seriously as the British or the Americans. You will find, though, that when they do turn up, they will be elegantly and appropriately dressed for the occasion. Don't make the mistake of not dressing up for appointments or for dinner; in France, it is better to be over- rather than under-dressed. On the other hand, you don't need to turn up in a three-piece pin-striped suit either! In other words, you don't have to be conventional to be elegant – if the creased look is in, the French business man or woman will be wearing it!

It is also good manners, if you are invited out, to take a bunch of flowers for your hostess. Don't take a bottle of wine – French people don't believe that the British take food or wine seriously, so it is better to be duly impressed by what your host offers than to try to compete in the gourmet league! It is also likely that your host will already have chosen an appropriate wine to accompany the meal. Your wine may not be suitable and will certainly not be at the correct temperature.

Progress check

1 Say that you don't know:
    a) Paris
    b) France
    c) Jean-Paul
    d) how to swim.
2 Ask if it is expensive to visit museums in France.
3 Say you would enjoy it a lot.
4 Say it would be very interesting.

5 What do the following mean?
    a) Fermé le lundi et jours fériés.
    b) C'est le même système qu'à Londres?
    c) Il est ouvert de 10 h à 20 h le weekend.
6 Say:
    a) Beaubourg is more interesting than the Louvre
    b) London is bigger than Paris
    c) the metro is faster than the bus.

12 En cas de maladie

In this unit you will learn how to ...

- make an appointment for the doctor
- describe your symptoms
- understand medical instructions.

Dialogue 1: **Rendez-vous chez le médecin**

One day Paul did not feel well. Before going to see the doctor (**le médecin**), he telephoned for an appointment.

Paul	Bonjour. Je voudrais prendre rendez-vous pour aujourd'hui.
Réceptionniste	Un instant, s'il vous plaît... Pouvez-vous venir à dix heures et demie?
Paul	Oui, ça ira.
Réceptionniste	Quel est votre nom?
Paul	Smith.
Réceptionniste	Ça s'écrit comment?
Paul	S-M-I-T-H.
Réceptionniste	Vous êtes anglais?
Paul	Oui.

Docteur Patrick BELLIARD
MEDECINE GENERALE
CONSULTATIONS TOUS LES JOURS
DE 8H A 9H ET DE 13H30 A 16H
LE SOIR SUR RENDEZ VOUS

Réceptionniste	Vous avez l'assurance médicale?
Paul	Oui.
Réceptionniste	La consultation coûtera 90 francs. Vous vous ferez rembourser plus tard.

Vocabulary

le médecin *doctor* **plus tard** *later*
l'assurance médicale *(f)*
   medical insurance

Notes

1 **Ça ira** *That will be fine.*   (Literally *that will go.*)
2 **Ça s'écrit comment?** *How is that spelt?* **Écrire** *to write*; **s'écrire** *to be spelt* (literally *written*).

3 **Vous vous ferez rembourser plus tard** *You will be reimbursed later.*   **Se faire rembourser** *to be reimbursed.*

Key phrases

Je voudrais prendre rendez-vous pour aujourd'hui/pour demain/pour la semaine prochaine

I'd like to make an appointment for today/ tomorrow/for next week

Exercise 1

1 You're ill in France: you ring up the doctor and try to make an appointment for the same day at 10.00 a.m. What do you say?

2 That space is not available. You are asked if you can make an alternative time: you suggest tomorrow at 9.00 a.m. What do you say?

L'alphabet en français

Listen to the tape and hear how the letters of the alphabet are pronounced in French before you do the next exercise.

Exercise 2

Now listen to the calls received by the doctor's receptionist and fill in the grid below.

	Nom	Heure du rendez-vous	Jour
1			
2			
3			

Dialogue 2: Chez le médecin

Paul arrives for his appointment with the doctor

Médecin	Alors, qu'est-ce que vous avez?
Paul	Eh bien, j'ai mal à la tête et un peu de fièvre. J'ai mal à la gorge depuis quelques jours.
Médecin	Et vous toussez?
Paul	Oui, un peu.
Médecin	C'est une grippe. Je vous donne une ordonnance pour des antibiotiques à prendre trois fois par jour et un sirop pour la toux. Mais faites attention. Le sirop vous endormira un peu. Ne conduisez surtout pas si vous avez sommeil. Prenez aussi des fortifiants, par exemple de la vitamine C.
Paul	D'accord.
Médecin	Je vais remplir une feuille de maladie. Allez à la Sécurité Sociale pour vous faire rembourser.

Vocabulary

tousser *to cough*
un peu *a bit*
la grippe *flu*
un sirop *cough mixture*

la toux *cough*
endormir *to send to sleep*
le sommeil *sleep*
le fortifiant *tonic*

remplir *to fill*
la feuille *piece of paper*
la maladie *illness, sickness*

Notes

1 **Alors, qu'est-ce que vous avez?** *So, what's wrong?* (Literally *what do you have?*)
2 **Je vous donne une ordonnance** *I'll give you a prescription.*
3 **Faites attention!** *Be careful!*

4 **Ne conduisez pas si vous avez sommeil** *Don't drive if you feel drowsy.* (The French say *to have sleep* not *to feel sleepy.*)
5 **Une feuille de maladie** This is the form you need to be reimbursed for any medical expenses you have incurred.

Key phrases

J'ai mal à la tête/mal à la gorge/un peu de fièvre/mal au ventre depuis une semaine/quelques jours/hier
Faites attention

I have (had) a headache/a sore throat/a slight temperature/a stomach ache for a week/a few days/since yesterday
Be careful

Exercise 3

Imagine the following scenario. You are in France and have been feeling unwell for several days. You are running a temperature and you have a cough. You also have a headache and a sore throat.

Tell the doctor:
a) how you feel
b) how long you've felt this way.

Don't forget to rehearse out loud.

 Then listen to the tape where you will hear someone describing the same symptoms to his doctor.

Comprehension 1 Look at these labels. If you were the doctor, which medicine would you prescribe for the following medical problems?

1 A sore throat
2 Toothache (**mal aux dents**)
3 Indigestion
4 A chest infection
5 A stomach upset.

Aspirine UPSA

Comprimés effervescents
Indications:
– états grippaux
– douleurs dentaires
– migraines

Maalox

Comprimés
Indications:
– gastrites
– dyspepsies
Posologie:
1 à 2 comprimés à sucer ou à croquer après les repas

---

ercéfuryl 200
nifuroxazide
Comprimés
Indications:
le traitement des diarrhées
Posologie:
– durée du traitement selon prescription médicale

---

oropivalone
bacitracine

Comprimés
Indications:
– laryngites
– angines
Posologie:
laisser fondre, sans croquer, 4 à 10 comprimés par jour

Oracéfal

Gélules à 500 mg
Indications:
– Infections respiratoires
Posologie:
2 g par jour
3 g à 4 g pour les infections plus sévères
avaler les gelules avec un peu d'eau

Vocabulary

comprimés *(m pl) tablets*
posologie *(f) dosage*

gélules *(f pl) capsules*
sucer *to suck*

Comprehension 2 · Garder la pleine forme au cours d'une journée de travail

Il suffit parfois de quelques «trucs» pour retrouver de bonnes habitudes et un dos droit, non douloureux, signe de bonne santé et d'épanouissement psychique.

Au téléphone
Pour éviter de courber votre colonne vertébrale et de tirer sur la nuque du côté de l'oreille collée au combiné, placez tout simplement une pile de livres ou de revues sous vos coudes.

A la machine à écrire
Pour ne pas trop arrondir votre dos, vos épaules et la nuque, placez quelques annuaires ou un petit banc sous vos pieds: cela suffit à tout redresser. N'oubliez pas, quand vous lisez assis, de placer vos avant-bras bien à plat jusqu'aux coudes.

Au bureau
Dos calé à la chaise, entre-croisez les doigts, paumes en l'air. Abaissez les doigts le plus bas possible. Tendez les jambes à l'horizontale, pointes vers vous. Votre dos vous «remerciera».

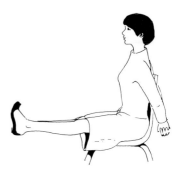

Au volant
Dans la voiture, mains sur le haut du volant, pieds à plat sous les pédales, repoussez fort les pieds et les mains en rentrant ventre et menton: finies les crampes. A l'extérieur, les pieds sur le bas de la caisse, les mains accrochées au toit, les paumes dirigées vers le ciel, tendez les jambes et baissez la tête le plus bas possible. C'est une mise en tension globale des bras, nuque, dos, fessiers, jambes et chevilles.

Look at the text and note down the French equivalent of these parts of the body:

1 palm _____   8 fingers _____

2 legs _____   9 back _____

3 feet _____   10 hands _____

4 head _____   11 arms _____

5 neck _____   12 hips _____

6 ankles _____   13 ears _____

7 elbows _____   14 shoulders _____

Exercise 4

At the chemist's while waiting for his prescription, Paul overheard several conversations. Complete the grid with the relevant information.

	Patient's problem	Medicine prescribed	Dosage instruction
1			
2			
3			

Dialogue 3: Un accident

While crossing France, Derek Jackson witnesses an accident between the driver of a car and a boy on a motorbike. He speaks to the driver who has got out of his car.

Derek	Qu'est-ce qui s'est passé?
Chauffeur	Eh bien, le garçon a pris le tournant sans regarder. Je n'ai pas pu m'arrêter. J'ai glissé et j'ai heurté le réverbère. Lui il est tombé de sa moto. Il ne bouge plus.
Derek	Il ne faut pas le déplacer. Il faut appeler le SAMU. Et vous? Vous n'êtes pas blessé?
Chauffeur	Eh bien, j'ai mal au bras. J'ai tourné un peu vite le volant et je me suis tordu le poignet. Ma femme n'est pas blessée, heureusement, mais elle souffre du choc. La voiture est bien abîmée quand même.
Derek	Restez-là. Je vais appeler l'ambulance.

Vocabulary

une voiture *car*	**le réverbère** *lamp post*	**le volant** *steering wheel*
une moto *motorbike*	**bouger** *to move*	**heureusement** *lucky*
le tournant *bend*	**déplacer** *to move*	**souffrir de** *to suffer from*
sans *without*	**les secours** *emergency*	**le choc** *shock*
regarder *to look*	*services*	**abîmé(e)** *damaged*
glisser *to slide*	**blessé(e)** *wounded*	**quand même** *nevertheless*
heurter *to run/crash into*	**vite** *quickly*	

Notes

1 **Je n'ai pas pu m'arrêter** *I was not able to stop (myself).* **Pu** is the past participle of **pouvoir.**

2 **Lui, il est tombé de sa moto** *He fell off his motorbike.*

3 **Le SAMU (service d'assistance médicale d'urgence)** *Mobile emergency medical service.*

4 **Je me suis tordu le poignet** *I twisted my wrist.* Note how the French say *I twisted the wrist to me.*

5 **Restez-là!** *Stay there!*

Key phrases

Qu'est-ce qui s'est passé?	*What has happened?*
Il (ne) faut (pas) le déplacer/appeler	*You must (not) move/call him*
J'ai mal au bras/au dos	*I have hurt my arm/back*
Je vais appeler...	*I am going to call ...*

Exercise 5	Unfortunately, you have been a witness at an accident on a French road. You immediately take charge.

1 Out loud, ask the woman involved:
   a) what happened
   b) whether she is hurt.
2 Then tell her:
   a) to stay where she is
   b) that you mustn't move the injured person
   c) that you will call the ambulance.

Comprehension 3

Derek has read through the section in the Highway Code which explains what to do in case of an accident. Try to get the general gist.

Alerter les secours

La survie d'un blessé dépend pour une large partie de la rapidité d'intervention des secours.

- On alerte de toute urgence au moyen du téléphone le plus proche:
  - la police (en ville) ou la gendarmerie (en campagne) en appelant le 17
  - les pompiers, si nécessaire, en appelant le 18
  - le SAMU en appelant le 15.
- Pour permettre une localisation rapide et une organisation efficace des secours, on indique:
  - en ville: le nom de la rue, le numéro de l'immeuble le plus proche
  - en rase campagne: des repères tels que les bornes kilométriques, les carrefours, les panneaux de direction, etc.
  - la nature de l'accident (dégâts matériels, blessés)
  - les véhicules impliqués: voitures de tourisme, camions, motocyclettes, etc.
  - le nombre des blessés et leur état apparent (respiration, hémorragie), les risques particuliers éventuels; chaussée encombrée, incendie, etc.
- A défaut de téléphone, on demande à un autre usager de donner l'alerte.

Now match the French with its English equivalent: we've done the first one for you:

1 les pompiers		**a)**	the fire service
2 les panneaux de direction		**b)**	a blocked road
3 un(e) blessé(e)		**c)**	a lorry
4 une incendie		**d)**	crossroads, junctions
5 une chaussée encombrée		**e)**	help, aid
6 le secours		**f)**	signposts
7 les carrefours (*m pl*)		**g)**	an injured person
8 un camion		**h)**	a fire

Exercise 6

Look at the sketch of this accident. Using information from the third dialogue work out what you would have said if you needed to explain what happened. Remember that you will have to change the first person **je** to the third person **il** and that each verb will change too.

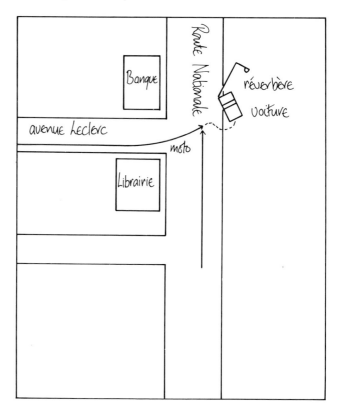

|| Pronunciation

Think about the rhythm of a French phrase or sentence. You will find that the voice rises at the end of a sentence if this is a question, or after each short phrase in a longer sentence. When doing oral work, try to imitate these rhythms as well as learning the correct structure and vocabulary. Sometimes it's worth listening for rhythm and intonation alone and not worrying about meaning.

Listen to the tape to hear the pronunciation of the examples given below.

1 Mais dis-donc!
2 C'est quoi ça?
3 Il n'est pas encore arrivé?
4 Salut les filles!
5 On est tous réunis? Alors on commence.

Language structures

Verbs The passive

You can often express the passive (when something is done to you rather than your doing it) by using a reflexive. The two examples we had were:

Ça s'écrit comment? *How is that written?*
Vous vous ferez rembourser plus tard *You will be reimbursed later*
(**se faire rembourser** literally *to make oneself reimbursed*)

Look out for other examples in your reading; at this stage you only need to recognise this usage.

The present participle

If you wish to translate an English verb ending in *ing* into French, do the following:

1 Take the **nous** form of the present tense (**parlons, finissons, attendons**).
2 Take off the ending **ons** and substitute **ant**.

en traversant	*while crossing*
en apprenant	*by telling, advising, teaching*
en appelant	*by calling*

Construction with verbs

This unit has introduced you to more verbs which require certain structures.

Téléphoner à Jean pour...	*To telephone John (in order) to ...*
Laisser fondre	*To allow to melt*
Répondre à cette question	*To reply to this question*
Empêcher de...	*To prevent from ...*
Dépendre de...	*To depend on ...*

Exercise 7

Look at the following verbs:

● **aimer**
● **rendre**
● **partir**
● **vouloir**
● **pouvoir**
● **aller**

1 Take the **nous** form of the present tense.
2 Make each verb into a present participle by removing the **ons** ending and adding **ant**.

Pronouns

Emphatic pronouns

If you wish to emphasise a pronoun, then make the following substitutions:

je	becomes	moi
tu		toi
il		lui
ils		eux
nous, vous and **elle(s)** remain the same		

You use this form when the pronoun occurs after a preposition such as **à**, **de**, **avec**, etc.

Look at these examples:

- **Moi**, je n'aime pas conduire (*driving*). Et toi?
- Ma femme et **moi**.
- **Lui**, il n'est pas blessé.
- Tu viens avec **moi**?

Cultural briefing

If you don't want to go to the doctor's, a visit to the chemist's always proves helpful. Chemists in Europe are very highly trained and will give you skilled advice about medical problems and what to do about them. Chemists are, of course, not open all day and everyday but there is usually a list of **pharmacies de garde** *chemists on duty* posted in the windows of chemist shops.

Before you go abroad make sure you have filled out form E111 which ensures that you will be reimbursed for any costs incurred through having visited a doctor. Remember though that you will have to pay on the spot and then claim back later. It's a good idea to get extra insurance if you want to be flown home in a medical emergency.

Progress check

1 At the doctor's:
   a) ask the receptionist for an appointment that day
   b) that's not possible: ask for one tomorrow instead
   c) spell out your first name and surname
   d) say you are English
   e) say you have insurance.
2 Later say:
   a) you have (had) a headache
   b) and a sore throat
   c) and a slight temperature
   d) for two days.

3 What do the following mean?
   a) Allez à la sécurité sociale pour vous faire rembourser.
   b) Je vais vous donner une ordonnance.
   c) Posologie – laisser fondre sans croquer 2 à 5 comprimés.
4 How do you say:
   a) What's happened?
   b) I couldn't stop.
   c) You must call emergency services.
   d) Stay there!
   e) I have hurt my arm.

13 Au boulot

In this unit you will learn how to …

- make simple telephone calls
- make contact with possible clients
- use informal everyday expressions.

Dialogue 1a: Conversation avec un futur client

Paul has begun work. He has made contact with several clients and is trying to find some more.

Réceptionniste	Allô. Société Dupont. J'écoute.
Paul	Bonjour. Pourrais-je parler au chef des achats, s'il vous plaît?
Réceptionniste	De la part de qui?
Paul	De Paul Smith, de la société Thompson France.
Réceptionniste	Je suis désolée. Le chef des achats est absent.
Paul	Quand est-ce que je pourrai le joindre?
Réceptionniste	Pas avant demain matin malheureusement.
Paul	Bon. Je rappellerai demain matin. Merci, Madame. Au revoir.
Réceptionniste	Au revoir, Monsieur.

Vocabulary

absent(e) *absent*   **malheureusement**   **rappeler** *to call back*
joindre *to join, contact*   *unfortunately*

Notes

1 **Pourrais-je...?** *Could I speak to?* This is the conditional tense and is usually translated by *would*. See Language structures.

2 **Pas avant demain matin** *Not before tomorrow morning.* Use **pas** to make a short phrase negative.

Key phrases

Pourrais-je parler au chef des achats/chef des ventes?
Could I speak to the purchasing manager/the sales manager?

De Paul Smith de la Société Thompson
Paul Smith from Thompson France speaking

Quand est-ce que je pourrai le joindre?
When will I be able to contact him?

Je rappellerai demain matin/la semaine prochaine/cet après-midi
I'll call back tomorrow morning/next week/this afternoon

Exercise 1

How's your memory? Without looking at the transcript or listening to the tape again, fill in the blanks in the following phrases. Then say each phrase out loud.

1 Pourrais-je _____ au chef des achats?

2 De la part de _____ ?

3 Le chef des achats est _____ .

4 Quand est-ce que je pourrai le _____ ?

5 Pas avant _____ matin.

6 Bon. Je _____ demain matin.

Dialogue 1b: Conversation avec un futur client

Paul rings up another company.

Réceptionniste	Legrand et Compagnie, bonjour.
Paul	Bonjour. Pourrais-je parler au chef des achats, s'il vous plaît? A propos, comment s'appelle-t-il?
Réceptionniste	Il s'appelle Monsieur Martin. C'est de la part de qui?
Paul	De Monsieur Paul Smith de la société Thompson France.
Réceptionniste	Je suis désolée. Monsieur Martin est en réunion.
Paul	Pourrais-je parler à son adjoint, alors?
Réceptionniste	Malheureusement, pas avant cet après-midi.
Paul	Bon. Je rappellerai plus tard. Merci, Madame. Au revoir.
Réceptionniste	Au revoir.

Vocabulary

en réunion *in a meeting*   **un adjoint** *assistant*

Exercise 2	Look at the dialogue and say your part out loud. Give your own details and those of your firm. When you've finished, write in your part and then listen to the complete conversation on tape.

Réceptionniste   Société Michaud, bonjour.

Vous   (*Ask to speak to the Production Manager.*)

_____

Réceptionniste   C'est de la part de qui?

Vous   (*Give your name and that of the company.*)

_____

Réceptionniste   Je suis désolée. Il est en réunion à ce moment.

Vous   (*Ask when you can contact him.*)

_____

Réceptionniste   Pas avant demain matin.

Vous   (*Say you will call back tomorrow morning, thank her and say goodbye.*)

_____

Dialogue 2:   La promotion discrète

Dialogue 2 introduces a more informal register, that is, a friendlier and more colloquial way of talking to others. You need to be able to recognise and use language appropriate to different situations.

Paul speaks to a client he knows very well.

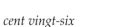

Paul	Salut, Jean-Pierre. Ça va?
Jean-Pierre	Ça va très bien. Et toi?
Paul	Très bien. Tu as passé un bon week-end?
Jean-Pierre	Impeccable.
Paul	Comment vont les affaires? Tu as reçu notre catalogue?
Jean-Pierre	Oui oui, je l'ai bien reçu.
Paul	Alors, qu'est-ce que tu vas commander? Je te propose notre dernier modèle... Allez, bon merci Jean-Pierre. A bientôt. Et bonne journée.

Vocabulary

salut *hi, hallo*
impeccable *super, great*
alors *well*

commander *order*
proposer *to suggest*
à bientôt *see you soon*

bonne journée *have a good day*

Notes

1 **La promotion discrète** *The soft sell.*
2 **Ça va?** *How are things?* Literally *how does it go?* Reply with **Ça va bien merci. Et toi/vous?**
3 **Comment vont les affaires?** *How is business?*   Another phrase using **aller**.

4 **Tu as reçu notre catalogue?** *Did you receive our catalogue?*   **Reçu** is the past participle of **recevoir** *to receive.*
5 **Allez** *Well then.*   Often used to bring a conversation to a close.

Key phrases

Salut   *Hi*
Ça va?   *How are things?*
Ça va (très) bien   *Fine*
Et vous/toi?   *And you?*
Tu as passé un bon week-end/de bonnes   *Have you had a good weekend/holiday?*
   vacances?
Comment vont les affaires?   *How is business?*
Je te propose...   *Let me suggest ...*
A bientôt   *See you soon*
Bonne journée/soirée   *Have a good day/evening*

Exercise 3

Comprehension 1

You are telephoning one of your French customers, Catherine. Complete your part of the dialogue on tape: you start. You will find the transcript and what you could have said on p. 194.

Paul has decided to translate the English description of the company into French for the new clients.

> Est-ce que vous nous connaissez? Notre entreprise s'appelle Thompson France. Nous fabriquons et vendons en gros des pièces pour les machines industrielles. Nous pouvons garantir une livraison rapide et des remises avantageuses.

Vocabulary

fabriquer *to make*
vendre *to sell*

en gros *wholesale*
la livraison *delivery*

la remise *discount*

What is the original version? You'll find it on p. 195.

Exercise 4

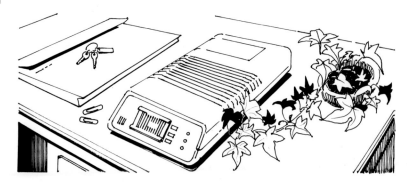

A number of salespeople have left messages on the answering machine at Thompson France. Listen to the tape and fill in the grid below.

	Name of company	Address/phone number	Contact name	Service offered
1				
2				
3				

Vocabulary

le papier *paper*
le bureau *office*

la commande *order*
la réparation *repair*

Exercise 5

Paul is compiling a register of contacts. He uses a standard form to record details of contacts. It looks like this.

```
Company name        _____
Address             _____
Telephone number    _____
Fax number          _____
Contact name        _____
Current suppliers   _____
Current discount    _____
```

Beside each detail, he jots down the question he wants to ask. What does he write? The questions will begin with **quel**, **quelle**, **quels** or **quelles**, depending on gender or number, or **qui**.

Example: **Quel est le nom de votre société?**

Here are some words to help:

Vocabulary

le télécopieur *fax machine*   **actuel(le)** *current, present*   **le fournisseur** *supplier*

||

Pronunciation

The double **l** sound in French can provide an English speaker with problems. The normal pronunciation is **ee-y** as in **juillet**, **travailler** and **fille**. Sometimes, however, the **ll** is pronounced as one **l** – as in **ville**, **rappeller** and **mille**.

Listen to the tape to hear the pronunciation of the examples given below.

1 Je te presente ma fille.
2 On ne travaille pas en juillet.
3 Ça coûte mille francs.
4 Je vous rappelle cet après-midi?

Language structures

Verbs   Conditional tense

Example: **prendre**

In this unit, we met the tense which translates the English *would* or *could*. To form add the following endings to the infinitive of the verb (for **re** verbs the final **e** of the infinitive is first deleted): **ais, ais, ait, ions, iez, aient**

je prendrais	nous prendrions
tu prendrais	vous prendriez
il/elle/on prendrait	ils/elles prendraient

Notice how similar the conditional is to the future tense (see Unit 9). Irregular verbs in the conditional take the same root, or main part of the word, as in the future.

je verrai	*I will see*
je verrais	*I would see*
je saurai	*I will know*
je saurais	*I would know*
je pourrai	*I will be able to*
je pourrais	*I would be able to, could*

Exercise 6	Using **Vous pourriez?** *Could you?* ask a colleague to do the following things:

1 Begin work at the factory tomorrow.
2 Contact some clients.
3 Try to contact the sales manager.
4 Speak to the accountant.
5 Call back tomorrow.

Remember to use an infinitive after **vous pourriez...**

Adjectives Possessive adjectives

You met **mon, ma, mes** in Unit 2. Here are the tables for all the possessive adjectives.

	My		**Your** (informal singular)		**His/her**	
	m	*f*	*m*	*f*	*m*	*f*
One object	mon	ma	ton	ta	son	sa
Several objects	mes		tes		ses	

	Our		**Your** (formal; also informal plural)		**Their**	
	m	*f*	*m*	*f*	*m*	*f*
One object	notre		votre		leur	
Several objects	nos		vos		leurs	

Remember that the possessive adjective agrees with the object – not with the possessor. Look at these examples:

Paul, voilà ta lettre!   *Paul, here's your letter!*

Anne attend son fils, mais il n'est pas encore arrivé.   *Anne is waiting for her son but he hasn't arrived yet.*

Voici vos papiers.   *Here are your documents.*

Leur bureau se trouve au troisième étage.   *Their office is on the third floor.*

Cultural briefing

However good you become at French, don't attempt to translate your sales literature into French yourself. Don't give it to your secretary to do either! Translating technical, commercial or marketing material is a job for a specialist and it is absolutely essential that it be done by a specialist. The French more than any other nation are proud of their linguistic heritage and reading the kind of **gaffes** which have appeared in some sales literature makes them dismiss the company rather than smile indulgently.

Be careful yourself when speaking French to keep within the formal register, that is, not to use the **tu** form, slang or colloquial expressions. You may think now that you will never acquire these, but it is easy enough to pick them up from French people speaking informally amongst themselves. The danger is that you use them inappropriately in a formal business setting. So stick with the language you learn in a business course, until you become absolutely sure of when and where you can use expressions picked up off the street.

Progress check _____

1 You are on the phone:
  a) ask to speak to the Purchasing Manager
  b) you don't know his name; ask the receptionist
  c) say who you are and whom you work for
  d) he is unavailable; ask when you can contact him again
  e) say you will call back next week/tomorrow.
2 You call a former colleague:
  a) greet her in a friendly way
  b) ask how she is

  c) ask if she has received the catalogue
  d) suggest she orders a fax machine, no. 22 in the catalogue
  e) say 'goodbye' and 'thank you'
  f) wish her a good evening.
3 What do the following mean?
  a) Nous vendons en gros des pièces pour des machines industrielles.
  b) Nous garantissons une livraison rapide.
  c) Nous offrons des remises avantageuses.

UNIT 14 Pourquoi travailler avec nous?

In this unit you will learn how to …

- talk more fully about a particular job
- ask about conditions of work
- write a short curriculum vitae.

Dialogue 1a: Entrevue avec une future employée

Claire is interviewing candidates for positions within the company. The first candidate is Fabienne Maréchal who has applied for a job as a secretary. Here is a part of the interview.

Claire	Pourquoi voulez-vous travailler pour nous?
Fabienne	Je fais actuellement un travail de secrétaire sténodactylo. Je fais plutôt un travail de sténo. J'ai une formation de secrétaire. Comme j'ai un peu d'expérience je voudrais faire quelque chose de plus intéressant, prendre plus de responsabilité.
Claire	Connaissez-vous notre entreprise?
Fabienne	Oui, j'ai obtenu des renseignements sur vos activités en Angleterre.
Claire	Vous savez que nous sommes une société anglaise. Verrez-vous un inconvénient à partir en déplacement en Angleterre de temps en temps?
Fabienne	Non, pas du tout. J'aimerais voyager.

Vocabulary

une entrevue *interview*
futur(e) *future*
pourquoi *why*
actuellement *at the moment*
sténodactylo *shorthand and typing*

plutôt *rather*
la sténo *shorthand (stenographer)*
une formation *training*
les renseignements (*m*) *information*

de temps en temps *from time to time*
pas du tout *not at all*

Notes

1 **Quelque chose de plus intéressant**
Something more interesting. Note the use of **de** in phrases like **quelque chose de joli** *something pretty.*
2 **J'ai obtenu des renseignements**
I obtained some information. **Obtenu** is the past participle of **obtenir.**

3 **Verrez-vous un inconvénient...?** *Would you mind …?* Literally *will you see an inconvenience in …?* **Verrez** is the future of **voir**. **Je verrai** *I will see,* **Je verrais** *I would see* (see Unit 13).
4 **J'aimerais voyager** *I would love to travel.*

Key phrases

Pourquoi voulez-vous travailler pour nous? *Why do you want to work for us?*
Je fais un travail de... *I am doing a … job*
J'ai une formation de... *I have a … training*
Connaissez-vous notre entreprise? *Do you know our company?*

Exercise 1

You are an accountant (**un(e) comptable**). Reply to Claire's question **Pourquoi voulez-vous travailler pour nous?** by saying:

1 That you have an accountant's training.
2 That you work in a small firm.
3 That you are looking for something more challenging (**plus stimulant**) …
4 … and which would give you more responsibility.
5 That you don't mind travelling for the firm.

Dialogue 1b: **Entrevue avec une future employée**

Claire asks Fabienne if she speaks any foreign languages.

Claire Quelles langues étrangères parlez-vous?
Fabienne Je parle anglais et espagnol.
Claire Vous savez que nous venons de nous implanter en France. Il y a beaucoup de travail en ce moment. Seriez-vous disposée à faire des heures supplémentaires?
Fabienne Aucun problème.
Claire Avez-vous des questions à me poser?

Vocabulary

une langue *language*   **s'implanter** *to set up*   **poser** *to put (questions)*

Notes

1 **Nous venons de nous implanter en France** *We have just set up in France.* Use **de** with **venir** to mean *to have just* (see p. 137).

2 **Beaucoup de** *A lot of.*

3 **Seriez-vous disposée?** *Would you be willing to?* **Je serai...**, *I will be;* **Je serais...**, *I would be.*

4 **Des heures supplémentaires** *Overtime* (literally *extra hours*).

Key phrases

Je parle anglais/espagnol/allemand   *I speak English/Spanish/German*
Aucun problème/pas de problème   *No problem*

Exercise 2

1 Imagine you are in Fabienne's place. Out loud, tell Claire:
  a) which languages you speak
  b) that you would be happy to do overtime.
2 Then ask her:
  a) what the hours of work are (**les heures du travail**)
  b) what the salary is (**la rémunération**)
  c) how many weeks' holiday (**semaines de vacances**) you will get.

Comprehension 1

When Fabienne wrote to Thompson about the secretarial post, she received the following description:

1 Fonction générale

  Titre: Secrétaire
  Lieu de travail: Angers

2 Description de l'activité

  • prises de rendez-vous
  • réservations d'hôtels et de billets d'avion
  • classement
  • frappe de documents confidentiels
  • traductions
  • facturation

3 Conditions offertes:

  Rémuneration: 8.500F par mois
  Horaires: 39 heures par semaine; 8h30 à 17h30 (16h30 le vendredi)
  Vacances: 5 semaines par an

Now, match the job functions with the French equivalents:

1 typing confidential documents
2 reserving hotels and plane tickets
3 invoicing
4 filing
5 translating
6 arranging appointments.

Comprehension 2

Here is Fabienne's job application (**la demande de poste**):

CURRICULUM VITAE

État Civil
Nom: MARÉCHAL
Prénom: Fabienne
Date de naissance: 24 juin 1964
Situation de famille: célibataire
Adresse: 39 rue du Marché, Meudon

Diplômes obtenus
1983: BAC A5
1985: B.T.S Option Secrétariat de Direction

Langues lues, parlées, et écrites
Anglais, espagnol

Expérience professionelle
Du 28 septembre 1985 à ce jour:
   Secrétaire sténodactylo
   bilingue chez C.D.F.G.
   Nanterre

Juillet à septembre 1985:
   Secrétaire dactylo chez
   Ballot, boulevard Haussman, Paris

Du 21 avril au 26 juin 1985:
   Stage de cours d'études effectué
   à Renault-Étoile, boulevard Péreire, Paris

Now write your own CV for a French company, adopting
Fabienne's format.

Comprehension 3

Fabienne received the following reply to her job application. Read it through.

Angers, le 22 janvier 199-

Madame,

Comme suite à notre entretien du 20 janvier, nous avons le plaisir de vous préciser les conditions de votre engagement, sous réserve de votre agrément, à compter du 1er mars.

Vous exercerez les fonctions de secrétaire. Vous vous conformerez à l'horaire de travail de notre entreprise, à savoir: lundi à jeudi de 8 h 30 à 17 h 30; vendredi de 8 h 30 à 16 h 30.

Votre salaire mensuel sera fixé à 8.500F. Vous bénéficierez des congés payés, soit 5 semaines par an.

Chacun aura la possibilité de mettre fin au contrat, à charge de prévenir l'autre de ses intentions par lettre recommandée avec accusé de réception au moins un mois à l'avance.

Nous vous prions de nous confirmer votre accord sur les termes de la présente lettre en nous retournant avant le 29 janvier la copie ci-jointe sur laquelle vous aurez indiqué la date et porté votre signature.

Veuillez agréer Madame, nos sentiments distingués.

Claire Stevenson

C. Stevenson

Vocabulary

comme suite à *as a result of*
sous réserve de votre agrément *subject to your agreement*
exercer *to carry out*
les congés payés *(m) paid leave*

la fin *end*
prévenir *to give notice of*
une lettre recommandée *registered letter*
accusé de réception *(m) acknowledgement of receipt*

la copie ci-jointe *enclosed copy*

Reply to these questions: first out loud, then, if you wish, writing out your replies.

1 Quand est-ce que Fabienne va commencer son nouveau travail?
2 Quel sera son horaire de travail?
3 Combien de semaines de vacances aura-t-elle?
4 Si Fabienne ne veut plus travailler chez Thompson, qu'est-ce qu'elle doit faire (*what must she do*)?
5 Qu'est-ce qu'elle doit faire maintenant pour accepter le poste?

Pronunciation

Take care with the pronunciation of **h** and **j**. **H** is never pronounced, but sometimes it prevents liaison: **l'homme** but **le haricot**. Listen to the examples on tape.

1 L'homme
2 Le haricot
3 La hâche

J is tricky too; pronounce it softly as you would the *s* in *leisure* or *pleasure*, as in **le jardin**.

Language structures

Prepositions   en

En is a sophisticated little word that replaces words preceded by **du**, **de la** or **des**. You can translate it by *of them* or *of it*.
Look at these examples:

> **Tu veux encore de la viande? Non, je n'en veux plus, merci.**
> *Do you want some more meat? No, I don't want any more thanks.*
>
> **Tu veux du vin? Non, je n'en veux pas.**
> *Do you want some wine? No, I don't want any (of it).*
>
> **Tu as beaucoup d'amis? Oui, j'en ai beaucoup.**
> *Do you have a lot of friends? Yes, I have a lot (of them).*

Verbs   venir de

This phrase means *to have just*. The verb following is always in the infinitive. Look at the following examples:

> **Je viens de voir ton collègue**   *I have just seen your colleague*
>
> **Il vient de rentrer de Thompson France**
> *He has just returned from Thompson France*
>
> **Elle vient de rappeler le client**   *She has just called the client back*

Exercise 3

Match up the French phrases, pronounced for you on tape, with their English translations.

1 Vous en voulez?
2 Ils viennent d'arriver en France
3 Prenez-en!
4 J'en ai assez
5 Je n'en vois pas
6 Elle vient de se doucher

a) She's just had a shower
b) I'm fed up!
c) I can't see any
d) They've just arrived in France
e) Would you like some?
f) Do have some!

Cultural briefing

As you may imagine, French company structure is quite different from the Anglo-Saxon model. There are two main types:

La Société à Responsabilité Limitée (SARL)
This type of company is privately owned and is suitable for small businesses. It is the most common type in France. To set one up, you need a minimum of two and a maximum of 50 shareholders. There is no Board of Directors; the company is run instead by one or more managers.

Small foreign companies can set up an **Entreprise Unipersonnelle à Responsabilité Limitée (EURL)**. You need only have one share, so decisions remain entirely within your own hands.

La Société Anonyme (SA)
This sort of company is a public company like the British PLC, with a minimum of seven shareholders and a share capital of 250.000F. It can be quoted on the stock exchange (**à la Bourse**) or not, with most shares being publicly owned.

Progress check

1 At interview say:
   a) you would like more responsability
   b) you would like something more interesting …
   c) … and something more stimulating.
2 Say you would love to travel in France and England.
3 Tell the interviewer you speak both French and Spanish.
4 Ask the following questions:
   a) What are the hours of work?
   b) What is the holiday entitlement?
   c) What is the starting date?
5 Say you have worked for:
   a) ICI in Scotland
   b) GEC Alsthom in France.

6 Jot down in French the duties of your new secretary:
   a) filing
   b) making appointments
   c) translating
   d) invoicing.
7 What do the following sentences mean?
   a) Vous bénéficierez des congés payés.
   b) Lettre recommandée avec accusé de réception.
   c) Votre salaire mensuel sera fixé à 9.000 francs.

UNIT 15 Dossiers

In this unit you will learn how to …

- use French in a number of practical situations
- practise the language in more open and less controlled conditions
- revise and consolidate the French learned in the previous units.

STUDY TIP

In this unit you are on your own! Language is no longer controlled and highly specific. You may prepare short answers or you may decide to pull out all the stops and use structures and vocabulary which are wider in scope. Don't be afraid to experiment; in the end, this is the only way you will push forward the boundaries of your language learning. On the other hand, keeping things simple is always productive. If you're not sure about how to render a complicated English phrase in French, reduce it to the bare French essentials and you will make yourself understood. Example dossiers are given on pp. 197–200.

Unit 15 takes a very different format from the preceding material. In this unit you will be applying the French language to a range of different tasks. Some of the tasks will be completed in English, as you would have to do if you were working in an English company. Others will involve your working in both languages. You may have to look back to the vocabulary and structures introduced in earlier units. We will indicate this where it will be helpful for you to do so. The key, though, is to use as much French as you can; now is your opportunity to draw together all your linguistic resources in order to complete each task in an efficient and elegant way. The order is not important: you can start on any dossier you like.

Dossier 1: A l'agence de tourisme

You work for a travel firm which acts as an agent for private individuals and companies. You work in the section which handles arrangements for clients travelling to French-speaking countries.

You have been assigned the following clients:

1 A business woman travelling alone who needs hotel accommodation in Paris. She wants a room in a comfortable hotel that has a restaurant nearby.
2 A company organising a promotional event in Belgium. They will need to reserve rooms for 30 people, one conference room to hold 250 people and a smaller one to hold up to 50 people. Parking facilities are essential. They will need to know about the catering facilities of any hotel you recommend.
3 A family looking for a holiday in a French-speaking part of the world other than France. They do not want a package holiday but are looking for accommodation which offers plenty of activities. They welcome suggestions and need maximum information about the holiday you recommend.

Study the extracts from the hotel brochures on the following pages and prepare a recommendation for each client. Do not forget to spell out details which could be important to them and which will encourage them to book through your agency.

(Look back to Unit 3 to refresh your memory on hotels in France.)

novotel

EN CENTRE VILLE

CHAMBRES AVEC LIT DOUBLE

PETIT DEJEUNER BUFFET

PARKING EXTERIEUR NON CLOS

PISCINE

TELEVISION (EQUIPEMENT TOTAL)

DU CENTRE VILLE

CHAMBRES AVEC LITS JUMEAUX

RESTAURANT GRILL

PARKING EXTERIEUR CLOS

PISCINE COUVERTE

TELEVISION (EQUIPEMENT PARTIEL)

TELEPHONE

CHAMBRES AVEC LIT DOUBLE ET CANAPE-LIT

-LA ROTISSERIE-

PARKING COUVERT GRATUIT

TENNIS

VIDEO

TELEX

CHAMBRES POUR HANDICAPE

RESTAURANT TRADITIONNEL

PARKING COUVERT PAYANT

EQUITATION

DIRECTEUR

SALLES DE REUNION

BAR

NAVETTE GRATUITE AVEC L'AEROPORT

GOLF(S) DANS UN RAYON DE 25 KM MAX

NOMBRE DE CHAMBRES

SUITES

novotel évasion

NAVETTE PAYANTE AVEC L'AEROPORT

NIGHT-CLUB DISCOTHEQUE

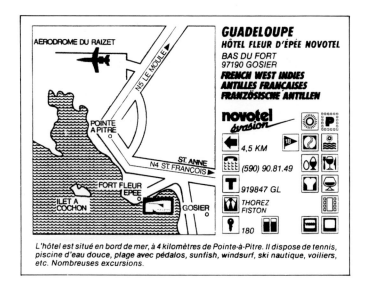

GUADELOUPE
HÔTEL FLEUR D'ÉPÉE NOVOTEL
BAS DU FORT
97190 GOSIER
FRENCH WEST INDIES
ANTILLES FRANÇAISES
FRANZÖSISCHE ANTILLEN

4,5 KM

(590) 90.81.49

919847 GL

THOREZ
FISTON

180

L'hôtel est situé en bord de mer, à 4 kilomètres de Pointe-à-Pitre. Il dispose de tennis, piscine d'eau douce, plage avec pédalos, sunfish, windsurf, ski nautique, voiliers, etc. Nombreuses excursions.

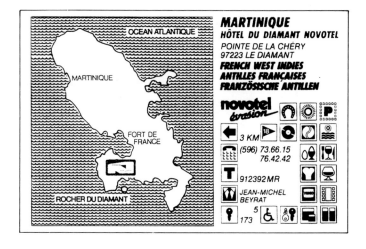

MARTINIQUE
HÔTEL DU DIAMANT NOVOTEL
POINTE DE LA CHÉRY
97223 LE DIAMANT
FRENCH WEST INDIES
ANTILLES FRANÇAISES
FRANZÖSISCHE ANTILLEN

3 KM

(596) 73.66.15
76.42.42

912392 MR

JEAN-MICHEL
BEYRAT

173   5

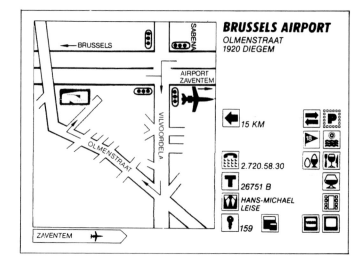

BRUSSELS AIRPORT
OLMENSTRAAT
1920 DIEGEM

15 KM

2.720.58.30

26751 B

HANS-MICHAEL
LEISE

159

Bienvenue chez Ibis

Avec plus de 250 hôtels et 200 restaurants en Europe, Ibis est le leader de l'hôtellerie-restauration. Les hôtels Ibis sont implantés en centre ville ou à proximité, le long des principaux axes routiers et près des aéroports dans des immeubles récents. Hôtellerie, restauration, location de salle de réunion: nous attachons une importance particulière à votre bien-être et mettons en œuvre tout notre professionnalisme pour vous garantir le meilleur service.

Bienvenue chez Urbis

Avec plus de 35 hôtels à votre disposition en Europe, Urbis vous offre un service impeccable et personnalisé.

PARIS BERCY

77, RUE DE BERCY
75012 PARIS
TEL: (1) 43.42.91.91   TLX: 216 391   FAX: (1) 43.42.34.79
DIRECTEUR: Gérard Biteau

368   7   7/180   Payant

Terrasse d'été sur parc.   *Piano-bar*

A 7 mn gare de Lyon. Métro Bercy ou gare de Lyon. Périphérique sortie porte de Bercy direc. P.O.P.B. face au parc de Bercy. A 5 mn du centre de Paris.

LIEGE OPERA

PLACE DE LA REPUBLIQUE FRANÇAISE 41
B-4000 LIEGE
TEL: 041/23.60.85   TLX: 42 369   FAX: 041/23.04.81
DIRECTEUR: Patrick Gengler

78   2   2/60   Payant

Restaurant à côté de l'hôtel.

SYMBOLES

 NOMBRE DE CHAMBRES

 PARKING

 CHAMBRES HANDICAPES

 RESTAURANT

 SALLES DE REUNIONS

 BAR

 VITABIS SP (SELON PERIODE)

 AEROPORT A PROXIMITE

 SOIREE ETAPE

 FRANCE: VIDEO-TRANSMISSION RECEPTION TV SPORT 5 CHAINES EUROPEENNES **EUROPE:** 5 CHAINES EUROPEENNES

LES CARACTÉRISTIQUES DES HÔTELS SOFITEL

Que vous soyez sportif, flâneur ou touriste, les hôtels Sofitel vous proposent, selon les cas :
• de profiter de la piscine, du sauna, des tennis et des diverses possibilités de loisirs à l'hôtel ou à proximité (golf, équitation, sports nautiques, sports d'hiver...) ;
• de passer la soirée à la discothèque ou au casino, ou simplement de vous détendre en prenant un verre au bar.

Quelques Sofitel sont situés dans de hauts lieux touristiques : Val d'Isère, Marrakech, la Polynésie ou l'Afrique de l'Ouest. Porticcio et Quiberon offrent en outre la possibilité de faire une cure de détente et de thalassothérapie.

 Location de voitures   Liaison gratuite avec l'aéroport   Sauna

 Boutiques   Piscine   Gymnase

 Agence de voyage   Tennis   Chambre pour handicapé

P Garage payant   Golf

P Parking gratuit   Planche à voile

FRANCE
PARIS

Hotel Sofitel Bourbon
32, rue Saint-Dominique
75007 Paris
Tél. : (1) 555.91.80
Oct. 85 : 4.555.91.80
Télex : 250 019

Directeur : M.-A. Potier

Au calme en plein Paris, à 100 m des Invalides et 200 m des quais de la Seine, tout près de la Place de la Concorde. Ambiance raffinée.

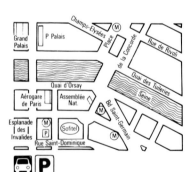

112 CHAMBRES
(dont 4 appartements), entièrement redécorées. Salle de bains (6 chambres avec douche), radio, TV couleurs, téléphone, mini-bar.

BELGIQUE

BRUXELLES

Hotel Sofitel Brussels Airport

Bessenveldstraat 15
B-1920 Diegem - Belgium
Tél. (32) (2) 720.60.50
Télex : 26 595

Directeur : B. Hummel

Près de l'aéroport international.
Navette gratuite.

125 CHAMBRES

dont 5 suites.
Salle de bains, radio, TV couleurs,
(15 programmes + films hôtel),
téléphone direct,
mini-bar.

RESTAURANTS ET BAR

"Diedeghem" : grande carte et
spécialités.
"Green Corner" : repas rapides et
soignés, ouvert du matin au soir.
"Golden Bar" : bar d'ambiance
avec terrasse-piscine.

10 SALONS RÉUNIONS ET RÉCEPTIONS

de 4 à 700 personnes.
Équipememt complet pour
conférences, congrès...
Traduction simultanée.

HÔTEL CLIMATISÉ ET INSONORISÉ

LOISIRS

Piscine chauffée intérieure/
extérieure, solarium, sauna, jardin
intérieur.

MAROC

MARRAKECH

Hotel Sofitel Marrakech

Avenue du Président Kennedy
Marrakech - Maroc
Tél. (212) (4) 346.26
Télex : 72 026 et 72 059

Directeur : J.-P. Claude

A proximité de la Koutoubia, à
2,5 km de la Place Djemaa-el-Fna,
au cœur d'un parc privé de 3,5 ha
aux arbres centenaires, hôtel 5 étoiles.

"N'Zaha" : tente caïdale dans le
jardin, restaurant marocain
(ouverture en saison).
"Le Sania" : bar d'ambiance.
"Le Derbouka" : club discothèque.

293 CHAMBRES

dont 8 suites et 3 chambres pour
handicapés, 75 chambres avec loggia.
Salle de bains, radio, TV vidéo,
téléphone, mini-bar.

RESTAURANTS ET BARS

"Laddah" : restaurant grande carte.
"Chahoua" : repas simples et rapides.
"El Boustane" : grill buffet autour
de la piscine.

7 SALONS RÉUNIONS ET RÉCEPTIONS de 50 à 750 m^2.

HÔTEL CLIMATISÉ

LOISIRS : 2 piscines (1 pour les
enfants). Hammam. Salles de jeux
et de gymnastique. 2 tennis en
terre battue, éclairés. Possibilité de
golf 18 trous (9 km), équitation à
proximité. Boutiques.

Dossier 2: Au bureau

You work for a branch of a French company in Britain. During the course of a week your firm received a number of answer-phone messages in French. It is your job to see that they are dealt with. Study the company structure below, then listen to the messages on the tape, decide who should deal with them and prepare a memo, in English, to that person, giving them full details.

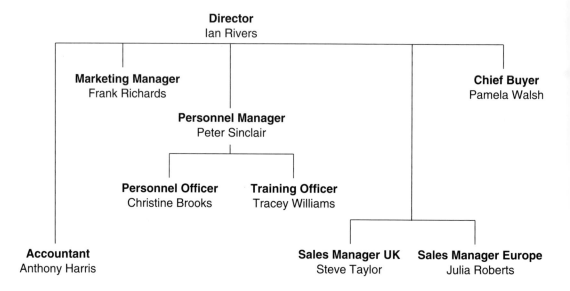

Director
Ian Rivers

Marketing Manager
Frank Richards

Chief Buyer
Pamela Walsh

Personnel Manager
Peter Sinclair

Personnel Officer
Christine Brooks

Training Officer
Tracey Williams

Accountant
Anthony Harris

Sales Manager UK
Steve Taylor

Sales Manager Europe
Julia Roberts

Use this model for your memo in each case:

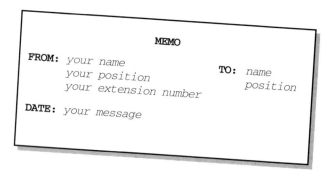

MEMO

FROM: *your name*
your position
your extension number

TO: *name*
position

DATE: *your message*

You will need the following vocabulary:

Vocabulary

l'annonce *(f) advertisement*   **la publicité** *publicity material*   **un formulaire** *form*

Dossier 3:   A la recherche d'un emploi

1 Read through each of the advertisements and identify:

   a) what the job is

   b) what kind of person the company is looking for

   c) how you should apply.

Oscar de la Renta
PARFUMS
PARIS

V

valentino
PARFUMS
ROME PARIS NEW YORK

Les PARFUMS STERN recherchent un

RESPONSABLE EXPORT
(aéroports, compagnies aériennes et maritimes...)

Les candidats devront justifier d'une expérience réussie d'au moins trois années dans la négociation, parler anglais et une deuxième langue, et être disponibles pour de fréquents déplacements à l'étranger.

Merci d'adresser votre dossier de candidature, en précisant la référence 160 Ex à
KEY MEN
10 rue de Rome – 75008 PARIS

MEMBRE DE SYNTEC

SOCIÉTÉ MÉTALLURGIQUE
recherche
CHEF COMPTABLE (H ou F)
il/elle sera responsable de l'élaboration des budgets, du contrôle de gestion, de la comptabilité reporting et des déclarations sociales et fiscales.
Ce poste conviendra à un jeune candidat diplômé ayant au minimum trois ans d'expérience.

Adresser lettre manuscrite, CV + photos sous réf. 42 à
MB DEVELOPPEMENT, BP 1, 69647 Caluire Cedex.

LES FEMMES ET LA FINANCE

Ce n'est pas encore très courant. Pourtant, notre clientèle leur fait autant confiance qu'aux hommes. Elles ont, chez nous, les mêmes chances qu'eux.

Joindre notre société séduira une personne d'expérience qui regarde au-delà de l'immédiat. Pendant 2 ans, il s'agira d'acquérir la maîtrise d'un nouveau métier par la formation que nous dispensons, de créer une clientèle.

Ecrire à

Matignon Conseil
57, rue de Richelieu – 75002 PARIS

HAVAS CONTACT

FABRICANT PRÊT-A-PORTER
Spécialisé été tee-shirt, polos, robes etc. 100% coton et hiver pulls acrylique/laine. Recherche

REPRÉSENTANTS
toutes régions

*Envoyer C.V. + références
sous réf. 11/846 à:*   61, avenue Hoche
75380 Paris Cedex 08

SPORT

ACHETEUR MATÉRIEL
Ses objectifs sont:
– négocier avec les fournisseurs;
– sélectionner les produits;
– assurer le suivi administratif.

Nous recherchons un candidat ayant une parfaite maîtrise de la négociation et étant fortement motivé par nos produits.

Candidature à adresser avec C.V. + photo à:
TEAM 5, *2–4, avenue de la Cerisaie, platane 304*
94266 FRESNES Cedex.

IMPORTANT GROUPE INDUSTRIEL
recherche
INGENIEUR COMMERCIAL

Charge:
- d'élaborer des solutions adaptées aux besoins des clients
- de mener les négociations à haut niveau concernant **les systèmes téléphoniques.** Aura la responsabilité d'une équipe de vente.

Adresser CV, rémunération souhaitée et photo sous réf. 19982 à CONTESSE PUBLICITE
20, avenue de l' Opéra 75040 Paris Cedex

2 a) Choose one of the jobs and prepare a covering letter.
Follow the model we have sketched out for you.

Madame, Monsieur

Comme suite à En réponse à Je me réfère à	votre annonce parue dans l'Express du (*date*).

J'ai l'honneur de poser ma candidature à Je pose ma candidature pour	l'emploi de... le poste de...

Je m'appelle... J'ai... ans, et je suis marié(e)/célibataire. J'ai été employé(e) à... Je suis étudiant(e) à...

J'ai l'honneur de vous adresser ci-inclus	mon curriculum vitae.	
Veuillez trouver ci-joint	certificats	concernant mes emplois précédents. délivrés par mes patrons successifs.

Dans l'attente de votre réponse

Veuillez agréer Je vous prie d'agréer	Madame, Monsieur,	l'expression de mes salutations distinguées.

b) Draw up a CV which will match the job specifications.
(Look back at Unit 13 for guidance.)

c) Some days later, you receive a reply to your letter of
application. Read it through.

Paris, le 4 juin

Madame, Monsieur

Nous avons bien reçu votre lettre pour un poste de...

Nous avons le plaisir de vous annoncer que votre curriculum vitae a attiré toute notre attention.

Toutefois, un entretien approfondi en nos bureaux serait souhaitable et ce si possible, avant le 30 juin.

Nous vous saurions donc gré de nous contacter afin de convenir d'un rendez-vous.

Dans l'attente du plaisir de vous recevoir.

Veuillez agréer, Madame, Monsieur l'expression de nos sentiments distingués.

M. Lasalle

M. Lasalle

Vocabulary

attirer *to draw*
souhaitable *desirable*
toutefois *however*
un entretien *interview*

nous vous saurions donc gré... *we would therefore be grateful ...*

d) In preparing for the interview, you expect to be asked some of the following questions. Prepare your answers and then rehearse them out loud.
   ● Que faites-vous actuellement?
   ● Quel aspect de votre travail vous plaît le plus?
   ● Quels sont vos buts (*goals*) dans la vie?

e) Now prepare some questions that you might ask. They could concern some of the following points:
   ● date d'embauche (*starting date*)
   ● lieu de travail (*place of work*)
   ● horaires de travail
   ● possibilités de formation
   ● avantages
   ● responsabilités
   ● salaire
   ● déplacements.

Remember to ask questions simply, using words like **quand, où, comment, quel(le)(s)**, etc. Again rehearse them out loud.

Dossier 4:   Accident à l'usine

 You are working in Belgium in the personnel department of a subsidiary of a British manufacturing company. A shop floor worker has had a slight accident and you are required to make a report. You speak to witnesses and the injured worker. Listen to these conversations on tape.

Write up a report in English including this information:

- the date of the accident
- who was injured
- how they were injured
- what their injuries are
- what action was taken.

You will need to look back to Unit 12 to refresh your memory on accident and injury. You may need this new vocabulary.

Vocabulary

un bruit *noise*
laisser tomber *to drop*

emmener *to take*
marcher *to walk*

l'entrepôt *(m) warehouse*

Dossier 5: Campagne de vente

You work as a member of a telephone sales team with a UK-based company which distributes computer software (**logiciels** (*m pl*)). The company has started exporting to France and is planning a trip to Paris to visit some prospective clients.

You are involved in both the planning stage and the visit.

Here are some of your contacts:

SUPERMICRO

89, bis rue Lamartine
75003 Paris

☎ 42 46 96 62

INFOTECHNO

Boîte Postale 3
75012 Paris

☎ 42 85 24 21

1 You telephone one of the companies:
   ● say you wish to speak to the purchasing manager
   ● ask his or her name
   ● say you are going to be in Paris on 3 or 4 May.
   Now write a fax to confirm your visit.
2 A week later, you arrive at the airport to pick up your ticket:
   ● give your name
   ● ask for your ticket
   ● give your flight number (**le numéro de vol**) AF 312.
3 You arrive at reception in the company and announce yourself. Give the following information:
   ● your name
   ● who your meeting is with
   ● at what time.
   You may need to look at Units 1 and 3 to refresh your memory.

Dossier 6: Implantation en Grande Bretagne

You are acting as agent for a French firm which is setting up a branch in the UK. They have asked you:

- to recommend office premises
- to give them a description of communications in your area: rail (**chemins de fer**), airports and motorways (**autoroutes**).

You recommend the offices whose details you see below. You write a specification for the firm, giving them all the relevant details. Don't forget to give them prices in francs (see exchange rate in Unit 8 or in a newspaper).

R.J COLLINS AND SON

Valuers ● Surveyors ● Estate Agents ● Commercial Property Specialists ●

OFFICE SUITES TO LET

Office J1	£185.000 per month
Office J2	£255.000 per month
Office J3	£255.000 per month
Office J4	£350.000 per month
Office J5	£399.000 per month
Office J6	£200.000 per month
Office J7	£185.000 per month
Office J8	£360.000 per month

Luxury office suites in modern town centre building available inclusive of: Furniture, Heating, Lighting, Reception, Cleaning, Parking, Electricity. Additional facilities include telex, fax, typing, photo-copying. Within easy reach of the motorway and mainline station.

Immediate occupation.

You may need the following vocabulary:

Vocabulary

meublé *furnished*
chauffage (à l'électricité, au gaz, central) *heating (electric, gas, central)*

éclairage *lighting*
nettoyage *cleaning*

This is the end of the dossier unit – and the end of the course. You should now be able to understand and manipulate basic business French, and the sort of French which will allow you to get by on future visits to France. Don't leave your French here though; it's very easy to forget a language if it's not practised regularly. Here are some tips for you to maintain and extend your knowledge.

1 Try to get to a class – even if it is not entirely appropriate, you will be getting some contact with the language on a regular basis.
2 You could advertise for a native speaker to come to your home and practise with you.
3 Try listening into French radio; it's quite easy to pick up in most areas of the UK.
4 More people now have access to satellite TV. Can you pick up a French channel?
5 Listen to Consolidation Cassettes 1 and 2 that accompany this course, whenever you have a spare moment. Play them at home, in the car or on a personal stereo.
6 Invest in the follow up to this course *Working with French* (Developmental level) and work your way steadily through it.

Good luck! Bonne chance!

Summary of language functions

Greeting people	Bonjour, Monsieur/Madame	Good morning/day, Sir/Madam
	Heureux(se) de faire votre connaissance	I'm pleased to meet you
	Enchanté(e)	Delighted (to meet you)
	Salut. Ça va?	Hello. How are you?
Leave taking	Au revoir	Goodbye
	A la prochaine	Till the next time
	A tout à l'heure	I'll see you later
	A un de ces jours	See you sometime
	A bientôt	See you soon
	A la semaine prochaine	See you next week
	A demain	See you tomorrow
	Bonne journée	Have a good day
	Bonne soirée	Have a nice evening
	Bon week-end	Have a good weekend
Introductions	Je suis...	I am …
	Je m'appelle...	My name is …
Giving personal information	Je viens d'Angleterre	I'm from England
	Je suis anglais(e), etc.	I'm English
	Je suis directeur, etc.	I'm a director
Social niceties		
Expressing thanks	Merci	Thank you
	Merci à vous	Thank you
	Merci infiniment	Thank you very much
Receiving thanks	Je vous en prie	Don't mention it
Wishing someone a good journey	Bonne route	Have a good journey
Paying a compliment	Ça vous va très bien	That suits you
Asking for something	Je voudrais/Nous voudrions	I would like/We would like
In a restaurant	Je prends	I'll have
	Je veux	I want
	Apportez (du vin)	Bring (some wine)

In a shop	Je cherche...	I'm looking for ...
Expressing regret	Je suis désolé(e)	I'm sorry
Offering help	Qu'est-ce que je peux faire pour vous?	What can I do for you?/
	Vous désirez?	Can I help you?
	Est-ce que je peux vous aider?	
	Qu'est-ce que vous cherchez?	What are you looking for?
Telephone expressions	Allô, oui?	Hello
	J'écoute	Speaking (literally: I'm listening)
	Ici... de la société...	This is ... from ... (company)
	Pourrais-je parler à... s'il vous plaît?	Could I speak to ..., please?
	C'est de la part de...	It's ... (your name)
	Puis-je laisser un message?	Can I leave a message?
	Quand est-ce que je peux le joindre?	When can I speak to him?
	Puis-je parler à son adjoint?	Can I speak to his/her deputy/assistant?
	Je rappellerai	I'll call back
Attracting someone's attention	Pardon, Monsieur	Excuse me
	Excusez-moi	
Asking for directions	Pour aller à... s'il vous plaît?	How do I get to .... please?
Giving directions	C'est là-bas	It's over there
	en face	opposite
	à côté de...	next to ...
	Prenez la direction...	Follow the signs for .../the direction
	Il faut aller...	You'll have to go ...
	En sortant d'ici	When you go out of/leave here
Asking for information	Pouvez-vous me dire?	Can you tell me?
Asking the price	Ça fait combien?	How much is it?
	Je vous dois combien?	What do I owe you?
Asking about duration	Vous en avez pour combien de temps?	How long will it take?
Expressing likes and dislikes	C'est bien	It's good
	C'est horrible	It's awful

	J'aime assez	I quite like it
	J'adore...	I love ...
	Je déteste	I hate/can't stand
	J'aime beaucoup	I like ... a lot
	Je n'aime pas	I don't like
	Je préfère	I prefer
	Ça me dirait	I'd like that
	Ça me plaira énormément	That will be lovely

Getting things done

Changing money	Je voudrais changer cent livres en francs	I'd like to change £100 into francs
	Je veux changer des chèques de voyage	I'd like to cash some travellers' cheques
	Je voudrais ouvrir un compte courant	I'd like to open a current account
Getting a refund	Vous vous ferez rembourser	You will get a refund
Making an appointment	Je voudrais prendre rendez-vous	I'd like to make an appointment
Asking someone to do something	Voulez-vous...?	Will you?
Asking someone's opinion	Vous pensez que...?	Do you think that ...?
Expressing disbelief	Ce n'est pas vrai	It's not true
Expressing need	J'ai besoin de...	I need
Making suggestions	Je vous conseille...	I advise you
	Je vous propose	I suggest
	Si on allait... (à Paris)?	Shall we go ... (to Paris)?
	Pourquoi pas?	Why not?
	Il faut absolument	We absolutely must ...
	Ça vous dit?	Would you like that?
Comparing and contrasting	Ce n'est pas tout à fait pareil	It's not quite the same
Asking what is wrong	Qu'est-ce que vous avez?	What's wrong?/What's the matter?

Grammar summary

Verbs

The present tense

Regular verbs

er verbs *Example:* **chercher** *to seek, to look for*
je cherche, tu cherches, il/elle cherche, nous cherchons, vous cherchez, ils/elles cherchent
ir verbs *Example:* **remplir** *to fill (in)*
je remplis, tu remplis, il/elle remplit, nous remplissons, vous remplissez, ils/elles remplissent
re verbs *Example:* **vendre** *to sell*
je vends, tu vends, il/elle vend, nous vendons, vous vendez, ils/elles vendent

Irregular verbs

aller *to go*
je vais, tu vas, il/elle va, nous allons, vous allez, ils/elles vont

apprendre *to learn*
j'apprends, tu apprends, il/elle apprend, nous apprenons, vous apprenez, ils/elles apprennent

avoir *to have*
j'ai, tu as, il/elle a, nous avons, vous avez, ils/elles ont

boire *to drink*
je bois, tu bois, il/elle boit, nous buvons, vous buvez, ils/elles boivent

connaître *to know*
je connais, tu connais, il/elle connaît, nous connaissons, vous connaissez, ils/elles connaissent

devenir *to become*
je deviens, tu deviens, il/elle devient, nous devenons, vous devenez, ils/elles deviennent

devoir *to have to, must*
je dois, tu dois, il/elle doit, nous devons, vous devez, ils/elles doivent

être *to be*
je suis, tu es, il/elle est, nous sommes, vous êtes, ils/elles sont

faire *to do, make*
je fais, tu fais, il/elle fait, nous faisons, vous faites, ils/elles font

mettre *to put*
je mets, tu mets, il/elle met, nous mettons, vous mettez, ils/elles mettent

obtenir *to obtain*
j'obtiens, tu obtiens, il/elle obtient, nous obtenons, vous obtenez, ils/elles obtiennent

payer *to pay*
je paie, tu paies, il/elle paie, nous payons, vous payez, ils/elles paient

pouvoir *to be able, can*
je peux, tu peux, il/elle peut, nous pouvons, vous pouvez, ils/elles peuvent

prendre *to take*
je prends, tu prends, il/elle prend, nous prenons, vous prenez, ils/elles prennent

recevoir *to receive*
je reçois, tu reçois, il/elle reçoit, nous recevons, vous recevez, ils/elles reçoivent

savoir *to know*
je sais, tu sais, il/elle sait, nous savons, vous savez, ils/elles savent

suivre *to follow*
je suis, tu suis, il/elle suit, nous suivons, vous suivez, ils/elles suivent

venir *to come*
je viens, tu viens, il/elle vient, nous venons, vous venez, ils/elles viennent

voir *to see*
je vois, tu vois, il/elle voit, nous voyons, vous voyez, ils/elles voient

vouloir *to want, wish*
je veux, tu veux, il/elle veut, nous voulons, vous voulez, ils/elles veulent

Reflexive verbs

Example: **s'appeler** *to be called*
je m'appelle, tu t'appelles, il/elle s'appelle, nous nous appelons, vous vous appelez, ils/elles s'appellent
Use of the reflexive infinitive:
The reflexive pronoun changes according to the subject.

Example: **se rendre** *to go*

Vous devrez **vous rendre** au commissariat.	You will have to go to the police station.
Je devrai **me rendre** au commissariat.	I will have to go to the police station.

The perfect tense with avoir

j'ai, tu as, il/elle a, nous avons, vous avez, ils/elles ont + past participle.

Past participle

er verbs
réser**ver** → réser**vé**
ir verbs
chois**ir** → chois**i**
re verbs
répon**dre** → répon**du**

Irregular past participle

avoir, eu
apprendre, appris
boire, bu
connaître, connu
devoir, dû
être, été
faire, fait
mettre, mis
obtenir, obtenu
pouvoir, pu
prendre, pris
recevoir, reçu
remettre, remis
reconnaître, reconnu
savoir, su
suivre, suivi
voir, vu
vouloir, voulu

The perfect tense with être

je suis, tu es, il/elle est, nous sommes, vous êtes, ils/elles sont + past participle.
The past participle must agree with the subject in the same way that adjectives do.
Example: **arriver** *to arrive*
je suis arriv**é(e)**
tu es arriv**é(e)**
il est arriv**é**
elle est arriv**ée**
nous sommes arriv**é(e)s**
vous êtes arriv**é(e)(s)**

ils sont arriv**és**
elles sont arriv**ées**

Other verbs in this category (with past participle):
partir (parti) *to depart*
aller (allé) *to go*
venir (venu) *to come*
entrer (entré) *to enter*
sortir (sorti) *to go out*
tomber (tombé) *to fall*
rester (resté) *to stay*
retourner (retourné) *to return*
revenir (revenu) *to come back*
monter (monté) *to go up*
descendre (descendu) *to go down*
naître (né) *to be born*
mourir (mort) *to die*

Reflexive verbs form the perfect with être:
Example: **s'arrêter** *to stop*
je me suis arrêté(e)
tu t'es arrêté(e)
il s'est arrêté
elle s'est arrêtée
nous nous sommes arrêté(e)s
vous vous êtes arrêté(e)(s)
ils se sont arrêtés
elles se sont arrêtées

The immediate past: to have just done something

This is expressed with venir de + infinitive.

je viens de téléphoner au chef des achats.	I have just telephoned the chief buyer.

The future tense

Formation: infinitive + endings **ai**, **as**, **a**, **ons**, **ez**, **ont**.

er verbs

Example: **trouver** *to find*
je trouverai, tu trouveras, il/elle trouvera, nous trouverons, vous trouverez, ils/elles trouveront

ir verbs

Example: **choisir** *to choose*
je choisirai, tu choisiras, il/elle choisira, nous choisirons, vous choisirez, ils/elles choisiront

re verbs

Example: **répondre** *to reply*
je répondrai, tu répondras, il/elle répondra, nous répondrons, vous répondrez, ils/elles répondront

Irregular forms
_____

aller, j'irai
avoir, j'aurai
devenir, je deviendrai
devoir, je devrai
être, je serai
faire, je ferai
obtenir, j'obtiendrai
payer, je paierai
pouvoir, je pourrai
rappeler, je rappellerai
recevoir, je recevrai
relever, je relèverai
savoir, je saurai
venir, je viendrai
voir, je verrai

The immediate future: going to

This is expressed by aller + infinitive.
Je vais passer six mois ici.   I am going to spend six months here.

The passive

This is formed with the appropriate tense of être + past participle.
Le salaire minimum est   The minimum salary is …
   régi par...   regulated by …

The conditional tense

Formation: infinitive + endings **ais, ais, ait, ions, iez, aient**.

Verbs in the conditional tense have the same stem, or basic form
as verbs in the future tense, whether regular or irregular; it is only
the endings that change.

Example: **Je trouverai**   *future*
              Je trouverais   *conditional*

               Nous serons   *future*
               Nous serions   *conditional*

The present participle

Formation: **nous** form of present tense minus **ons** ending, + **ant**.
Example: signer → nous sign**ons**, → sign**ant**
en signant   by signing

The imperative (commands)

Formation: the **tu** and **vous** forms of the verb are used without
the subject pronoun.
Example: **Signez ici.**   *Sign here.*

Verb constructions

Verbs which take the infinitive
_____

désirer
Si vous désirez recevoir votre   If you wish to receive your
   salaire   salary

devoir
Vous devez payer... You have to pay …

pouvoir
Vous pouvez retirer cinq cents
  francs. You can withdraw 500 francs.

vouloir
Je veux changer cent livres. I want to change £100.

se faire
Vous vous faites rembourser. You get a refund (get yourself
  refunded).

laisser
laisser fondre to let dissolve

Verbs which take **à**

répondre à
J'ai répondu à la lettre. I answered (to) the letter.

téléphoner à
Paul a téléphoné au chef des
  achats. Paul telephoned (to) the chief
  buyer.

Verbs which take **de**

décider de + infinitive, decide to
empêcher de + infinitive, prevent
dépendre de + noun, depend on

Verbs which take **à** and **de**

demander à quelqu'un de faire
  quelque chose ask someone to do something

proposer à quelqu'un de faire
  quelque chose suggest someone does
  something

Example: **Il a proposé à Paul d'aller à Paris.**

conseiller à quelqu'un de faire
  quelque chose advise someone to do
  something

Example: **Il a conseillé à Paul d'aller au musée du Louvre.**

pour + infinitive = in order to
pour simplifier la vie to make life easier

Impersonal verbs

Il faut, must
With the infinitive:
Il faut partir. I/you/he/she/we/they,
  etc. must go.

depuis + present tense

J'ai mal à la gorge depuis deux jours.	I have had a sore throat for two days.

The articles

Definite article: the

le (masculine singular)
la (feminine singular)
les (plural)
Used with parts of the body:

Je me suis tordu le poignet.	I have sprained my wrist.

Indefinite article: a/an

un (masculine singular)
une (feminine singular)
The indefinite article is omitted before names of professions.

Example: Je suis ingénieur.	I am an engineer.

Partitive article

du, de la, de l', des, some
de is used before an adjective and after a negative.

Adjectives

Adjectives agree with the noun, whether masculine or feminine, singular or plural.

Regular forms

	singular	plural	
masculine	enchanté	enchantés	delighted
feminine	enchanté**e**	enchanté**es**	
	petit	petits	small
	peti**te**	peti**tes**	

Irregular forms

	singular	plural	
masculine	nouveau, nouvel	nouveaux	new
feminine	nouve**lle**	nouve**lles**	
	blanc	blancs	white
	blan**che**	blan**ches**	
	heureux	heureux	happy
	heureu**se**	heureu**ses**	
	premier	premiers	first
	premi**ère**	premi**ères**	
	ce, cet	ces	this, these
	ce**tte**	ces	
	beau, bel	beaux	beautiful, handsome
	be**lle**	be**lles**	

NB **ce** is used before a noun beginning with a consonant:
ce journal, this newspaper.
cet is used with a masculine noun beginning with a vowel:
cet homme, this man.
Similarly: un **nouvel** homme, un **bel** homme.

Possessive adjectives	mon, ma, mes	my
	ton, ta, tes	your
	son, sa, ses	his/her
	notre, nos	our
	votre, vos	your
	leur, leurs	their

The comparative Formation: **plus** + adjective.
Examples:

plus avantageux	more advantageous
plus cher	more expensive, dearer
moins cher	less expensive

Irregular forms
bon (good) becomes **meilleur** (better).

The superlative Formation: using **le/la/les plus** + adjective.
le plus célèbre du monde   the most famous in the world

Pronouns

Subject pronouns

je	I	nous	we
tu	you	vous	you
il	he	ils/elles	they
elle	she	on	one

On often replaces **nous** in the spoken language.
Example: **On pourrait aller au musée du Louvre.**   *We could go to the Louvre.*

Object pronouns

le	
la	it
les	them

Emphatic pronouns moi, toi, lui, elle, nous, vous, eux, elles
These are used for emphasis and after prepositions.
Examples:

chez moi	at my house
pour nous	for us
c'est moi	it's me

Interrogatives

Qui?	Who?
Où?	Where?
Quel?/Quelle?/Quels?/Quelles?	What?

Combien?	How many?
Comment?	How?
Pourquoi?	Why?
Quand?	When?
Qu'est-ce que?	What?

Est-ce que? used before any statement will convert it into a question.

Negatives

ne... pas	not
ne... plus	no longer
ne... ni... ni...	neither ... nor
ne... rien	nothing
ne... jamais	never
ne... aucun(e)	not one
ne... personne	no-one

Prepositions

à	to, at
au, à la, à l', aux	
de	of, from
du, de la, de l', des	

Prepositional uses

muni de	equipped with
grâce à	thanks to
signalé par	indicated by
accompagné de	accompanied by

Vocabulary list

A

à cause de because of
à côté (de) next door (*to*)
à l'étranger abroad
à la mode fashionable
à long terme in the long term
à partir de as from
abaisser to pull down
abîmé(e) damaged
abri (*m*) **inviolable** safe place
absent(e) away/out
accéder à to gain access to
accepter to accept
accès (*m*) access
accord (*m*) agreement
accroché(e) à gripping
accusé (*m*) **de réception** acknowledgement
achat (*m*) purchase
acheter to buy
achèvement (*m*) completion
activité (*f*) operation
actuellement now/at the moment
adapter to adapt
addition (*f*) bill
adhérence (*f*) grip
adjoint (*m*) assistant
adorer to love
adresse (*f*) address
aérogare (*f*) air terminal
aéroport (*m*) airport
affaires (*f pl*) business
affecté(e) assigned to
affiché(e) displayed
afficher to display
afin de in order to
âge (*m*) age
agréé(e) recognised/approved
agrément (*m*) acceptance
aider to help
ail (*m*) garlic
ailleurs elsewhere
aimer to like
aîné(e) elder/eldest
alerter to alert/warn
allait: on allait one/we went
Allemagne (*f*) Germany
aller to go
aller-retour (*m*) return ticket
aller simple (*m*) single ticket
allocations (*f pl*) **familiales** family allowance
allonger to lie down
allouer to allocate (a sum)
allumer to switch on
alors so/then/therefore
ambiance (*f*) atmosphere
ambulance (*f*) ambulance

aménagé(e) fitted out
amende (*f*) fine
ami/amie (*m or f*) friend
amoureusement lovingly
ampoule (*f*) bulb
ampoule de rechange spare bulb
an (*m*) year
anchois (*m pl*) anchovies
ancien(ne) ancient/former
anglais(e) English
Angleterre (*f*) England
année (*f*) year
annonce (*f*) announcement/advert
annuaire (*m*) directory
antibiotiques (*f pl*) antibiotics
antiquité (*f*) antiquity
appareil (*m*) equipment
apparent(e) apparent
appartement (*m*) flat
appel (*m*) call
apporter to bring
apprendre to learn
approfondi(e) in depth
après after
après-midi (*m or f*) afternoon
argent (*m*) money
argent liquide cash
arrêt (*m*) stop
arrière (*m*) back
arrivée (*f*) arrival
arriver to arrive
arrondir to round
artichaut (*m*) artichoke
article (*m*) article/goods
ascenseur (*m*) lift
assez quite
assis(e) seated
assurance (*f*) insurance
assuré(e) insured
assurer to insure
atelier (*m*) workshop
attendre to wait
attente (*f*) waiting
attention: fais/faites attention! be careful!
attester to testify
attirer to attract/draw (attention)
au hasard by chance
au moyen de by means of
au revoir goodbye
auberge (*f*) inn
augmenter to increase
aujourd'hui today
auprès de at/next to
aussi also
autobus (*m*) bus
autocollant (*m*) sticker

autorisé(e) allowed
autoroute (*f*) motorway
autre (*m* or *f*) other
autrefois previously
Autriche (*f*) Austria
avance: à l'avance in advance
avant before
avant-bras (*m*) forearm
avant: pas avant not until
avantages (*m pl*) perks
avantageux/avantageuse worthwhile
avec with
avion (*m*) plane
avocat (*m*) solicitor
avoir to have
avoir besoin to need
avoir mal to ache/to be in pain

B
bagages (*m pl*) luggage
baguette (*f*) French stick
balcon (*m*) balcony
banane (*f*) banana
banc (*m*) bench
banlieue (*f*) suburbs
banque (*f*) bank
bas/basse low
basculer to rock
baskets (*m pl*) trainers, basket-ball boots
bateau-mouche (*m*) river boat
bâtiment (*m*) building
beau/belle beautiful
beaucoup a lot/very much
bébé (*m*) baby
belge Belgian
Belgique (*f*) Belgium
bénéficier to beneflt/profit
bénéficier de to be entitled to
beurre (*m*) butter
bibliothèque (*f*) bookcase/library
bien well/good
bien sûr of course
biens (*m pl*) property
bière (*f*) beer
bilingue bilingual
billet (*m*) ticket/bank note
blanc/blanche white
blessé (*m*) **blessée** (*f*) injured person
blessé(e) injured
bleu(e) blue
boeuf (*m*) beef
bois (*m*) wood
boisson (*f*) drink
boîte (*f*) can/tin; night club
bon/bonne good/right
bon marché cheap
bonjour Good morning
bonsoir Good evening
bord (*m*) edge
boulevard (*m*) avenue/boulevard
boulot (*m*) work (slang)
bout (*m*): **au bout de** end: at/to the end of

boutique (*f*) shop
bras (*m*) arm
brochure (*f*) brochure
brouillard (*m*) fog
bruit (*m*) noise
bulletin (*m*) report
bureau (*m*) desk/office
but (*m*) goal/aim

C
cabinet (*m*) **de toilette** toilet
cadeau (*m*) (*pl: cadeaux*) gift
cadet/cadette younger/youngest
café (m) coffee
café crème white coffee
caisse (*f*) cash desk: body (of vehicle)
cale (*f*) clamp
calé(e) propped against
camion (*m*) lorry
Canada (*m*) Canada
canadien/canadienne Canadian
canapé (*m*) sofa
candidat (*m*) candidate
carafe (*f*) carafe/decanter
carnet (*m*) book (of tickets)
carnet de chèques cheque book
carrefour (*m*) crossroads
carrière (*f*) career
carte (*f*) menu/card
carte de crédit credit card
carte de paiement charge card
catalogue (*m*) catalogue
cathédrale (*f*) cathedral
caution (*f*) guarantee/security
cave (*f*) cellar
ce/cet, cette; ces this: these
ceinture (*f*) belt
ceinture de sécurité seat belt
célèbre famous
célibataire single
cellier (*m*) cellar
cent hundred
centre (*m*) **d'affaires** business centre
cérémonie (*f*) special occasions
cerise (*f*) cherry
certain(e) certain/some
certificat (*m*) **d'immatriculation** registration document
chacun(e) each one/either party
chaise (*f*) chair
chambre (*f*) room/bedroom
champignon (*m*) mushroom
changer to change
chantier (*m*) building site
chapeau (*m*) (*pl: chapeaux*) hat
chargement (*m*) load
charges comprises including service charges
charmant(e) charming
chasseur (*m*) hunter
chaud(e) hot
chauffage (*m*) heating
chauffeur (*m*) driver
chaussée (*f*) roadway

chaussettes (*f pl*) socks
chaussure (*f*) shoe
chef (*m*) **de production** production manager
chef des achats purchasing manager
chef des ventes sales manager
chef du personnel personnel manager
chemin (*m*) way
chemise (*f*) shirt
chemisier (*m*) blouse
chèque (*m*) **de voyage** traveller's cheque
chéquier (*m*) cheque book
cher/chère expensive
chercher to seek/look for
cheville (*f*) ankle
chez at the house/shop/firm of
chocolat (*m*) chocolate
choisir to choose
choix (*m*) choice
choux (*m pl*) **de Bruxelles** Brussels sprouts
ci-contre opposite
ciel (*m*) sky
cigare (*m*) cigar
cinéma (*m*) cinema
cinquième fifth
circulation (*f*) traffic
circuler to run (transport)/move about
clair/claire clear
classement (*m*) filing
clef (*f*) key
clémentine (*f*) clementine
client (*m*)/**cliente** (*f*) customer
climatisé(e) air conditioned
code (*m*) code
coeur (*m*) heart
coin (*m*) corner
coin touristique tourist spot
col (*m*) collar
collant (*m*) pair of tights
collation (*f*) snack
collé(e) glued to
collège (*m*) school
collègue (*m* or *f*) colleague
colonne (*f*) **vertébrale** spine
combien how much/many
combiné (*m*) receiver (telephone)
commande (*f*) order
commander to order
comme as/like
commerce (*m*) business
commissariat (*m*) police station
commode convenient
communauté (*f*) community
Communauté Européenne European Community
compagnie (*f*) **aérienne** airline
compétence (*f*) ability
complémentaire complementary
complet full (hotel)
compléter to complete
compliqué(e) complicated
comporter to include
comprendre to understand/comprise
comprimé (*m*) tablet

compris included
comptabilité (*f*) accounting
comptable (*m/f*) accountant
compte (*m*) account
compte courant current account
compte-chèques (*m*) cheque account
compte-joint (*m*) joint account
compter: à compter du as from/commencing
concerner to concern
concevoir: conçu to create: created
concombre (*m*) cucumber
concurrence (*f*) competition
conducteur (*m*) driver
conduire to drive
conduite (*f*) driving
confirmer to confirrn
conformer à to abide by
confortable comfortable
congé (*m*) day off/holiday
conjoint (*m*) spouse
connaître to know (information)
connu(e) well-known
consécutif/consécutive consecutive
conseiller to advise
conserve (*f*) tinned food
consommer to consume
construction (*f*) building
contrat (*m*) contract
consultation (*f*) consultation
contre against
contrôle (*m*) test/service (car)
convenir to agree upon
copie (*f*) copy
correctement correctly
correspondance (*f*) connection
correspondant(e) corresponding
correspondre to correspond
costume (*m*) suit
cotisation (*f*) contribution
coton (*m*) cotton
coude (*m*) elbow
couleur (*f*) colour
coup (*m*) **de téléphone** phone call
courant(e) common
courrier (*m*) post/letter
cours (*m pl*) lessons
court (*m*) **de tennis** tennis court
coûter to cost
couvert cloudy
couvrir to cover
crampe (*f*) cramp
crêpe (*f*) pancake
crevette (*f*) shrimp
cuisine (*f*) kitchen/cooking
cuisiné(e) cooked
cuit(e) cooked

D
d'abord first
d'accord okay
dame (*f*) lady
Danemark (*m*) Denmark

dangereux/dangereuse dangerous
dans in
danser to dance
date (*f*) date
de of
déclarer to declare
dédommager to compensate
défaut: à défaut de téléphone if there's no phone
dégâts (*m pl*) damage
déjà already
déjeuner to have lunch
déjeuner (*m*) lunch
délai (*m*) delay/time limit
demain tomorrow
demande (*f*): **sur demande** upon request
demande de poste job application
demander to ask
démarche (*f*) claim
dents (*m pl*) teeth
dépanneur (*m*) breakdown mechanic
département (*m*) department (equivalent of county in England)
dépassement (*m*) overtaking
dépendre de to depend on
dépenses (*f pl*) expenses
déplacement: en déplacement travelling on business
déplacer to move
déposer de l'argent to pay in money
dépression (*f*) depression
depuis since/for
dernier/dernière last/latest
derrière behind
description (*f*) description
désirer to wish for
désolé(e) sorry
dessert (*m*) dessert
desserte (*f*) railway line
desservir to serve (of train service)
détenteur (*m*)/**détentrice** (*f*) holder
détester to detest/hate
deuxième second
devis (*m*) estimate
devises (*f pl*) foreign currency
devoir to have to/must
devrait: il devrait it should be
digestif (*m*) liqueur
diminué(e) diminished
diminuer to diminish
dîner (*m*) dinner
diplôme (*m*) qualification
dire to say
directeur (*m*) director/manager
directeur-général (*m*) managing director
direction (*f*) direction; management
directrice (*f*) female manager
dirigé(e) pointed towards
dis-donc! say
disposé(e) à willing to
disposer de to have available
disposition (*f*): **à votre disposition** at your disposal
disque (*m*) disc
disque compact compact disc

distance (*f*) **de sécurité** safe distance
distractions (*f pl*) entertainment
distributeur (*m*) **automatique** cash machine
doigt (*m*) finger
domicile (*m*) residence
domiciliations (*f pl*) domiciliations (of bills of exchange)
dominer to predominate
donc so
donner to give
donner sur to look out onto
dont of which
dos (*m*) back
doubler to overtake
douche (*f*) shower
douloureux/douloureuse painful
doux/douce mild
droit (*m*) law
droit/droite straight
droite right
dur/dure hard
durabilité (*f*) durability

E
eau (*f*) water
échange (*m*) exchange
échantillon (*m*) sample
éclairage (*m*) lighting
éclaircies (*f pl*) bright intervals
écossais(e) Scottish
écouter to listen
écru cream (colour)
effectué(e) carried out
effectuer to carry out
efficace effective/efficient
également equally
église (*f*) church
électricité (*f*) electricity
embauche (*m*) hiring
empêcher to prevent
emploi (*m*) job
employé (*m*) employee, clerk
en cas de in case of
en face opposite
en fin de semaine at the weekend
en moyenne on average
en pleine nuit in the middle of the night
encaisser to cash
enchanté(e) delighted
encolure (*f*) collar size
encombré(e) blocked, busy, packed
endive (*f*) chicory
endormir to put to sleep/make sleepy
endroit (*m*) place
endroit: par endroits in places
enfant (*m*) child
enfin lastly/at last
engagement (*m*) employment
ensemble together
ensemble: dans l'ensemble in general
ensoleillé(e) sunny
entre between

entrecroiser to interlock
entrée (*f*) entrance (building); starter (meal)
entrepôt (*m*) warehouse
entreprise (*f*) **familiale** family business
entrevue (*f*) interview
envisager to plan/arrange
envoyer to send
épanouissement (*m*) **psychique** mental well-being
épaule (*f*) shoulder
épinard (*m*) spinach
équipé(e) equipped/fitted
équitation (*f*) horse riding
escalier (*m*) staircase
escalier **roulant** escalator
escargot (*m*) snail
Espagne (*f*) Spain
espagnol(e) Spanish
espèces (*f pl*) cash
espérer to hope
esprit (*m*) spirit
essayer to try/try on
essence (*f*) petrol
essuyer to wipe/clean
est (*m*) East
et and
établir to draw up
établissement (*m*) establishment
étage (*m*) floor
étaient: **ils étaient** they were
état (*m*) state
Etats Unis (*m pl*) United States
étendu(e) extensive
étranger/étrangère foreign
être to be
être enrhumé(e) to have a cold
études (*f pl*) studies
étudiant(e) student
éviter to avoid
excusez-moi excuse me
exécuté(e) carried out
exemple: **par exemple** for example
exempté(e) exempt
exercer to carry out
expédier to forward/dispatch
expertise (*f*) valuation/appraisal
expertise **préalable** assessment (of damage)
extérieur (m) exterior

F
fabricant (*m*) manufacturer
fabrique (*f*) factory
fabriquer to manufacture
face: **en face de** opposite
facilement easily
faciliter to make easier
facturation (*f*) invoicing
facture (*f*) invoice/bill
faible weak
faire to do/make
faire le plein to fill up (petrol)
faire partie de to be a part of
familial(e) family (adj.)

fauteuil (*m*) armchair
favorable advantageous
femme (*f*) wife/woman
fenêtre (*f*) window
fermé(e) closed
fessier (*m*) buttocks
fête (*f*) holiday
feu (*m*) fire
feuille (*f*) **de maladie** sickness form
feux (*m pl*) rear lights
fiche (*f*) form
fièvre (*f*) temperature
fille (*f*) daughter
fils (*m*) son
fin (*f*) end
financier(ère) financial
fini(e) finished/ended
Finlande (*f*) Finland
fixé à fixed at
fixer to fix
flocon (*m*) **de neige** snowflake
fois (*f*) time
fonction: **en fonction de** in terms of
fonctionnement (*m*) working/operation
fonctions (*m pl*) duties
fond (*m*) background
fonder to found, create
formalité (*f*) formality
formation (*f*) training
forme (*f*) form, shape
formulaire (*m*) form
formulé(e) formulated
formuler to formulate
fort(e) strong/large
fortement strongly
fortifiant (*m*) tonic
fouiller to search
fournisseur (*m*) supplier
frais (*m pl*) expenses
frais/fraîche fresh
France (*f*) France
français(e) French
franchise (*f*) franchise
frappe (*f*) typing
frauduleux/frauduleuse fraudulent
frein (*m*) brake
frère (*m*) brother
froid(e) cold
fromage (*m*) cheese
fruits (*m pl*) **de mer** sea food

G
galerie (*f*) gallery
gallois(e) Welsh
gamme (*f*) range (of goods)
garage (*m*) garage
garanti(e) guaranteed
garantir to guarantee
garçon (*m*) waiter; boy
garder to keep to
gare (*f*) station
garer to park (vehicle)

gâteau (*m*) cake
gauche left
gaz (*m*) gas
gélule (*f*) capsule
gêner to obstruct
généralement usually
gérant (*m*) manager
gérante (*f*) female manager
gérer to manage
geste (*m*) gesture/movement/action
glace (*f*) ice cream
glissant(e) slippery
glisser to slip/slide/skid
gorge (*f*) throat
grâce à thanks to
grand(e) large
Grande-Bretagne (*f*) Great Britain
grands-parents (*m pl*) grandparents
gras: en gras in bold lettering
gratuitement free
Grèce (*f*) Greece
grève (*f*) strike
grillé(e) grilled
grippe (*f*) influenza
gris(e) grey
gros: en gros wholesale
groupe (*m*) group
groupement (*m*) group (of companies)
guichet (*m*) ticket office
gymnase (*m*) gym

H
habiter to live
habitude (*f*) habit
habitué(e) à used to
hall (*m*) **d'entrée** entrance hall
handicapé (*m*) disabled person
haricots (*m pl*) **blancs** haricot beans
haricots (*m pl*) **verts** green beans
haut (*m*) top
hebdomadaire weekly
héler to hail (taxi)
hémorragie (*f*) bleeding
heure (*f*) time/hour
heures (*f pl*) **supplémentaires** overtime
heureusement fortunately
heureux/heureuse happy
heurter to crash into
homard (*m*) lobster
homme (*m*) man
hôpital (*m*) hospital
horaire (*m*) timetable
horizontal(e) horizontal
hospitalisation (*f*) hospitalisation
hôtel (*m*) **de ville** town hall
huile (*f*) oil

I
ici here
il y a there is
imagination (*f*) imagination
imaginer to imagine

immatriculé(e) registered
immeuble (*m*) building/block of flats
immobilisé(e) immobilised
impeccable great
implanté(e) established/set up
implanter to establish/set up
impliqué(e) involved
important(e) large/important
importateur (*m*) importer
importation (*f*) importing
impôts (*m pl*) taxes
incendie (*m*) fire
indépendant(e) independent
indiquer to indicate
industriel/industrielle industrial
informer to inform
ingénieur (*m*) **commercial** commercial engineer
insonorisé(e) sound proofed
instant (*m*) moment
interdiction (*f*) prohibition
interdit forbidden
intéressant(e) interesting/lucrative
intérieur (*m*) interior
international(e) international
intersection (*f*) intersection
intervention (*f*) intervention
interviewer to interview
invariablement invariably
irlandais(e) Irish
Irlande (*f*) Ireland
Italie (*f*) Italy

J
jamais never
jambe (*f*) leg
jambon (*m*) ham
Japon (*m*) Japan
jardin (*m*) garden
jaune yellow
jeter to throw
jeter un coup d'oeil to glance
jeu (*m*) (*pl:* **jeux**) game
jeune young
jeunesse (*f*) youth
joindre to contact
joint(e) attached/enclosed
joli(e) pretty
jouer to play
jouet (*m*) toy
jour (*m*) day
jour férié holiday
journal (*m*) newspaper
journée (*f*) day
jupe (*f*) skirt
juridique legal
jus (m) **de fruit** fruit juice
jus d'orange orange juice
jusqu'à until
justement exactly/precisely

L
là there

Vocabulary list

la plupart de most of
là-bas over there
laisser tomber to drop
lait (*m*) milk
langue (*f*) language
large broad/wide (spread)
laver to wash
léger/légère light
légume (*m*) vegetable
lequel/laquelle which
lettre (*f*) letter
lettre recommandée registered letter
leur/leurs their
libérer to free
libre free
librement freely
lieu (*m*) place
ligne (*f*) line
limité(e) limited
limité à limited to
lingerie (*f*) laundry
lire to read
liste (*f*) *list*
lit (*m*) bed
littoral (*m*) coastal region
livraison (*f*) delivery
livre (*f*) pound (weight/money)
livre (*m*) book
local (*m*) (*pl* locaux) premises
localisation (*f*) location
location (*f*) rental
location de voitures car hire
logement (*m*) somewhere to live
loin far
loisirs (*m pl*) leisure pursuits/pastimes
longtemps a long time
lors de on the occasion of
lorsque when
louer to hire
lourd/lourde heavy
loyer (*m*) rent
lune (*f*) moon

M

madame Madam
magasin (*m*) shop/store/warehouse
main (*f*) hand
maintenant now
mais but
maison (*f*) house/firm
maladie (*f*) illness
malheureusement unfortunately
manger to eat
manière (*f*) manner
marchand (*m*) dealer
marchand(e) commercial
marchandises (*f pl*) goods
marcher to work/walk
marié(e) married
mariée (*f*) bride/bridal
marquage (*m*) antivol security engraving (on a car)
marque (*f*) make

marron brown
matériel (*m*) (*pl* matériaux) material
matin (*m*) morning
matinée (*f*) morning
mauvais(e) bad/wrong
McDo McDonalds
médecin (*m*) doctor
médical(e) (*pl:* médicaux) medical
médicament (*m*) medicine
méditerranéen/méditerranéenne Mediterranean
meilleur(e) better
meilleur marché cheaper
melon (*m*) melon
membres (*m pl*) limbs
même even/same
mensuel/mensuelle monthly
menton (*m*) chin
menu (*m*) menu/dish of the day
merci thank you
mère (*f*) mother
message (*m*) message
météo (*f*) weather forecast
métier (*m*) trade/craft
métro (*m*) underground railway
mettre to put
mettre fin à to end
meublé furnished
meubles (*m pl*) furniture
Mexique (*m*) Mexico
midi midday/lunchtime
mieux better (adverb)
mille thousand
minimum minimum
minuit midnight
mode (*f*) fashion
mode: à la mode fashionable
modèle (*m*) style/model
modique moderate
moins less
moins: au moins at least
mois (*m*) month
monde (*m*) world
monnaie (*f*) change
monsieur Sir
moto/motocyclette (*f*) motorbike
moyen (*m*) means
moyen: au moyen de by means of
moyenne (*f*) average
mur (*m*) wall
musculation (*f*) weight training
musée (*m*) museum
musique (*f*) music
myrtille (*f*) bilberry

N

naissance (*f*) birth
natation (*f*) swimming
national(e) national
nationalité (*f*) nationality
navette (*f*) shuttle
nécessaire necessary
neige (*f*) snow

n'est-ce pas isn't it, aren't they, etc.
nettement distinctly/noticeably
nettoyage (*m*) cleaning
neuf/neuve new
ni... ni neither … nor
nom (*m*) name/surname
nombreux/nombreuses numerous
non no
nord (*m*) North
normalement usually
Norvège (*f*) Norway
noter to note down
notre/nos our
nouveau/nouvelle new
nuage (*m*) cloud
nuageux/nuageuse cloudy
nuit (*f*) night
numéro (*m*) number
nuque (*f*) nape of neck

O

objets (*m pl*) **de valeur** valuables
obligatoire compulsory
obligé(e) forced
obtenir to obtain
oeuf (*m*) egg
oeuf dur hard-boiled egg
oeuf miroir fried egg
office (*m*) **de tourisme** tourist office
offrir to offer
oignon (*m*) onion
olive (*f*) olive
on allait one/we went
optimale: une date optimale a date limit
orange (*f*) orange
ordonnance (*f*) prescription
oreille (*f*) ear
organisation (*f*) organisation
où? where?
oublier to forget
ouest (*m*) West
oui yes
outre in addition to
ouvert(e) open
ouvrir to open

P

panique (*f*) panic
panneau (*m*) (*pl* **panneaux**) sign
pantalon (*m*) trousers
papier (*m*) paper
par semaine per week
parc (*m*) park
parce que because
parcmètre (*m*) parking meter
pardon excuse me
pare-brise (*m*) windscreen
pareil/pareille the same
parents (*m pl*) parents/relatives
parfait(e) perfect
parfum (*m*) perfume
parisien/parisienne Parisian

parking (*m*) car park
parler to speak/talk
parmi among
partager to share
particulièrement particularly
partie (*f*) part
partiel/partielle partial
partir to depart
partout everywhere
paru(e) appearing
passage (*m*) passage way/visit
passant (*m*), **passante** (*f*) passer-by
passeport (*m*) passport
passer to spend (time)/go past
pâtisserie (*f*) pastry/cake/cake shop
paume (*f*) palm
payé(e) paid
payer to pay
pays (*m*) country
Pays Bas (*m pl*) Netherlands
pêche (*f*) peach
pédale (*f*) pedal
peint(e) painted
peluche (*f*) soft toy
pendant during
penser to think/consider
père (*m*) father
permanent(e) permanent
permettre to permit/allow
permis (m) **de conduire** driving test/driving licence
permis(e) allowed
persil (*m*) parsley
persister to persist
personne (*f*) person
perte (*f*) loss
petit déjeuner (*m*) breakfast
petits pois (*m pl*) peas
peu: un peu a little
photo (*f*) photograph
pichet (*m*) jug
pièce (*f*) coin; part (machinery)
pièce d'identité identification
pièce de théâtre play
pièces (*f pl*) **détachées** spare parts
pied (*m*) foot
pile (*f*) pile/battery
piscine (*f*) swimming pool
piste (*f*) **à double voie** dual carriageway
place (*f*) square (in town)
placer to place
plaire: cela me plaît I like that
plaisir (*m*) pleasure
plat (*m*) dish
plat(e) flat
plein(e) full
plomb (*m*) lead
pluie (*f*) rain
plus more
plus: un peu plus a little more
plusieurs several
plutôt rather
pluvieux/pluvieuse rainy

pneu (*m*) tyre
poids (*m*) weight
poignet (*m*) wrist
point: à point medium rare
pointe (*f*) point
pointure (*f*) size (shoes)
poire (*f*) pear
poivre (*m*) pepper
poivron (*m*) pepper
pomme (*f*) apple
pomme de terre potato
pompiers (*m pl*) fire service
pompiste (*m*) pump attendant
pont (*m*) bridge
porc (*m*) pork
port (*m*) port
porte (*f*) door
porter to carry/wear
Portugal (*m*) Portugal
poser sa candidature to apply
poser un problème to pose a problem
posséder to possess
possibilité (*f*) possibility
poste (*m*) post/job
poste de télévision (*m*) television set
poulet (*m*) chicken
pour for
pourquoi why
pouvoir to be able to
pratique useful/practical
précaution (*f*) care
préciser to specify
préférer to prefer
préjudice (*m*) harm, loss
premier/première first
prendre to take
prendre contact to make contact
prénom (*m*) first name
présenter to present/introduce
pression (*f*) pressure
prêt (*m*) loan
prévenir to give notice
prévisions (*f pl*) forecast
prévoir to provide for/allow for
principe (*m*) principle
principe: en principe in theory
prise (*f*) **de rendez-vous** booking appointments
prix (*m*) price
prochain(e) next
proche nearby
produit (*m*) product
professeur (*m*) school teacher
profession (*f*) profession
promotion (*f*) sales promotion
propos: à propos by the way
proposer to offer/suggest
propre clean
propre own (adj.)
propriétaire (*m/f*) owner
publicité (*f*) publicity/advertising
puis next
pull (*m*) pullover

Q
quai (*m*) platform
qualification (*f*) qualification
qualité (*f*) quality
quand when
quant à as for
quartier (*m*) district
quatrième fourth
quel/quelle what/which
quelque/quelques a few/some
quelque chose something
qu'est-ce que what
question (*f*) question
qui who
quittance (*f*) receipt

R
radiateur (*m*) radiator
ramener to bring
rapatriement (*f*) repatriation
rapide rapid/fast
rapidité (*f*) speed
rappeler to call back
rase: en rase campagne in the open country
rayon (*m*) shelf/department
réception (*f*) reception
recette (*f*) recipe
recevoir to receive
recherche (*f*) research
recommandé(e) recommended/registered (letter)
réconforter to comfort
reconnaître to recognise
reconnu(e) recognised
reçu (*m*) receipt
redresser to put right
réduire to reduce
réduit(e) reduced
réflexion (*f*) reflection/time for thought
regarder to look at
régional(e) regional
règlement (*m*) regulation/rule
regretter to regret/be sorry
régulier/régulière regular
reine (*f*) queen
relier to link
remboursement (*m*) refund
rembourser to refund
remercier to thank
remise (*f*) discount
remorque (*f*) trailer
remorquer to tow
remorqueur-dépanneur (*m*) breakdown/ recovery vehicle
remplir to fill in
rémunération (*f*) pay
rencontrer to meet
rendez-vous (*m*) meeting/appointment
rendre to return/give back
rendre visite à to pay a visit to
renseignements (*m pl*) information
rentrée (*f*) **d'argent** deposit
rentrer to go in/pull in

répandu(e) widespread/common
réparation (*f*) repairs
repas (*m*) meal
repas d'affaires business lunch
repère (*m*) landmark
répondeur (*m*) **automatique** answering machine
répondre to answer
repos (*m*) rest
repousser to push back
représentant (*m*)/**représentante** (*f*) representative
réservation (*f*) reservation
réserve: sous réserve de subject to
réserver to reserve
respiration (*f*) breathing
respiratoire breathing/respiratory
responsabilité (*f*) responsibility
responsable (*m/f*) **du personnel** personnel officer
retirer to withdraw
retour (*m*) return journey
retourner to return
rétréci(e) narrowing
retrouver to rediscover
réunion (*f*) meeting
réverbère (*m*) lamp-post
révision (*f*) service (car)
revoir: au revoir goodbye
revue (*f*) magazine
rez-de-chaussée (*m*) ground floor
rien nothing
risque (*m*) risk
risquer de to risk
robe (*f*) dress
roi (*m*) king
rose pink
rôti(e) roast
roue (*f*) wheel
rouge red
roulant: escalier (*m*) **roulant** escalator
rouler to run (transport)
route (*f*) road
routier (*m*) lorry driver
rue (*f*) road/street

S
s'appeler to be called
s'arrêter to stop
s'écrire to be spelt
s'il vous plaît please
s'installer to set up a practice
s'occuper de to bother about
sabot (m) **de Denver** clamp
saignant rare (steak)
salade (*f*) lettuce
salaire (*m*) salary
salle (*f*) room
salle à manger dining room
salle d'eau shower room
salle de bains bathroom
salon (*m*) living room
salon (*m*) **de coiffure** hairdresser's
salon d'essayage fitting room
salon de thé tea room

salsifis (*m*) salsify
sans without
sans plomb unleaded
santé (*f*) health
sauf except
saumon (*m*) salmon
saviez: vous saviez you knew
savoir to know (information)
savoir: à savoir namely
se détendre to relax
se développer to develop
se diriger vers to go towards
se passer to happen
se prémunir de to take precautions
se rendre à to go to
se renforcer to get stronger
se retrouver to meet
se tenir to be
séance (*f*) performance
secourir to help
secours (*m pl*) emergency services
secret/secrète secret
secrétaire secretary
sécurité (*f*) security
Sécurité sociale Social Security
séjour (*m*) stay/living room
selon according to, depending on
semaine (*f*) week
seminaire (*m*) seminar
sens (*m*) direction
sensiblement noticeably
sentait: il se sentait he felt
séparé(e) separate
service (*m*) **du personnel** personnel department
service en chambre room service
servir to serve
seul(e) single/only
seulement only
si if
signature (*f*) signature
signer to sign
simplement simply
simplifier to simplify
sirop (*m*) syrup
société (*f*) company
sœur (*f*) sister
soir (*m*) evening
soit namely
soit... ou either … or
soleil (*m*) sun
somme (*f*) sum (money)
sommeil (*m*) sleep
son (*m*) sound
sortie (*f*) outing/exit
souffrir to suffer
souhaitable desirable
sous underneath
souterrain(e) underground
souvent often
spacieux/spacieuse spacious
spécialiste (*m/f*) specialist
spécialité (*f*) speciality

sport (*m*) **d'équipe** team game
sportif/sportive keen on sport
stage (*m*) training course
standing (*m*) standing, prestige
station (*f*) **service** service station
stationnement (*m*) parking
steak (*m*) steak
sténodactylo (*f*) shorthand typist
stimulant(e) stimulating
studio (*m*) bedsit
style (*m*) style
subir to undergo
substantiel/substantielle substantial
sud (*m*) South
Suède (*f*) Sweden
suffire: il suffit it is enough
Suisse (*f*) Switzerland
suisse Swiss
suivre to follow
supérieur à greater than
supplémentaire additional
sur on
sûr/sûre sure
surtout above all
survie (*f*) survival
système (*m*) system

T
table (*f*) table
taille (*f*) size
tapisserie (*f*) tapestry
tard late
tard: plus tard later
tarif (*m*) rate/price list
tarte (*f*) **aux pommes** apple tart
tatouage (*m*) **sécurité automobile** security engraving
   (on a car)
taux (*m*) **de change** exchange rate
télécopieur (*m*) fax machine
téléphoner to telephone
téléphoniste (*m/f*) telephonist
téléviseur (*m*) television
télévision (*m*) television
témoin (*m*) witness
temps (*m*) time/weather
temps: de temps en temps from time to time
tendre to hold out
tenez here you are
tenir to hold
termes (*m pl*) terms
tête (*f*) head
thé (*m*) tea
théâtre (*m*) theatre
thon (*m*) tuna
tirer to pull
toit (*m*) roof
tomate (*f*) tomato
tomber en panne to break down
tordre to twist/sprain
toucher to cash (a cheque)
toujours always/still
tournant (*m*) turning/corner

tourner to turn
tous risques fully comprehensive
tousser to cough
tout à fait quite
tout(e) all/every
toutefois however
toux (*f*) cough
traditionnel/traditionnelle traditional
traduction (*f*) translation
trajet (*m*) trip/journey
transport (*m*) **routier** transport of goods
travail (*m*) work
travailler to work
traveller (*m*) traveller's cheque
très very
triangle (*m*) **de panne** hazard warning triangle
troisième third
trouver to find
truc (*m*) thing/trick
T-shirt (*m*) T-shirt
tuile (*f*) roof tile

U
unité (*f*)**: à l'unité** singly
unité monétaire currency
urgence: de toute urgence without delay
urgent(e) urgent
usine (*f*) plant factory
utiliser to use

V
vacances (*f pl*) holidays
vague (*f*) wave
valable valid
valeur (*f*) value
varier to vary
vaste huge
véhicule (*m*) vehicle
véhicule articulé articulated vehicle
vendre to sell
venir to come
vent (*m*) wind
vent: le vent d'autan South wind
vente (*f*) sale
ventre (*m*) stomach
verglas (*m*) black ice
vérifier to check
vers towards/about (time)
vert(e) green
veste (*f*) jacket
vêtements (*m pl*) clothes
viande (*f*) meat
vie (*f*) life
vieux/vieille old
vignette (*f*) tax disc/sticker
vigueur: en vigueur in force
ville (*f*) town
vin (*m*) wine
virage (*m*) bend (road)
virer to transfer
visibilité (*f*) visibility
visiter to visit

vitesse (*f*) speed
vitrine (*f*) shop window
voie (*f*) way/pathway
voilà there you are
voir to see
voiture (*f*) car
vol (*m*) theft
volant (*m*) steering wheel
votre/vos your
vôtres: les vôtres yours

vouloir to want
vous saviez you knew
voyage (*m*) **d'affaires** business trip
voyageur (*m*) traveller
vrai true
vue (*f*) view

Y
yaourt (*m*) yogurt

Unit key

UNIT 1

Dialogue 1:   At reception

Monsieur Leclerc arrives at reception.

M. Leclerc	Do you speak French?
Receptionist	Yes sir.
M. Leclerc	Good morning. I have a meeting with John Davidson.
Receptionist	May I ask your name?
M. Leclerc	I'm Gérard Leclerc, the director of Thompson France.

The lady at reception phones John Davidson.

Receptionist	Mr. Davidson is coming.
M. Leclerc	Thank you.
Mr. Davidson	Good morning, I'm John Davidson. Pleased to meet you.
M. Leclerc	Pleased to meet you.

Exercise 1

1 Je suis anglaise; je suis chef des ventes. **2** Je suis écossais; je suis ingénieur. **3** Je suis irlandais; je suis gérant. **4** Je suis galloise; je suis secrétaire. **5** Je suis anglais; je suis chef des ventes. **6** Je suis américaine; je suis chef des achats.

Exercise 3

1b); 2d); 3a); 4c)

Exercise 4

1 a) J'habite Manchester
b) Je travaille à Twyford Chemicals.

Exercise 5

Bonjour, Monsieur./Bonjour, Madame./C'est de la part de qui?/Je m'appelle Chris James./Bonjour, Monsieur./Bonjour, Madame./Je suis Monique Leblanc, chef des achats./Moi, je suis Chris James de Booth Brothers./Heureuse de faire votre connaissance./Enchanté.

Comprehension 1

Suzanne   Réceptionniste; française; Angoulême/**Paul**   Ingénieur commercial; français; Bordeaux/**Jean-Pierre**   Ingénieur; français; Paris/**Monique**   Secrétaire; française, Boulogne

Transcript
Suzanne   Je suis Suzanne Albin, je suis française bien sûr, j'habite Angoulême et je suis réceptionniste./**Paul**   Bon, je suis Paul Bernard, je suis français et j'habite Bordeaux. Je suis ingénieur commercial./**Jean-Pierre**   Moi, je m'appelle Jean-Pierre Champigny, j'habite Paris et je suis ingénieur aussi. Oh, et je suis français!/**Monique**   Moi, je suis Monique Legrand, je suis française, j'habite Boulogne et je suis secrétaire. Et voilà!

Progress check

1 Bonjour. Je suis...
2 Je suis anglais(e) et je suis... avec Marley Transport.
3 I am happy to make your acquaintance.
   a) A woman because the word is **heureuse** (*f*) and not **heureux** (*m*).

b) Enchanté(e).
4 J'habite (Manchester).
5 Je travaille à/pour Agrichem.

UNIT 2

Dialogue 1: **On the telephone**

Secretary	Hallo, yes. Personnel department.
Candidate	Good afternoon. I'm looking for a job with your company.
Secretary	What is your name, sir?
Candidate	I'm called Dubois.
Secretary	And your first name?
Candidate	Pierre.
Secretary	What is your profession?
Candidate	I'm an engineer.
Secretary	What is your nationality?
Candidate	I'm French.
Secretary	Where do you live?
Candidate	I live in Saumur.

Exercise 1

```
Nom:            Truscott
Prénom:         Sandra
Profession:     Professeur
Nationalité:    Britannique
Domicile:       Manchester
```

Comprehension 1

F. Voisine Canadian, 32, production engineer/**G. Leclerc** Swiss, 22, secretary/**D. Berrogain** French, 30, manager/**M. Bérous** French, 23, purchasing manager.

Transcript
‹‹Eh bien, j'ai une liste de candidats qui cherchent un emploi dans la société. D'abord il y a Frédéric Voisine. Il est canadien. Il a trente-deux ans. Il est chef de production. Puis, Geneviève Leclerc. Elle est suisse, elle a vingt-deux ans. Elle est secrétaire. Ensuite, Daniel Berrogain. Il est français. Il a trente ans. Il est gérant. Enfin Martine Bérous. Elle est française, elle a vingt-trois ans. Elle est chef des achats.››

Comprehension 2

1a) faux **b)** vrai **c)** faux **d)** vrai **e)** vrai
2a) vrai **b)** faux **c)** faux **d)** vrai **e)** vrai

Translation
1 I am called Dominique Dupont. I am French and I am from Fontainebleau. I am married and I have one daughter. She is called Claudine. My husband is called Yves. He is an engineer. He is production manager at a car manufacturer's. I work in a restaurant.

2 I am called Patrick Joubert. My firm is called Créations Joubert. It is a little family firm, a little hat factory. I am married. My wife is called Chloé. She works with me. My sister works with me too. She is called Martine and is unmarried.

| **Exercise 6** | **1** le frère **2** la fille **3** le mari **4** le fils **5** la mère **6** la soeur |

| **Exercise 7** | **1** John **2** Stephen **3** John/Monica **4** John/Monica **5** Monica |

| **Exercise 8** | 1a), 2f), 3h), 4b), 5c), 6d), 7j), 8e), 9g), 10i) |

| **Exercise 9** | **1** M. Leclerc est français. **2** Mme Vandenberghe est belge. **3** Mlle Dubois est canadienne. **4** Mme Vasquez est espagnole. **5** M. O'Donnell est irlandais. **6** Mlle Kohl est suisse. |

| **Exercise 10** | **1** Où habitez-vous? **2** Où travaillez-vous? **3** Êtes-vous marié? **4** Êtes-vous chef de production? **5** Cherchez-vous un emploi ici en France? |

Progress check

1 a) Je suis marié(e)/célibataire.
   b) Il est/s'appelle/William.
       Elle s'appelle/est Janet.
2 J'ai une soeur. Elle s'appelle Claire.
   Ma mère s'appelle Sheila.
3 Suisse, Belge, Canadien.

4 Il s'appelle Robert Martin, il est gérant, il est irlandais et il
   habite Stockport.
5 a) espagnole b) français c) belge d) espagnol
   e) irlandais f) française g) anglaise.
6 a) le fils b) la fille c) le père d) la femme e) le mari.

UNIT 3

| **Exercise 1** | C'est bien l'Hôtel France?/Je voudrais réserver une chambre s'il vous plaît/Pour une personne/Pour quatre nuits à partir du seize décembre/Au nom de Monsieur Paul Smith/C'est le zéro huit, douze, vingt-huit, dix-neuf, dix-huit/Parfait. Merci, Madame./Merci, et au revoir Monsieur. |

| **Exercise 2** | **1** C'est bien l'Hôtel France?/Je voudrais réserver une chambre/Pour une personne/Pour quatre nuits à partir du seize décembre/Au nom de (*your name*)/C'est le (*your phone number – if you don't know the numbers, use ones you do!*)/Merci, au revoir. **2** C'est bien l'Hôtel France?/Je voudrais réserver une chambre/Pour deux personnes/Pour deux nuits à partir du vendredi soir (le dix-neuf décembre) au dimanche matin (le vingt et un). |

| **Exercise 3** |

```
1 Je confirme ma réservation d'une chambre
  pour une personne avec salle de bains
  pour quatre nuits du seize au dix-neuf
  décembre au nom de...

2 Je confirme notre réservation d'une
  chambre pour deux personnes avec salle
  de bains pour deux nuits du dix-neuf au
  vingt et un décembre au nom de
  M./Mme/Mlle...
```

| **Exercise 5** | 29–38–59–22; 44–37–51–33; 58–46–35–42 |

| **Exercise 6** | **1** The word **désolée** agrees with its noun – it has an extra **e** to show it is feminine. |

2 Une chambre pour deux personnes.

3 **C'est bien l'Hôtel Anjou?** *This is the Hôtel Anjou isn't it?* **Bien** is used to check on the information.
Merci bien. *Thank you very much.* **Bien** is used for emphasis.

Comprehension 1

1 2 nights, 1 person, bathroom and telephone, one room.
2 A fortnight, 4 people, bathroom, 3 rooms.
3 1 night, 1 person, bathroom, television and telephone.
4 4 nights, 20 people, restaurant and car park, 20 rooms.

Transcript

1 Bonjour, Madame. Je voudrais réserver une chambre d'hôtel pour deux nuits à partir du 14 février. Je voudrais une chambre avec salle de bains et téléphone.

2 Bonjour. Nous cherchons un hôtel pour notre famille pour quinze jours. Une chambre pour deux personnes avec salle de bains, et deux chambres pour une personne pour les enfants.

3 Je voudrais réserver une chambre pour une personne pour une nuit au nom de Legrand. Il voudrait une chambre avec salle de bains, télévision et téléphone.

4 Je voudrais réserver des chambres pour vingt personnes de notre société pour quatre nuits. Ils voudraient un hôtel avec un restaurant et un parking est essentiel.

Comprehension 2

1 vrai **2** vrai **3** faux **4** faux **5** faux **6** vrai

Translation

```
Sir,

I am coming to London in August. I would like to
book a hotel room for my family. There are four
of us: my wife and me and our two children, a
boy and a girl. We are looking for a little
hotel with a car park. We would like a double
room with a bathroom and two singles for the
children. Will you please send us a list of hotels
and prices (literally do you wish to send ...)?
Thanking you in advance, Yours faithfully ...
(literally I pray you to accept the expression
of my best wishes).
```

Progress check

1 L'Hôtel du Cerf s'il vous plaît.
2 Je voudrais deux chambres, une avec douche et une avec salle de bains.
3 I am sorry.
4 Une chambre pour deux personnes avec salle de bains.

5 Pour trois nuits, s'il vous plaît.
6 Quarante-deux, cinquante-sept, trente et un.
7 Douze, cinquante-cinq, quarante.

UNIT 4

Exercise 1

1 No capitals; you need the article (**le**); you don't need to say *of.* **2** Because **heure** is feminine. **3** *I am* telephoning; *I am* a secretary; they *will be* arriving; they *will* take. (The French present tense can be translated by continuous tenses, in the present and future, and by the straight present and future.)

Exercise 3	**Anne** dimanche, à quinze heures trente; **Paul** mercredi, à sept heures quinze; **Clare** lundi, à neuf heures quarante; **Debbie** vendredi, à dix-sept heures cinquante; **John** samedi, à quatre heures dix; **Kathy** mardi, à dix-huit heures cinq; **Tim** jeudi à vingt et une heures quarante-cinq.

Exercise 4

1 Bonjour Madame, je suis la/le secrétaire de Thompson Angleterre. M. Leclerc part vendredi à huit heures; il prend l'avion à onze heures et il arrive à Paris à treize heures. Il prend le train de Montparnasse à quatorze heures cinquante et il arrive à Angers à seize heures vingt et une.

2 Bonjour chérie! Je pars à huit heures et je prends l'avion à onze heures. J'arrive à Paris à treize heures et je prends le train de Montparnasse à quatorze heures cinquante. J'arrive à Angers à seize heures vingt et une.

3 Je pars de Manchester à sept heures trente. J'arrive à Glasgow à onze heures cinquante. J'ai un rendez-vous avec McLaren Associates à douze heures trente. Je pars de Glasgow à seize heures quinze et j'arrive à Manchester à vingt heures trente.

Exercise 6

2 le six janvier **3** le vingt et un mai **4** le trente septembre **5** le cinq novembre **6** le dix-huit août **7** le huit février **8** le onze juin.

Comprehension 1

Mme Pinot	Monday at 10.00
M. Michel	Tuesday at 14.00
Chef des Achats	Wednesday at 10.30
Chef de Production	Thursday at 15.30
Chef de Production et Chef des Ventes	Friday, midday

Transcript

D'abord lundi, vous avez une réunion à dix heures avec Madame Pinot. Mardi, vous avez une réunion avec Monsieur Michel à quatorze heures. Mercredi à dix heures et demie, le chef des achats de la société Leroy; jeudi à quinze heures trente, le chef de production; vendredi à midi le chef de production et le chef des ventes.

Comprehension 2

1 13 April **2** 13.40 **3** BA 657 **4** TGV (train de grande vitesse, *high speed train*) **5** Hotel Biarritz, rue Pont-Lévy **6** 2 nights **7** 15 April **8** In the afternoon.

Translation

Hallo, good morning …. Yes? Um, I am called Louise Hetherington: I am the secretary of John Baker of Permatour in Brighton. I am phoning to tell you that everything is arranged for Mr. Baker's visit to you next week. I am going to write to you today with all the details but I just wish to confirm to you on the phone that Mr. Baker will be arriving in France on Monday 13 April at 13.40. His flight number is BA 657 which leaves Heathrow at 12.45 and which arrives at Orly at 13.40. After that, he will be catching the TGV directly to Lyons and arrives in Lyons at about 19.00 – the exact arrival time is 19.05. I have reserved a room for him at the Biarritz Hotel, in Pont-Levy street – that's for two nights. He is returning to England on Wednesday, 15 April in the afternoon. I hope that is convenient for you. Is that all right?… Fine. I will tell him that everything is all settled for his visit then. Thank you very much and goodbye.

Exercise 8

1 Question **2** Statement **3** Question **4** Question **5** Statement **6** Statement

Progress check

1 a) Bonjour, je suis Debby James...
   b) ... de Porter Ladouce en Angleterre.
2 a) J'arrive à Paris, jeudi le treize février.
   b) Je prends le train de Paris à Saumur.

c) J'arrive à six heures du soir.
d) J'ai une chambre réservée à l'Hôtel du Cerf pour deux nuits.

3   Je pars pour l'Angleterre samedi, le quinze février à 8.00 le matin.
4   a)   John Smith et Marie Anderson prennent l'avion le 2 mars
     b)   Ils arrivent à Saumur à 15.00 mardi, le 4 mars.

5   a)   J'ai rendez-vous avec M. Paul Roger, vendredi, le 14 février à 14.00.
     b)   J'ai rendez-vous avec Sandrine Bernard, samedi, à 9.30.

UNIT 5

Exercise 1

Un billet pour Nice s'il vous plaît/ Un aller-retour: ça fait combien?/Je suis désolé(e), je n'ai pas de monnaie/Le train est à quelle heure?/Quel quai, s'il vous plaît?

Exercise 2

1 35 minutes **2** Every fifteen minutes **3** In all the RER stations **4** In all stations on the B line in Paris

Exercise 3

valid **valable**; *singly* **à l'unité**; *sold* **en vente**; *a trip* **un trajet**; *the suburbs* **la banlieue**; *unlimited* **illimité**; *enquire* **renseignez-vous** from **se renseigner**; *reduced rate* **des tarifs réduits.**

Exercise 4

1 Pour aller à Odéon s'il vous plaît? **2** Pour aller à la Gare du Nord s'il vous plaît? **3** Pour aller à la Gare de Lyon s'il vous plaît? **4** Pour aller à Concorde s'il vous plaît?

Comprehension 1

1 18.55 **2** Platform 5 **3** 20.30

Transcript
Le train en partance pour Versailles partira dans cinq minutes du quai numéro deux. Le train en partance pour Chartres, partira à dix-huit heures treize du quai numéro trois. Attention s'il vous plaît. Le train au quai numéro cinq en partance pour Angers partira à 18.55 au lieu de 18.45. Il arrivera avec dix minutes de retard vers 20.30. La SNCF vous prie de bien vouloir l'excuser.

Exercise 6

1 72, soixante-douze **2** 86, quatre-vingt-six **3** 91, quatre-vingt-onze **4** 89, quatre-vingt-neuf **5** 92, quatre-vingt-douze **6** 88, quatre-vingt-huit **7** 94, quatre-vingt-quatorze **8** 81, quatre-vingt-un **9** 75, soixante-quinze **10** 71, soixante et onze.

Exercise 7

You should have circled: 75, 81, 99, 77, 63, 96.

Exercise 8

1 64, soixante-quatre **2** 79, soixante-dix-neuf **3** 92, quatre-vingt-douze **4** 85, quatre-vingt-cinq **5** 93, quatre-vingt-treize **6** 97, quatre-vingt-dix-sept **7** 78, soixante-dix-huit **8** 83, quatre-vingt-trois **9** 76, soixante-seize **10** 80, quatre-vingts.

Exercise 9

1 Everyone **2** Each company **3** All the boys and girls

Exercise 10

L'Hôtel Concorde s'il vous plaît/Oui, je suis anglais(e)/Non, c'est un voyage d'affaires/Merci, je suis des cours de français depuis six mois.

Exercise 11

1 The departure times of trains arriving in Versailles in the evening.
2 The departure times of trains to Nantes on Friday evenings in June.
3 The departure times of trains from Versailles to Chartres, tomorrow, Saturday.
4 The evening departure times of trains from Paris to Le Mans in June.

Transcript

1 Bonjour, Mademoiselle. Je veux aller à Versailles. Je voudrais arriver le soir. A quelle heure est-ce qu'il y a un train? **2** Je veux aller en vacances à Nantes un vendredi soir en juin. A quelle heure sont les trains? **3** Nous voudrions aller de Versailles à Chartres demain, samedi. A quelle heure sont les trains? **4** Je vais au Mans au mois de juin. Quand est-ce qu'il y a un train de Paris? J'arrive à Paris le soir.

Exercise 12	**1a)** Mais non, je ne suis pas américain, je suis anglais. **b)** Non, je ne suis pas de York, je suis de Manchester. **c)** Non, je ne suis pas avec ma femme, je suis avec une collègue. **d)** Non, je ne suis pas chef des achats, je suis chef des ventes. **e)** Mais non, je ne parle pas bien français, je suis des cours depuis six mois seulement!

2 Je travaille chez Thompson depuis six ans. J'habite Londres depuis six ans. Je suis des cours de français depuis neuf mois et je viens en France depuis six mois.

Exercise 13	(on tape): Elle finit son cours en France. Nous finissons notre travail à Angers.

Progress check

1 Un aller-retour à Saumur, s'il vous plaît.
2 Je n'ai pas de monnaie.
3 Le train est à quelle heure?
4 Où est le quai s'il vous plaît?
5 a) C'est ma troisième visite en France.
   b) C'est un voyage d'affaires.
   c) J'ai appris le français à l'école.

   d) Nous suivons des cours de français chez... depuis trois mois.
   e) La rue Jean-Jacques Rousseau s'il vous plaît.
6 Le quatre-vingt-deux, quatre-vingt-douze, soixante-quinze.
7 a) Have a good stay!
   b) You're welcome!
   c) I am not on holiday.

UNIT 6

Exercise 1	Bonjour, j'ai une chambre reservée au nom de Smith./Oui, je suis ingénieur commercial avec Thompson Manufacturing./Oui, voilà mon passeport./Bien sûr./Est-ce qu'il y a un bar?/A quelle heure est le dîner?/Merci. Bonsoir.

Exercise 2	**1** f) **2** d) **3** b) **4** c) **5** g) **6** j) **7** i) **8** k) **9** h) **10** e)

Exercise 3	*You could say sentences such as:* À l'hôtel, il y a soixante-treize chambres et un restaurant et un salon pour les seminaires. Dans la chambre il y a un téléviseur et un téléphone. Ils acceptent des cartes de crédit.

Exercise 4	**1** 2:10 **2** 18:45 **3** 16:21 **4** 11:11 **5** 21:25 **6** 5:15

Exercise 5	**1** From 7.00 a.m. **2** Between 12.00 and 14.00. **3** Between 19.00 and 22.30. **4** All day.

Transcript

1 Et voilà votre clef, Madame. Chambre numéro 36./Merci, Madame. Pouvez-vous me dire à quelle heure est le petit dejeuner le matin?/A partir de sept heures, Madame.

2 Bonjour, Monsieur./Bonjour, Madame. Le déjeuner est à quelle heure?/Le restaurant est ouvert entre midi et quatorze heures./Et le soir?/Vous pouvez dîner entre dix-neuf heures et vingt-deux heures trente, Monsieur./Merci, Madame.

3 Voilà votre passeport, Monsieur. C'est la chambre numéro cinq cent avec salle de bain./Merci. J'ai un rendez-vous ce soir. A quelle heure est-ce que le bar ouvre?/Il est ouvert toute la journée.

Exercise 6

J'arrive à Angers lundi à vingt et une heures. Mardi à neuf heures j'ai une réunion avec le chef des ventes à Thompson France et je déjeune avec Claire et Marianne à midi. A treize heures je visite l'usine. Mercredi, à neuf heures trente j'ai un rendez-vous avec le chef de production à Silex, et à quatorze heures et demie je visite l'usine de Silex avec Gérard. Jeudi matin, je prends le petit déjeuner avec le P.-D.G de Lamarche et Cie, et à quinze heures, je visite le chantier avec Robert Bernier. Vendredi à huit heures du matin je pars de l'hôtel pour Paris et j'arrive à Paris à dix heures quarante cinq. Je prends l'avion pour Londres à treize heures.

Comprehension 1

The hotel in the brochure on the right would be most appropriate.

Exercise 7

Some possibilities are: Celui-ci est spacieux et ensoleillé et il a un balcon. Ce n'est pas trop cher. Celui-là est petit avec un parking. Celui-ci donne sur le parc – il est tout neuf et il a un parking couvert. Celui-ci est trop petit avec un cabinet de toilette seulement mais ce n'est pas cher.

Exercise 8

In order of intensity: J'adore (1) C'est bien (2) J'aime assez (3) C'est horrible (4) Je déteste (5). There is little difference between 4 and 5.

Comprehension 2

1 Large 2 Yes 3 The sitting room 4 A sofa, a table, chairs and a TV set 5 In the car park opposite

Transcript
Paul   C'est ici, au premier étage. Voilà, Mesdames./**Claire**   Mais c'est grand. Le salon est immense. J'aime ça./**Marianne**   Il est confortable. J'aime beaucoup ce canapé./**Claire**   Une petite table, et des chaises... et tu as un poste de télévision!/**Paul**   Bien sûr!/**Claire**   Qu'est ce que c'est? C'est la douche? Tu n'as pas de salle de bains alors./**Marianne**   La chambre donne sur le parc. La vue est très belle. Il y a un parking?/**Paul**   Oui. En face./**Marianne**   C'est bien. J'aime beaucoup.

Comprehension 3

1a) l'entrée b) l'escalier c) le jardin d) donne sur e) les murs f) la salle à manger g) la cuisine h) le cabinet de toilette.
2 En Haute Provence

Transcript
In Charente
Building in an olde-worlde style, traditional materials, whitewashed walls and pink roof tiles. It comprises a ground floor, first floor and garage. The dining room is next to the kitchen. The entrance hall, stairs and store room are to the back of the house. On the first floor there are three bedrooms, a bathroom and gallery.

In Haute Provence
A house built in regional style with a garden and balcony on the bedroom floor. The ground floor has a very large sitting room with a separate dining room and kitchen. The dining room, shower room, laundry and cloakroom give on to the entrance hall. A corridor gives access to the garage.
On the first floor there are two bedrooms with a bathroom and separate lavatory. The bedroom gives on to a balcony.

Exercise 9

1 Il est ouvert de huit heures trente à midi, et de quatorze heures à dix-huit heures. Il est fermé de midi à quatorze heures.
2 Il est ouvert de neuf heures à une heure, et de deux heures à cinq heures et demie. Il est fermé d'une heure à deux heures.

Progress check

1 a) J'ai une chambre reservée au nom de...
   b) Je suis *Anne Baker* de *Maupas Ltd.*
   c) Voilà mon passeport.
   d) Est-ce qu'il y a un bar et un restaurant à l'hôtel?
   e) Est-ce qu'il y a un téléviseur dans ma chambre?
   f) A quelle heure est le petit dejeuner?
   g) Le restaurant est ouvert?

2 a) L'hôtel a un sauna et une piscine.
   b) Il a un grand gymnase.
   c) Il a une petite boutique.

3 a) J'ai rendez-vous avec le chef des ventes à 9.30 du matin à Tratex, à Angers.
   b) Je visite le chef des achats à onze heures.
   c) Je déjeune/mange avec le P.-D.G à une heure.

4 L'appartement est petit et bon marché. C'est très confortable avec une cuisine, deux chambres et un salon. L'appartement est bien meublé. Il donne sur un parc charmant et il y a un parking à côté.

UNIT 7

| Exercise 1 |
Bonsoir Monsieur, je voudrais réserver une table pour ce soir/Pour quatre personnes/A sept heures et demie/Au nom de (your name).

| Exercise 2 |
Bonjour Monsieur, je voudrais réserver une table pour cet après-midi/Pour trois personnes/A une heure/Au nom de (*your name*).

| Exercise 3 |
Société Leroy   20 personnes, samedi le 2 juin, dix-neuf heures./
M. Legrand   2 personnes, vendredi, midi./**Mme Dufour**   6 personnes, samedi soir, dix-neuf heures.

Transcript
1 Restaurant 'Chez Henri'. J'écoute./Je voudrais réserver une table pour samedi soir./Oui, Madame. Pour combien de personnes?/Nous sommes six./A quelle heure, Madame?/Dix-neuf heures./Et c'est à quel nom?/Dufour./C'est noté, Madame. Au revoir./Au revoir.
2 Allô. Restaurant 'Le Relais'./Je voudrais réserver une table pour vendredi midi./Oui, Monsieur. Pour combien de personnes?/Deux. Au nom de Legrand./D'accord, merci. Au revoir./Au revoir.
3 Allô, oui./Je voudrais réserver une table pour le samedi 2 juin./Pour combien de personnes, Madame?/Un groupe de vingt personnes./Oui. C'est possible. C'est à quel nom?/Au nom de le Société Leroy./Vous arriverez vers quelle heure?/Pour l'apéritif à dix-neuf heures./C'est noté, Madame. Merci et au revoir./Au revoir.

| Exercise 4 |
1 J'aime le melon **2** J'adore le melon **3** Je préfère le steak **4** Je n'aime pas le cocktail de crevettes.

| Exercise 6 |
1e), 2c), 3a), 4b), 5d)

| Exercise 7 |
Jean-Luc   J'ai bu un café. Je dois payer 6F80. **Bernard**   J'ai pris un thé et une tarte aux cerises. Je dois payer 16F10. **Nicole**   J'ai pris un thé et un baba au rhum. Je dois payer 16F30.

Comprehension 1

1b), 2c), 3a) under-done.

Transcript
Garçon   Messieurs – Dames. Vous avez choisi?/**Homme**   Madame Dufour, qu'est-ce que vous prenez?/**Dame**   Alors, moi je prends le poulet flambé à l'Armagnac./**Homme**   Et Anne-Marie, tu as choisi?/**Anne-Marie**   Pour moi, c'est la sole à la Normande./**Homme**   Apportez–moi un steak au poivre./**Garçon**   Saignant ou bien cuit, Monsieur?/**Homme**   Saignant, s'il vous plaît.

Comprehension 2   **1** Ils ont appris les recettes de leurs parents. **2** Le midi, le repas d'affaires vous est servi en trois quarts d'heure. **3** Ils les aiment comme ils aiment leur pays, leur région et leur métier. **4** Dans toutes les villes le voyageur peut bien manger sans payer très cher.

Translation

Cooking is very important for the French and French cooking is known throughout the world. In all towns, the traveller can eat well without paying too much. In country inns, the owners (*male or female*) do the cooking. They learnt the recipes from their parents or grand parents when they were young. They know them well. They love them as they love their country, region or trade. On their menu or in their modestly priced set meal you find products which have been lovingly cooked for you. At Angers, Eric, the owner of Saint Gourmand is 25. His wife, Carole, is 22. Eric feels the same passion for cooking that others feel for music. He has no specialities. All the dishes he makes are specialities. At lunch time, the businessmens' lunch at 59 francs is served up to you in three quarters of an hour.

Exercise 8   *You can write sentences such as:* J'ai réservé une table à La Calèche. J'ai pris le poulet et Gérard le steak. Gérard a payé. Nous avons pris un pichet de vin et après j'ai bu un thé. Claire a mangé du poisson. *(Use* **du**, **de la** *or* **des** *if you want to say* some *and* **le** *or* **la** *if you wish to say* the. *In French you say* he chose the fish, *not* he chose fish.*)*

Progress check

1   Une table pour quatre personnes à sept heures et demie samedi, le 14 mars.

2   **a)** Le poulet pour moi, le melon pour ma femme et le cocktail de crevettes pour mon/ma collègue.
    b) Le steak pour tous trois, deux bien cuits et un saignant, et pour boire, du vin rouge.
    c) Un café noir pour moi et deux crèmes.

3   **a)** Un thé au lait
    b) Un jus d'orange

    c) Un sandwich au jambon
    d) Un baba au rhum
    e) Une tarte aux pommes

4   **a)** Je préfère le steak à point. **b)** Je préfère le vin blanc.

5   **a)** J'aime le jambon. **b)** J'aime le steak au poivre.

6   Je dois quatre-vingt-seize francs.

7   J'ai bu un café et j'ai mangé un baba au rhum. Nous avons bu du vin. Caroline a mangé un sandwich au jambon, etc.

UNIT 8

Exercise 1   **a)** toucher un chèque **b)** changer de l'argent (or required amount, i.e. cent livres, cent cinquante dollars, etc.) **c)** quel est le taux d'échange?

Exercise 2   **a)** 5000 francs **b)** 100 franc notes **c)** passport or an ID card **d)** Thursday at 3.00 p.m.

Transcript

Bonjour, Monsieur. Je voudrais des chèques de voyage pour partir en Angleterre vendredi matin./Combien voulez-vous changer?/Je voudrais changer cinq mille francs./Voulez-vous des chèques de cent ou cinq cents francs?/Cent francs./Quand est-ce que vous comptez passer les chercher?/Jeudi, à trois heures de l'après-midi./Oui, il faut un passeport ou une carte d'identité.

Comprehension 1   **1** un compte **2** retirer de l'argent **3** quand les banques sont fermées **4** payer le téléphone et l'eau **5** en signant simplement une facture **6** une cotisation modique **7** gérer votre budget

Translation

The ability to withdraw money on Sunday or at midnight one evening when the banks are shut … The certainty of finding money wherever you are on holiday … Not having to think about paying the telephone bill, the water and gas bills, the electricity … Having an easy way of accessing your salary and all your regular cash deposits … Paying for your purchases by simply signing a bill, in France as well as abroad … Doing more towards the security of your family through a modest payment … Depositing your documents and your valuables in a safe place. These are some of the services which you can draw on at Crédit Lyonnais thanks to your Checking Account and your Blue Card. These services have been designed to simply your life, to help you manage your money better and to guarantee you better security.

Exercise 3

Je vais travailler ici pendant une année et je voudrais ouvrir un compte courant./A partir du mois de septembre./Oui, bien sûr, voilà mon permis de conduire./Mon adresse c'est 49, rue Aristide Briand./Oui, je voudrais déposer mille francs sur le compte.

Comprehension 2

1 Pay for purchases in many different establishments all over the world; withdraw money in France and all over the world.
2 Your spouse may use it; a member of your family may use it.

Translation

In France as abroad DINERS CLUB is your financial passport. **An international credit card:** You settle your account by a simple signature in more than a million and a half establishments: shops, restaurants, hotels, airlines – throughout the entire world! **Cashpoints all over the world:** You can withdraw up to 4000 francs with your card in France over a period of seven days in branches of BNP, BARCLAYS, BANQUE WORMS and CHEQUE POINT. And abroad, the equivalent of 1000 US dollars in local currency at more than 27,000 cash dispensers in Canada, Japan, England and the US as well as in all Diners Club offices throughout the world. **Protection in case of loss or theft:** You need only telephone (1) 47.62.75.75 and you are entirely protected against unlawful use of your Diners Club card. **A money reserve thanks to permanent credit:** Diners Club offers you credit of 3000 to 140.000 francs that you can use quite safely. You will therefore have the choice each month of settling the bill, in cash, for your purchases in France and throughout the world in three payments (with 45 francs administration charge) or on credit. If you wish to use this service, you need only mention it on your card request (form). **Your second Diners Club card:** For 285 francs per year you can have it made out in the name of your spouse or other member of your family.

Exercise 4

1 Wants to know if it's possible to take out money when the banks are shut.
2 Wants to pay for bills and taxes other than by cheque. **3** Wants to know how much money can be taken out with a Blue Card. **4** Wants a joint account with her husband but also wants her own cheque book.

Transcript

Je travaille de neuf heures à six heures. Je voudrais retirer de l'argent quand les banques sont fermées. Est-ce possible?/Je n'aime pas faire de chèque pour mes quittances et mes impôts. J'aimerais un moyen de paiement plus pratique./Combien d'argent peut-on retirer avec une Carte Bleue?/Mon mari et moi voudrions un compte-joint. Mais je voudrais mon propre chéquier. C'est possible?

Exercise 5

1 Je vais toucher un chèque de voyage **2** Je vais retirer de l'argent **3** Je vais ouvrir un compte **4** Je vais toucher un chèque **5** Je vais payer l'éléctricité.

Progress check

1 a) Quel est le taux d'échange aujourd'hui?
   b) Je voudrais changer deux cents livres en francs.
   c) Je voudrais toucher dix chèques de voyage.
   d) Voilà mon passeport.
   e) Je peux ouvrir un compte courant?
   f) J'habite 16, rue de Rennes, Vincennes.

   g) Je voudrais remettre sept cents francs.
   h) Mon salaire va être viré directement sur mon compte.
2 a) Vous pouvez retirer de l'argent quand les banques sont fermées.
   b) Vous pouvez payer le téléphone, l'eau et l'éléctricité.
   c) Vous pouvez payer les achats en signant la facture.

UNIT 9

Exercise 1

1 Il faut aller à Sport 2000, rue St. Jean 2 Il faut aller à Madeleine Lambert, 29, Place Bilange (*or various other possibilities*) 3 Il faut aller à Maison Lelogeais, 6 Avenue du Général de Gaulle 4 Il faut aller à Caves de Grenelle, 20 rue Marceau

Exercise 3

1 The Hospital 2 Place Verdun 3 Pont Cessart 4 The church of Nantilly

Transcript
1 Je suis à l'office du tourisme. Je tourne à droite et puis à gauche. Je suis dans une grande rue. Je prends la cinquième rue à gauche, puis la deuxième à droite. Je suis devant un grand bâtiment. Qu'est-ce que c'est?/2 Je suis devant l'église de Nantilly, je prends la Rue Hoche. Je prends la troisième à droite. Je suis sur une place. Comment s'appelle cette place?/3 Je sors de la Maison du Vin, rue Beaurepaire, je tourne à droite, puis à gauche. Je traverse une place et j'arrive sur un pont. Comment s'appelle ce pont?/4 Je suis à la gare routière. Je tourne à droite dans la rue Carnot. Je prends la première rue à droite et la cinquième à gauche. Ensuite, je prends la troisième rue à droite et la première à gauche. Un peu plus loin il y a une église. Où suis-je?

Exercise 4

Je cherche un/je fais du/je préfère le…

Exercise 5

1e); 2d); 3b); 4c); 5a)

Comprehension 1

a) un chéquier b) l'argent liquide c) une carte de crédit d) un remboursement e) un prêt
The card works as a credit card giving you the right to borrow a certain sum of money. It also works as a 'payment' card to pay for goods directly in shops.

Translation
The Pass card has two functions. It is a card you can pay with. You need neither cash nor chequebook. You simply show your card and by using your secret code, you can make up to 3000 francs worth of purchases in a week. It is also a permanent credit card. If you contribute between 150 and 450 francs per month, you are eligible for a loan from 3000 to 9000 francs.

Comprehension 2

1 He is a hat importer. 2 He is exploring the possibility of working with him and importing his products. 3 To send a brochure or photos of the hats together with a price list.

Translation
Dear Sirs,
We import formal and wedding hats directly (into France). We visit, and are established in, the whole of France. In order to complete our range of products we are seeking new manufacturers.

Could you send us a brochure or photos of your products together with prices, so that we can familiarise ourselves with your products and consider a meeting on our next visit to Great Britain? We await a reply. Yours faithfully, etc.

Comprehension 3   **a)** grey and pink; 546; 54 francs **b)** blue; 550; 62 francs **c)** white and black; 321; 71 francs **d)** red and cream; 210; 75 francs **e)** green; 142; 115 francs **f)** yellow; 236; 134 francs

Transcript
Bonjour Monsieur Johnson. Je voudrais commander les marchandises suivantes. D'abord, article numéro 546 à 54 francs en gris et rose. Puis, article numéro 550 à 62 francs en bleu. Ensuite, article numéro 321 à 71 francs en blanc et noir. Ensuite, article numéro 210 à 75 francs en rouge et écru. Ensuite article numéro 142 à 115 francs en vert. Et enfin, article numéro 236 à 134 francs en jaune.

Progress check

1 a) La Place Bilange s'il vous plaît.
   b) Où est l'Avenue Charles de Gaulle?
   c) Où se trouve la rue St. Jean?
2 a) Je cherche les/des vêtements.
   b) Je cherche du vin.
   c) Je cherche des disques.
   d) Nous cherchons des livres.
   e) Nous cherchons des jouets.
3 a) You must go to Prisunic.
   b) Take the escalator on the ground floor.

   c) Go towards the town centre, as far as Place Bilange and then turn left.
4 a) Je fais du *quarante-deux*.
   b) Je préfère le *vert*.
   c) Il y a un pantalon bleu en vitrine...
   d) Je peux l'essayer?
5 a) Je visiterai Tours demain.
   b) Je trouverai du parfum à Euromarché.
   c) Je demanderai à la réceptionniste.

UNIT 10

Exercise 1   1b); 2e); 3g); 4f); 5a); 6d); 7c)

Exercise 2   Le plein s'il vous plaît/Sans plomb s'il vous plaît/Oui, vérifiez l'huile et l'eau et essuyez le pare-brise aussi.

Comprehension 1   **a)** Centre de Contrôle **b)** Pole Position **c)** Caravaning Loisirs Saumurois

Exercise 3   1b); 2i); 3h); 4f); 5e); 6a); 7c); 8d); 9g)

Comprehension 2   **1** faux **2** vrai **3** faux **4** vrai **5** vrai **6** vrai

Translation
A number of agencies in Paris offer French or foreign cars. Local agencies offer cheaper rates than international agencies but you usually have to return the car where you hired it and not in another town. You must show a valid driving licence and some form of identity. The minimum age can be between 21 and 25 years old. You will be asked for a substantial deposit, a formality which will be waived usually if you are the holder of a recognised credit card.

Exercise 4   Les voilà/Je vais à Paris. C'est un voyage d'affaires/Oui, des cigares/J'ai une réunion à deux heures de l'après-midi. Ça va durer longtemps?

Comprehension 3   **1** He has broken down. **2** He is going to be towed to the next town.

Transcript

Bonjour, Monsieur. Alors, qu'est-ce qui s'est passé?/La voiture... elle s'est arrêtée/Vous avez de l'essence?/Oui, j'ai fait le plein ce matin./Eh bien, il n'y a plus d'eau dans le radiateur Monsieur/C'est pas vrai!/Bon, je vais vous remorquer jusqu'à la prochaine ville. Il y a un garage là-bas.

Progress check

1 a) Le plein, s'il vous plaît... b) ... sans plomb. c) Je vous dois combien? d) Vous me donnez un reçu?
2 a) Voilà mon permis de conduire, carte grise et certificat d'assurance. b) Je n'ai rien à déclarer.
3 a) No entry. b) Stopping and parking forbidden.
   c) Bend to the right.

4 a) We have to search your car. b) Park over there.
   c) Will it take you a long time?
5 a) Je suis allé à Lille la semaine dernière.
   b) Je me suis levé(e) à huit heures ce matin.

UNIT 11

Exercise 1

Non, je n'y suis jamais allé/Ça sera très intéressant/Ça coûte chère la visite?/Ça me plairait beaucoup.

Comprehension 1

Le Louvre: jeudi, samedi, dimanche 9.00–18.00; lundi, mercredi 9.00–21.45; mardi – closed all day.
Beaubourg: lundi–vendredi 12.00–22.00; samedi, dimanche 10.00–22.00.

Translation
The Louvre, a former royal palace, is the most famous museum in the world. There you will find Leonardo da Vinci's Mona Lisa, Venus de Milo and Egyptian and Oriental Antiquities. It is open on Thursday, Saturday and Sunday from 9.00 to 18.00, Mondays and Wednesdays from 9.00 to 21.45 and it is closed on Tuesdays. Beaubourg, the Georges Pompidou National Centre of Art and Culture, is open from 12.00 to 22.00 during the week and from 10.00 to 22.00 at the weekend and on holidays. It is known for its modern architecture. Inside, you will find a reference library, a laboratory for musical research and the national museum of modern art.

Exercise 3

1 Pour aller au Louvre, il faut prendre la direction Château de Vincennes jusqu'au Louvre. 2 Pour aller aux Champs-Elysées il faut prendre la direction Pont de Neuilly, jusqu'aux Champs Elysées. 3 Pour aller à la cathédrale de Notre Dame il faut prendre la direction Château de Vincennes jusqu'à Châtelet, et puis la direction Porte d'Orléans jusqu'à la Cité. 4 Pour aller dîner au Boulevard Saint-Michel, il faut prendre la direction Porte d'Orléans jusqu'à Saint-Michel. 5 Pour rentrer il faut prendre la direction Porte d'Orléans jusqu'à Montparnasse, et puis la direction Etoile jusqu'au bout de la ligne.

Comprehension 2

3; 7; 6; 5; 1; 4; 2

Transcript
Vous avez les Invalides sur votre droite. Maintenant, sur votre gauche, vous voyez le Jardin des Tuileries et à droite, le musée d'Orsay. Le musée du Louvre est sur votre gauche. Maintenant nous passons sous le Pont Neuf. Le Châtelet et un peu plus loin, l'Hôtel de Ville, sont à gauche. Et maintenant nous arrivons à la cathédrale de Notre Dame.

Comprehension 3

1 Le métro parisien est l'un des plus efficaces et des plus propres du monde. 2 En moyenne, vous paierez 25,80 francs le kilomètre. 3 Il est particulièrement pratique pour la banlieue. 4 Certains roulent jusqu'à minuit et demi. 5 Les lignes de RER relient les banlieues au centre de la ville en un temps record.

Translation

The RATP bus service is efficient and widely spread but not always very fast because of the traffic. It is particularly practical for use in the suburbs. The stops are shown by red and yellow signs with the number of the route. Most buses run from 7.00 in the morning to 20.30. Some run till 12.30 in the morning. Depending on your itinerary, you will pay for one, two, or three tickets which you can buy on the bus.

The metro in Paris is one of the most efficient and cleanest in the world. It is also one of the cheapest. The RER routes link the suburbs and the town centre in record time. You can buy metro tickets singly (5F) or in books of ten (31F29). The RER tickets are a bit more expensive. The first metro train leaves at 5.30, the last one about one o'clock in the morning.

You can flag down a taxi or take one from a taxi stand. You pay, not only the price fixed by the meter, but also a tarif which is indicated on the taxi window – a luggage supplement, for example. On average, you pay 25,80F per kilometre.

Exercise 4

1 Je **connais** un petit restaurant très sympathique. **2** Vous **savez** si Paul est déjà parti? **3** Il **sait** nager maintenant. **4** Je le **connais** très bien. **5** Je **connais** très bien l'Italie. **6** On ne **sait** jamais.

Comprehension 4

Transcript

Oui, tu sais, Jean-Pierre est beaucoup plus intelligent que Marc. Il travaille plus aussi. Mais je trouve qu'il n'est pas très sympathique. Marc est beaucoup plus sympa que lui – et plus beau aussi!

Progress check

1   a)   Je ne connais pas Paris.
   b)   Je ne connais pas la France.
   c)   jJe ne connais pas Jean-Paul.
   d)   Je ne sais pas nager.
2   Ça coûte cher la visite aux musées?
3   Ça me plairait beaucoup.
4   Ça sera très intéressant.

5   a)   Closed on Mondays and holidays.
   b)   Is it the same system as in London?
   c)   It's open from 10 a.m. to 8 p.m. at weekends.
6   a)   Beaubourg est plus intéressant que le Louvre.
   b)   Londres est plus grand que Paris.
   c)   Le métro est plus rapide que l'autobus.

UNIT 12

Exercise 1

1   Bonjour. Je voudrais prendre rendez-vous pour aujourd'hui à 10 h.
2   Je peux venir demain à neuf heures?

Exercise 2

1 Mme Berthon, 14.00, today **2** M. Benoit, Wednesday, 15.00 **3** Mme Jeanlin, this evening, 19.00.

Transcript

1   Allô, oui?/Bonjour. Je voudrais prendre rendez-vous avec le médecin./Oui, Madame. Pouvez-vous venir aujourd'hui à deux heures?/Oui, ça ira./Quel est votre nom?/C'est Madame Berthon (B-E-R-T-H-O-N)./Très bien, Madame. Alors, à plus tard. Au revoir Madame.
2   Ici le cabinet du docteur Martin. J'écoute./Je voudrais prendre rendez-vous avec le médecin mercredi après-midi si possible./Mercredi après-midi. A trois heures?/Oui, ça ira./C'est quel nom? C'est Monsieur Benoît (B-E-N-O-I-T)./Merci Monsieur. Au revoir.
3   Allô, oui?/Je voudrais prendre rendez-vous pour mon fils. Il a eu un petit accident et il a mal au genou./Pouvez-vous venir demain matin à neuf heures?/Je préfère venir ce soir. Il a très mal./Si c'est urgent, le médecin va vous voir à sept heures./Merci, Madame/C'est quel nom?/Jeanlin (J-E-A-N-L-I-N)./Et le prénom de votre fils?/Pierre./Merci, Madame. Au revoir.

Exercise 3

Bonjour docteur. Je ne me sens pas tres bien (*I don't feel very well*) – j'ai de la fièvre depuis hier et je tousse depuis mardi. J'ai mal à la tête et mal à la gorge depuis le weekend. Vous croyez que c'est la grippe? (This is just one of several possibilities.)

Comprehension 1

1 oropivalone 2 aspirine upse 3 maalox 4 oracéfal 5 ercéfuryl 200.

Translation
Aspirine upse. Effervescent tablets. Directions: 'flu symptoms, toothache, migraines.
Maalox. Tablets. Directions: gastritis, dyspepsia. Dosage – 1 or 2 tablets to suck or chew after meals.
Ercéfurly 200 nifuroxacide. Tablets. Directions: treatment of diarrhoea. Dosage – length of treatment according to medical prescription.
Gropivalone bacitracine. Tablets. Directions: laryngitis and tonsillitis. Dosage – 4 to 10 tablets per day. Allow to dissolve. Do not chew.
Oracéfal. 500 mg. capsules. Directions: respiratory infections. Dosage: 2 grams per day, 3 to 4 grams for more severe infections. Swallow the capsules with water.

Comprehension 2

1 la paume 2 les jambes 3 les pieds 4 la tête 5 le cou 6 les chevilles 7 les coudes 8 les doigts 9 le dos 10 les mains 11 les bras 12 les hanches 13 les oreilles 14 les épaules.

Translation
Sometimes a few tricks are sufficient to encourage good habits and a straight, painless back, which is a sign of good health and mental strength. **On the telephone** In order to avoid rounding your spine and pulling the nape of the neck towards the side where your ear is resting on the receiver, simply put a pile of books or magazines under your elbows. **At the typewriter** So as not to round your back, shoulders and neck too much, put a few directories or a little stool beneath your feet. That will be enough to pull everything upwards. Do not forget when you are sitting reading to keep your forearms (as far as your elbows) flat. **At the office** With your back supported by the chair, interweave your fingers with your palms upwards. Push your fingers as far down as possible. Push your legs straight out, toes pointing towards you. Your back will thank you. **At the steering-wheel** In the car, with your hands on the top part of the steering-wheel, and feet flat under the pedals, push your feet and your hands forward, pulling in your stomach and chin. That will be the end of your cramp! Outside, with your feet on the lower part of the bodywork, your hands holding the roof, your plams upwards, stretch your legs and lower your head as far as possible. This will tense your arms, neck, back, buttocks and ankles.

Exercise 4

1 Sore throat; tablets; suck no more than eight per day.
2 Flu, aspirin four times a day; effervescent vitamin C tablets.
3 Indigestion; tablets; one or two after each meal.

Transcript
1 J'ai mal à la gorge depuis quatre jours. Avez-vous quelque chose pour le mal de gorge?/J'ai ces comprimés. Vous les sucez quand vous avez mal. Mais il ne faut pas en prendre plus de huit par jour.
2 Mon mari à la grippe. Il ne veut pas voir le médecin. Qu'est-ce que vous conseillez?/Il a de la fièvre?/Oui. Depuis le week-end./Bon je vous donne de l'aspirine à prendre quatre fois par jour. Et des comprimés effervescents à la vitamine C. Si ça continue il faut aller voir le médecin.
3 Mon fils a une indigestion. Il a très mal. Qu'est-ce qu'il faut faire?/Essayez ces comprimés. Il faut en sucer un ou deux après les repas.

Exercise 5	**1a)** Qu'est-ce qui s'est passé? **b)** Vous êtes blessée? **2a)** Restez là, ne bougez pas. **b)** Il ne faut pas le/la bouger. **c)** Je vais appeler l'ambulance.

Comprehension 3   1a); 2f); 3g); 4h); 5b); 6e); 7d); 8c)

Translation
The survival of an injured person depends in large part on the speed at which help arrives.
- As quickly as possible get to the nearest phone and alert
  - the police (in town) or the gendarmes (in the country) by dialling 17
  - the fire brigade if necessary, by calling 18
  - SAMU by calling 15.
- To allow for speedy localisation and efficient organisation of the rescue services, indicate
  - in town, the name of the street, the number of the nearest building
  - in the country, markers such as boundary stones, crossroads, signposts, etc.
  - the nature of the accident (damage, injuries)
  - vehicles involved – private cars, lorries, motorbikes, etc.
  - the number of injured and their apparent state (breathing, bleeding)
  - possible risks – blocked roads, fire, etc.
- If no telephone is available, ask another road user to give the alert.

Exercise 6	Bonjour, c'est la police? Il y a eu un accident sur la Route Nationale. Un garçon à moto est sorti de l'avenue Leclerc sans regarder. Une voiture n'a pas pu s'arrêter et a heurté le réverbère. Le garçon ne bouge pas et le conducteur est blessé aussi. Sa femme souffre du choc.

Exercise 7	aimant; rendant; partant; voulant; pouvant; allant.

Exercise 8	(on tape) **a)** moi **b)** eux

Progress check

1. a) Je voudrais prendre rendez-vous pour aujourd'hui.
   b) Bon, alors pour demain s'il vous plaît.
   d) Je suis anglais(e).
   e) J'ai l'assurance médicale.
2. a) J'ai mal à la tête.
   b) J'ai mal à la gorge.
   c) J'ai un peu de fièvre...
   d) ... depuis deux jours.
3. a) Go to Social Security to be reimbursed.

   b) I am going to give you a prescription.
   c) Dosage – allow 2–5 pills to melt (in your mouth) without biting them.
4. a) Qu'est-ce qui s'est passé?
   b) Je n'ai pas pu m'arrêter.
   c) Il faut appeler les secours.
   d) Restez-là!
   e) Je me suis fait mal au bras *or* J'ai mal au bras.

UNIT 13

Exercise 1	**1** Pourrais-je *parler* au chef des achats, s'il vous plaît? **2** De la part de *qui*? **3** Le chef des achats est *absent*. **4** Quand est-ce que je pourrai le *joindre*? **5** Pas avant *demain* matin. **6** Bon. Je *rappellerai* demain matin.

Exercise 2	Pourrais-je parler au chef de production s'il vous plaît?/John Barclay de la Société Marshall et Cie. (*Substitute your own details.*)/Quand est-ce que je pourrai le joindre?/Bien. Je rappellerai demain matin. Merci, Madame. Au revoir.

<table>
<tr><td>

Exercise 3
</td><td>

Salut Catherine! Ça va?/Ça va très bien merci. Et toi?/Ça va très bien. Tu as passé un bon weekend?/Superbe/Comment vont les affaires?/Excellent. A propos, j'ai reçu le catalogue que tu m'as envoyé./Excellent. Qu'est-ce que tu vas commander alors? Je propose.../Bon, merci Pascale. A la prochaine.
</td></tr>
</table>

Comprehension 1

Translation

Do you know who we are? Our company is called Thompson France. We are manufacturers and wholesalers of parts for industrial machines. We can guarantee speedy delivery and generous discounts.

<table>
<tr><td>

Exercise 4
</td><td>

1 Leroy; 7, rue St. Jacques, 42, 55, 29, 47; Marc; Office goods, stationery
2 Duchesne; 41 44 81 81; Jean-Claude Thibault; Lifts and escalators
3 Marcel and Sons; 54, Avenue Charlebois, 45 68 93 42; André Marcel; Gifts.
</td></tr>
</table>

Transcript

1 Ici la Société Leroy. Nous sommes marchand de papier et d'articles de bureau. Nous sommes au numéro 7, rue St. Jacques. Notre numéro de téléphone est le 42 55 29 47. Demandez à parler à Marc.

2 Bonjour. Ici Jean-Claude Thibault (T-H-I-B-A-U-L-T) de l'entreprise Duchesne (D-U-C-H-E-S-N-E). Nous sommes spécialistes en réparations d'ascenseurs et d'escaliers roulants. Notre numéro de téléphone est le 41 44 81 81.

3 Bonsoir. Ici Marcel et fils. Nous vous avons envoyé notre catalogue de cadeaux et nous attendons votre commande. Nous sommes au 54 Avenue Charlebois (C-H-A-R-L-E-B-O-I-S); téléphone 45 68 93 42; demandez André Marcel.

<table>
<tr><td>

Exercise 5
</td><td>

Quel est le nom de votre société?/Quelle est l'adresse?/Quel est votre numéro de téléphone?/Quel est votre numéro de télécopie?/Quel est le nom de la personne à contacter?/Qui sont vos fournisseurs actuels?/Quelle est la remise actuelle?
</td></tr>
</table>

<table>
<tr><td>

Exercise 6
</td><td>

1 Vous pourriez travailler à l'usine demain? **2** Vous pourriez contacter quelques clients? **3** Vous pourriez essayer de contacter le chef des ventes? **4** Vous pourriez parler au comptable? **5** Vous pourriez rappeler demain?
</td></tr>
</table>

Progress check

1 a) Est-ce que je peux parler au chef des achats?
  b) Comment s'appelle-t-il?
  c) Je suis... et je travaille pour/chez/à *Mechanem*.
  d) Quand est-ce que je peux le joindre?
  e) Je vais rappeler la semaine prochaine/Je rappellerai demain.
2 a) Salut!
  b) Ça va?

  c) Tu as bien reçu le catalogue?
  d) Je te propose le télécopieur numéro vingt-deux dans le catalogue.
  e) Allez, au revoir et merci.
  f) Bonne soirée.
3 a) We are wholesalers of machine parts.
  b) We guarantee a speedy delivery.
  c) We offer large discounts.

UNIT 14

<table>
<tr><td>

Exercise 1
</td><td>

1 J'ai une formation de comptable. **2** Je travaille pour une petite entreprise. **3** Je cherche quelque chose de plus stimulant... **4** ...qui me donnerait plus de responsabilité (quelque chose de plus responsable). **5** Je ne vois pas d'inconvénient à partir en déplacement pour l'entreprise.
</td></tr>
</table>

<table>
<tr><td>

Exercise 2
</td><td>

1a) Je parle anglais et français. **b)** Je serais disposé(e) à faire des heures supplémentaires.
2a) Quelles sont les heures du travail? **b)** Quelle est la rémunération? **c)** On a combien de semaines de vacances?
</td></tr>
</table>

Comprehension 1

1 frappe de documents confidentiels **2** réservation d'hôtels et de billets d'avion **3** facturation **4** classement **5** traductions **6** prises de rendez-vous.

Translation

1 General description
   Job title: secretary
   Place of work: Angers.
2 Job description
   – organising meetings
   – hotel and air reservations
   – filing
   – typing confidential documents
   – translations
   – invoicing
3 Conditions (offered)
   Salary: 8500 francs per month
   Hours: 39 hours per week: 8.30 to 17.30 (16.30 on Fridays)
   Holidays: five weeks per year.

Comprehension 2

```
Civil status
Surname:              MARÉCHAL
Christian name:       Fabienne
Birthday:             24 June 1964
Marital status:       Single
Address:              39 rue du Marche, Meudon.
Diplomas obtained
1983:                 Bac (calauréat) A5
1985:                 BTS Option Executive Secretary
Languages read, spoken and written
English and Spanish.
Professional experience
From 28 September 1985    bilingual secretary (shorthand
till the present:         and typing) with CDFG, Nanterre.
July to September 1985:   Typist with Ballot, boulevard
                          Haussman, Paris
21 April to 26 June 1985: Placement at Renault-Étoile,
                          boulevard Péreire, Paris.
```

Comprehension 3

1 Elle va commencer son nouveau travail le 1er mars. **2** Son horaire de travail sera de 8 h 30 à 17 h 30 lundi à jeudi et de 8 h 30 à 16 h 30 vendredi. **3** Elle aura cinq semaines de vacances. **4** Elle doit envoyer une lettre recommandée avec accusé de réception au moins un mois à l'avance. **5** Elle doit signer la lettre, mettre la date et la renvoyer à Thompson France.

Translation

```
Dear Madam
As a result of our interview on 20 January, we have pleasure in
detailing the conditions of your employment, which, if you agree
to them, will take effect from 1 March.
You will carry out the duties of a secretary. Your hours of work
in the company will be Monday to Thursday from 8.30 to 17.30 and
on Friday from 8.30 to 16.30. Your monthly salary will be 8500
francs. You will be entitled to paid leave of five weeks per
year. Each party has the right to terminate the contract by
advising the other of their intention by registered letter to be
received at least one month in advance. We would urge you to
confirm your agreement to the terms set out in the letter by
returning before 29 January the enclosed copy which you will have
signed and dated.
Yours sincerely, etc. C. Stevens
```

Exercise 3	1e); 2d); 3f); 4b); 5c); 6a)

Progress check

1 a) Je voudrais (prendre) plus de responsabilité
  b) et quelque chose de plus intéressant
  c) et de plus stimulant.
2 J'aimerais voyager en France et en Angleterre.
3 Je parle (le) français et (l') espagnol.
4 a) Quelles sont les heures du travail?
  b) On a combien de semaines de vacances (congé)?

  c) Quelle est la date d'embauche?
5 a) J'ai travaillé pour ICI en Écosse.
  b) J'ai travaillé aussi pour GEC Alsthom en France.
6 a) classement b) prises de rendez-vous c) traduction
  d) facturation
7 a) You will be entitled to paid leave. b) A registered letter with receipt. c) Your monthly salary will be 9000 francs.

UNIT 15

Dossier 1

1 Je vous recommande L'Hôtel Ibis dans la rue de Bercy. C'est un quartier tout près de la gare de Lyon et du centre de Paris. Il y a un restaurant dans l'hôtel et il y a un piano-bar aussi.

2 Je vous recommande l'Hôtel Sofitel Brussels Airport. Tout d'abord, c'est près de l'aéroport international de Bruxelles. Il y a 125 chambres toutes avec salles de bains, radio, poste de télévision, etc. Il y a 10 salons pour des réunions et ils sont tous équipés pour les conférences et les congrès. Il y a deux restaurants, un plus élégant que l'autre: le Diedeghem sert plutôt des spécialités: le Green Corner sert des repas rapides et il est ouvert toute la journée du matin au soir. Il y a aussi un grand parking pour ceux qui viennent en voiture.

3 Je vous recommande l'Hôtel Sofitel Marrakesh au Maroc. Tout d'abord, l'hôtel est climatisé, ce qui est important au Maroc où il fait chaud. L'hôtel est situé dans un grand parc privé où il y a beaucoup de facilités, surtout pour les enfants, comme, par exemple, des piscines, des salles de jeux, deux tennis éclairés où vous pouvez jouer la nuit. Il y a aussi un terrain de golf tout près. Vous avez beaucoup de choix pour les repas: il y a des restaurants élégants, des restaurants plus simples, un grill autour de la piscine, même un restaurant marocain sous une tente dans le jardin.

Dossier 2

1 **To:** Ian Rivers
      Director

Françoise Renault rang to change M. Lamaire's appointment with you to 14 September.

Transcript
Bonjour. Ici Françoise Renault la secrétaire de Monsieur Lemaire (L-E-M-A-I-R-E). J'ai un message pour votre directeur. C'est pour dire que Monsieur Lemaire a changé la date de sa visite. Il arrive le 14 (quatorze) septembre.

2 **To:** Julia Roberts
      Sales Manager Europe

Please phone Monsieur Maurois 36 95 05 05. He would like information about article AB 2007 in the catalogue.

Transcript
Ici Monsieur Maurois, téléphone 36 95 05 05. Je voudrais des renseignements sur votre produit référence AB 2007 dans votre catalogue. Voulez-vous me téléphoner?

3 **To:** Christine Brooks
Personnel Officer

Please send an application form for the receptionist's position, to Mlle Vandestoc, 14 Rue de la Madeleine.

Transcript
Bonjour, euh, j'ai vu votre annonce dans le journal, et je voudrais un formulaire de demande de candidature pour votre poste de réceptionniste. C'est Mademoiselle Vandestoc (V-A-N-D-E-S-T-O-C), 14 rue de la Madeleine (M-A-D-E-L-E-I-N-E).

4 **To:** Julia Roberts
Sales Manager Europe

A message from Jacques Vignault 48 98 01 01 to thank you for the delivery and to order 5 parts (number Y-Z4015).

Transcript
Ici Jacques Vignault (V-I-G-N-A-U-L-T), téléphone 48 98 01 01. Nous avons bien reçu la livraison, merci. Nous voulons commander cinq pièces numéro Y-Z4015.

5 **To:** Christine Brooks
Personnel Officer

A Mlle Février called you to confirm that she will be attending the interview next Tuesday.

Transcript
Bonjour, c'est Mademoiselle Février. C'est pour confirmer que je viens à l'entrevue mardi prochain. Merci.

6 **To:** Julia Roberts
Sales Manager Europe

The Danuc factory would like you to send them a catalogue.

Transcript
Voulez-vous nous envoyer votre catalogue? C'est l'usine Danuc.

7 **To:** Frank Richards
Marketing Manager

A message from Martine to say she would like to speak to you about the latest publicity material.

Transcript
Ici Martine. Je voudrais parler à Frank à propos de la nouvelle publicité.

8 **To:** Anthony Harris
Accountant

Alain François (35 24 52 11) rang to say he would like to talk to someone in accounts about our account with them.

Transcript
Nous voudrions parler à un représentant de votre service de comptabilité à propos de votre compte avec nous. Demandez Alain François au numéro 35 24 52 11.

Dossier 3

1
Parfums Stern: **a)** Export manager. **b)** Someone with at least 3 years experience of negotiation, who can speak English and a second language and who is able to make frequent trips abroad. **c)** Send candidates dossier (CV, references and letter) quoting reference 160 Ex.

Matignon Conseil:	**a)** Financial adviser. **b)** Woman looking to develop her career. **c)** Apply in writing.
Team 5:	**a)** Materials buyer. **b)** Experienced negotiator with belief in the product. **c)** Apply in writing with CV and photo.
MB Développement:	**a)** Accounts manager. **b)** Young graduate with at least 3 years experience. **c)** Send handwritten letter with CV and photos.
L'Express:	**a)** Salesman of ready-to-wear clothes. **b)** Wanted for all areas. **c)** Send CV and references.
Contesse Publicité:	**a)** Sales engineer. **b)** Capable of conducting high-level negotiations (concerning telephone systems) and of taking responsibility for a sales team. **c)** Send CV with salary expectations and photo.

2a)

```
Messieurs,
En réponse à votre annonce parue dans l'Express du 5 octobre
1992 j'ai l'honneur de poser ma candidature au poste du
responsable export. Je m'appelle Robert Brown, j'ai trente ans
et je suis célibataire. J'ai été employé à Thompson Angleterre
mais je cherche maintenant un emploi en France. Veuillez
trouvez ci-joint mon curriculum vitae. Dans l'attente de votre
réponse, je vous prie d'agréer Messieurs, mes salutations
distinguées.
```

b)

```
CV
Etat civil
Nom                      Brown
Prénom                   Robert
Date de naissance        3 juin 1961
Situation de famille     Célibataire
Adresse                  24, Maple Drive, Hazel Grove, Stockport

Diplômes obtenus
1982:          BA (Licence) français, espagnol
1983:          PGCE (diplôme d'enseignement)

Langues lues, parlées et écrites
Français, anglais, espagnol

Expérience professionelle
Du 15 octobre 1987 à ce jour      Traducteur chez Thompson
                                  Angleterre
De septembre 1982 à juillet, 1987  Professeur de langues à
                                  Moortop High School
```

Transcript of letter

```
Dear Sir(s)
With reference to your advertisement which appeared in the
Express on the (  ), I should like to apply for the post of
(  ). My name is (  ), I am (  ) years old and I am single. I
have been working for (  ). Please find enclosed my curriculum/
testimonials concerning my previous employment. I await your
reply. Yours faithfully, etc. …
```

c)   **Translation of second letter**

```
Dear Sir/Madame
We received your application for the post of …
We are pleased to inform you that your CV was of great interest
to us. However, an in-depth interview at our offices would be
desirable, to be held before 30 June if possible. We would
therefore be grateful if you could contact us in order to
arrange an interview. We look forward to hearing from you.
Yours faithfully, etc.
```

d) These are some possible answers

- Actuellement je suis secrétaire chez Branson et Fils
- J'aime la responsabilité et l'indépendance du travail. Mais je préfère ne plus travailler à Paris. Je veux quitter Paris pour aller m'installer en province – à Angers, par exemple!
- Je voudrais continuer à faire carrière et peut-être à long terme fonder ma propre entreprise.

e) Possible questions:

- C'est quand la date d'embauche?
- Est-ce que je travaillerais ici dans ces bureaux ou ailleurs?
- Quel est l'horaire du travail?
- Est-ce que je pourrais faire des stages?
- Quelles sont les avantages de travailler ici en province?
- Vous pourriez me parler un peu des responsabilités du poste?
- Et quel est le salaire?
- Je dois faire des déplacements pour l'entreprise?

Dossier 4

Transcript

Vous   François, vous avez vu l'accident la semaine dernière. Jean Bénard a été blessé... mardi dernier, le trois./**François**   Oui, alors, c'était dans l'entrepôt. Je n'ai pas tout vu mais j'ai entendu un bruit. Il s'est blessé au pied, mais je ne sais pas comment./**Vous**   Philippe, vous avez appelé les urgences?/**Philippe**   Oui, il s'était blessé au pied. Nous avons appelé les urgences et une ambulance l'a emmené à l'hôpital./**Vous**   Jean, qu'est-ce qui s'est passé?/**Jean**   J'étais dans l'entrepôt. Je me suis laissé tomber une des pièces sur le pied droit. Depuis une semaine je ne peux plus marcher. Je suis allé à l'hôpital. J'ai rendez-vous mercredi prochain.

Accident report

Jean Bénard was injured on Tuesday, the third. He dropped a part on his right foot while in the warehouse. The emergency services were called and an ambulance took him to hospital. He has another hospital appointment next Wednesday.

Dossier 5

1   Bonjour Monsieur, je voudrais parler au chef des achats. Comment s'appelle-t-il? (Il s'appelle comment?). Je viens à Paris le 3 ou 4 mai. Je peux passer le voir? Excellent. Quelle heure vous conviendrait? Dix heures du matin le trois mai? D'accord.

```
Je vous écris pour confirmer ma visite à Paris, lundi, le trois
mai à dix heures.
```

2   Excusez-moi, je suis Tom Brooks, vous avez mon billet d'avion? Le numéro de vol c'est le AF 312. Vous l'avez? Très bien.

3   Bonjour Mademoiselle. Je m'appelle Tom Brooks de Microtex à Londres. J'ai rendez-vous avec François Thomas à dix heures.

Dossier 6

Nous recommandons des bureaux complètement équipés dans un immeuble moderne de standing au centre ville et près des accès autoroutiers et de la gare centrale. Le loyer mensuel comprend chauffage, éléctricité, nettoyage, éclairage, etc. Parking à disposition. Libre tout de suite. Loyer à partir de 1.850 francs par mois jusqu'à 3.600 francs par mois.